DK LANGUAGE LEARNER

FRENCH

Everything you need to get talking

LONDON, NEW YORK,
MELBOURNE, MUNICH, and DELHI

REVISED EDITION 2011
DK LONDON
Editor Matilda Gollon
Designer Spencer Holbrook
Managing Editor Linda Esposito
Managing Art Editor Jim Green
Category Publisher Laura Buller
Production Controller Angela Graef
Production Editor Marc Staples
Design Development Manager
Sophia M Tampakopoulos Turner
Jacket Designer Natalie Godwin
Jacket Editor Matilda Gollon

DK DELHI
Senior Art Editor Govind Mittal
Editor Aparajita Kumar
Designers Nishesh Bhatnagar,
Ridhi Khanna
Managing Editor Suchismita Banerjee
Managing Art Editor Romi Chakraborty
DTP Manager Sunil Sharma
DTP Designer Manish Chandra Upreti

FIRST EDITION 2006
Senior Editor Hazel Beynon
Senior Art Editor Smiljka Surla
Editor Jenny Finch
Designers Mo Choy, Ralph Pitchford,
Marilou Prokopiou
Managing Editors
Linda Esposito, Camilla Hallinan
Managing Art Editor Diane Thistlethwaite
Written by Viv Lambert
Consultant Suzanne Gaynor

First published in Great Britain in 2006
This new edition published in 2011 by
Dorling Kindersley Limited,
80 Strand, London, WC2R ORL

6 8 10 9 7 5
013-LD055-May/2012

A CIP catalogue for this book is available from the British Library.

ISBN: 978-1-40536-660-1

Colour reproduction by
Media Development Printing Ltd, UK
Printed and bound by Hung Hing, China

Discover more at
www.dk.com

Contents

Activities

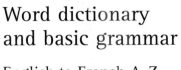

Picture dictionary

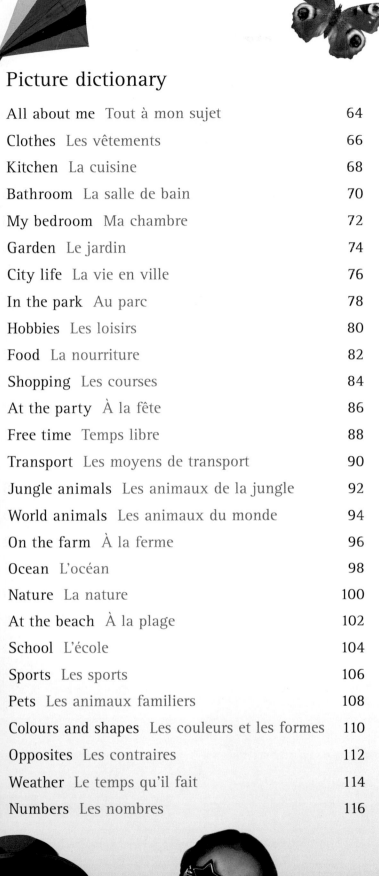

Word dictionary and basic grammar

What's in this pack

This DK Language Learner pack contains everything your child needs to start speaking French. All the components – the Activities, CD, Flash cards, Picture dictionary, Word dictionary and basic grammar – are designed to build children's confidence as they develop their language skills. Try to encourage your child to speak as much French as possible – and remember – it's much more fun to practise speaking French with a partner.

Activities

The Activities section is linked to the CD and consists of 26 themed topics. Each topic introduces children to useful, everyday words and phrases, and lets them practise what they have learned with fun activities.

Activities

Picture dictionary

The Picture dictionary includes 26 topic pages and brings key vocabulary to life with colourful images. Under each illustrated French word, children will see how to pronounce it and find the English translation.

Picture dictionary

CD

All the phrases and conversations in the Activities section are recorded on the CD, so that children can hear how the language is spoken and pronounced. A narrator leads the learner through each topic and encourages the children to repeat everything they read on the page. The CD also includes several listening activities and games.

Word dictionary and basic grammar

At the back of the book, a useful reference section provides learners with quick and clear access to all the vocabulary, basic grammar, and useful phrases covered in the rest of the book.

Word dictionary
and basic grammar

Flash cards

There are five sets of twelve flash cards covering the following topics: food, clothes, objects, numbers, and animals. Your child can use the flash cards to practise learning vocabulary and to play the games and puzzles in the Activities section.

Bringing language to life

This fun interactive section covers all the key words and phrases children will need to know in everyday situations like going to the doctor's or going shopping. All the French words and phrases are translated into English and are recorded on the CD, so children can hear how they are pronounced. Each topic includes games, puzzles, and activities for readers to try out what they have learned, and Top tips boxes to explain the basic grammar covered on the page.

CD-links show children when to play a track so that they can hear the language being spoken and repeat it for themselves

Thematic spreads show full-colour photographs of children using French in everyday situations

Speech bubbles introduce the key French words and phrases on each spread and provide the English translations

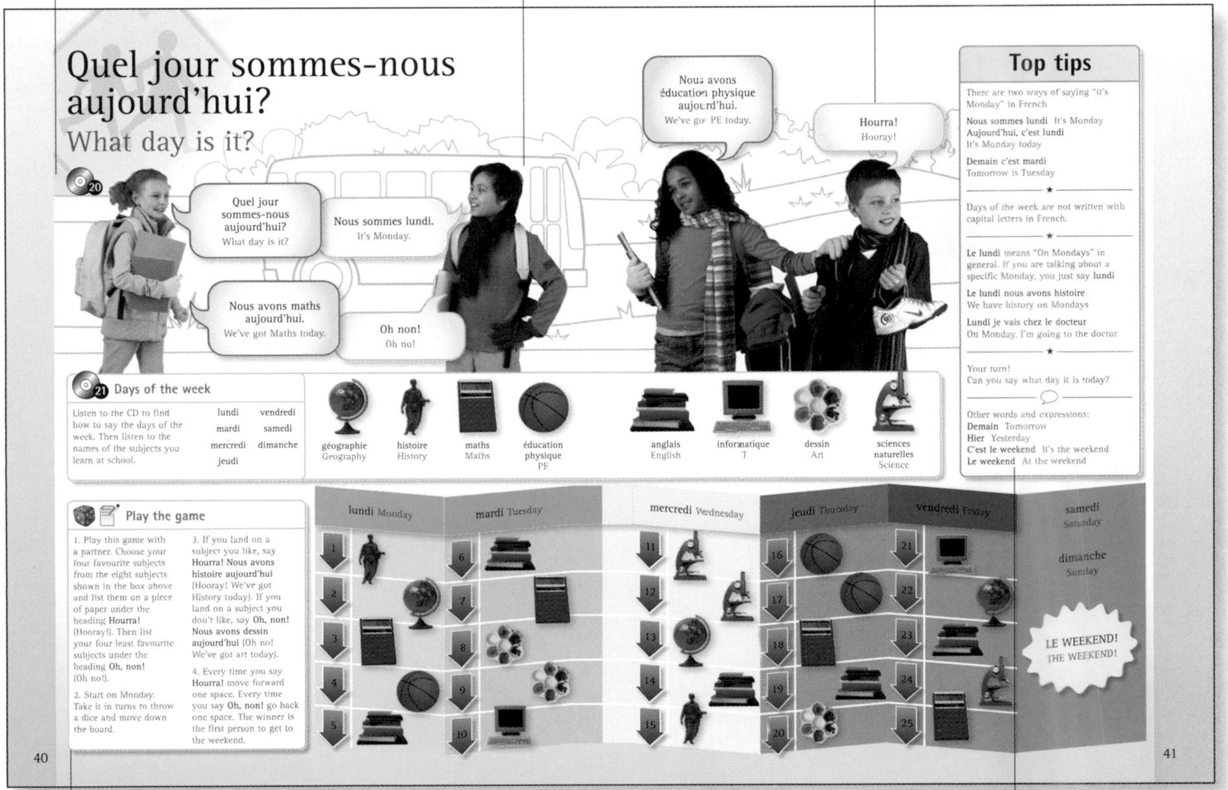

Quel jour sommes-nous aujourd'hui?
What day is it?
20
Quel jour sommes-nous aujourd'hui? What day is it?
Nous sommes lundi. It's Monday.
Nous avons maths aujourd'hui. We've got Maths today.
Oh non! Oh no!
Nous avons éducation physique aujourd'hui. We've got PE today.
Hourra! Hooray!
Top tips
There are two ways of saying "it's Monday" in French
Nous sommes lundi It's Monday
Aujourd'hui, c'est lundi It's Monday today
Demain c'est mardi Tomorrow is Tuesday
Days of the week are not written with capital letters in French.
Le lundi means "On Mondays" in general. If you are talking about a specific Monday, you just say lundi
Le lundi nous avons histoire We have history on Mondays
Lundi je vais chez le docteur On Monday, I'm going to the doctor
Your turn! Can you say what day it is today?
Other words and expressions:
Demain Tomorrow
Hier Yesterday
C'est le weekend It's the weekend
Le weekend At the weekend
21 Days of the week
lundi mardi mercredi jeudi vendredi samedi dimanche
géographie Geography
histoire History
maths Maths
éducation physique PE
anglais English
informatique IT
dessin Art
sciences naturelles Science
Play the game
lundi Monday
mardi Tuesday
mercredi Wednesday
jeudi Thursday
vendredi Friday
samedi Saturday
dimanche Sunday
LE WEEKEND! THE WEEKEND!
40
41

Games and puzzles give children an opportunity to practise the key words and phrases while they play

Top tips help explain the basic grammar covered on the spread

Numbers on the CD icons show which track to play for each topic

You can find more words relating to the topic in the Picture dictionary

You need to use a dice for these games and activities

You need to use the Flash cards to play these games

Other words and expressions give extra vocabulary for each topic

Words in pictures

The Picture dictionary brings vocabulary to life by illustrating key words from a variety of topics, such as hobbies, pets, and transport. Each French word has an English translation and information on how to pronounce it. In addition to the illustrated words, there is a list of extra words to help learners build their vocabulary, together with simple sentences containing words covered in the topic, and questions to help them practise their spoken French.

Headings introduce the theme of the vocabulary on the page

Questions encourage the reader to practise the words

Extra words on the subject help to expand vocabulary

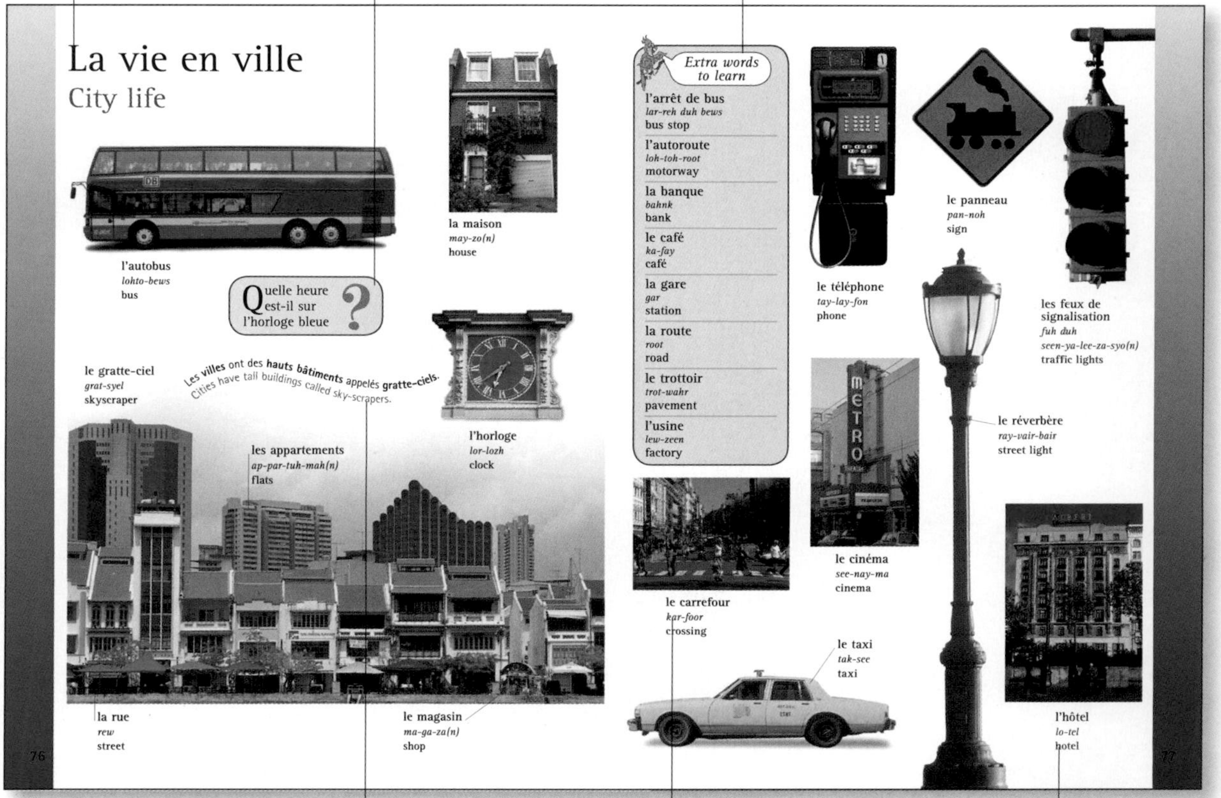

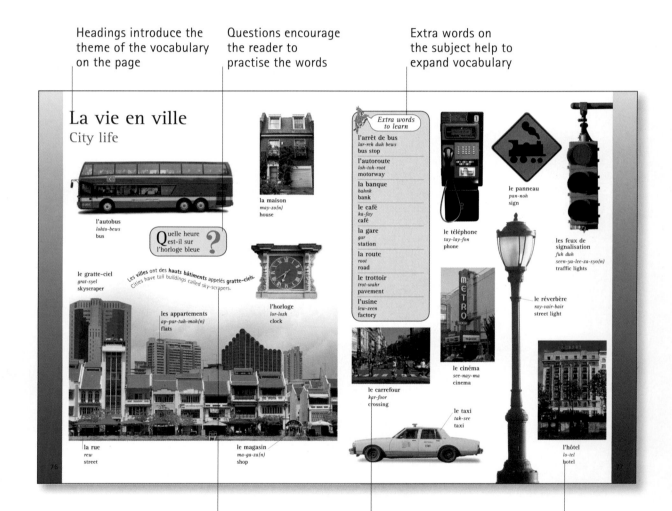

La vie en ville
City life
l'autobus
lohto-bews
bus
Quelle heure est-il sur l'horloge bleue ?
la maison
may-zo(n)
house
le gratte-ciel
grat-syel
skyscraper
Les villes ont des hauts bâtiments appelés gratte-ciels.
Cities have tall buildings called sky-scrapers.
l'horloge
lor-lozh
clock
les appartements
ap-par-tuh-mah(n)
flats
la rue
rew
street
le magasin
ma-ga-za(n)
shop
76
Extra words to learn
l'arrêt de bus
lar-reh duh bews
bus stop
l'autoroute
loh-toh-root
motorway
la banque
bahnk
bank
le café
ka-fay
café
la gare
gar
station
la route
root
road
le trottoir
trot-wahr
pavement
l'usine
lew-zeen
factory
le téléphone
tay-lay-fon
phone
le panneau
pan-noh
sign
les feux de signalisation
fuh duh seen-ya-lee-za-syo(n)
traffic lights
METRO
le réverbère
ray-vair-bair
street light
le cinéma
see-nay-ma
cinema
le carrefour
kar-foor
crossing
le taxi
tak-see
taxi
l'hôtel
lo-tel
hotel
77

Simple sentences show how to use topic vocabulary

French words are also written how they sound to help pronunciation

English translations are given for each French word

Word dictionary and basic grammar

The Word dictionary contains more than 2,000 words. In the first section, the English words are given in alphabetical order, with the French translation and pronunciation. A guide to French pronunciation is provided on page 137. In the second section, the French words are listed with their English translation. This is followed by an overview of basic grammatical rules, the most commonly used regular and irregular verbs, and a list of useful phrases.

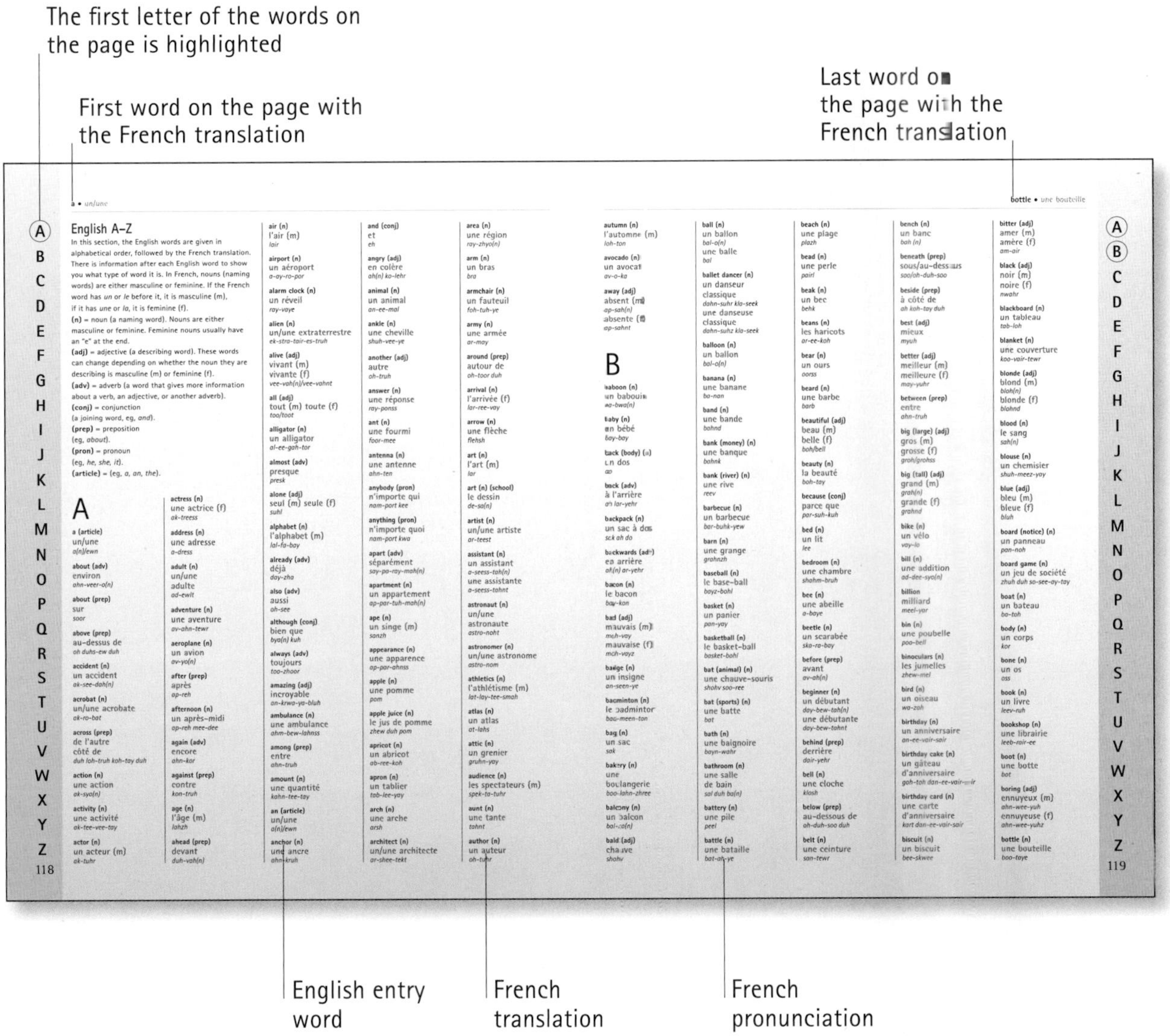

The first letter of the words on the page is highlighted
First word on the page with the French translation
Last word on the page with the French translation
English entry word
French translation
French pronunciation

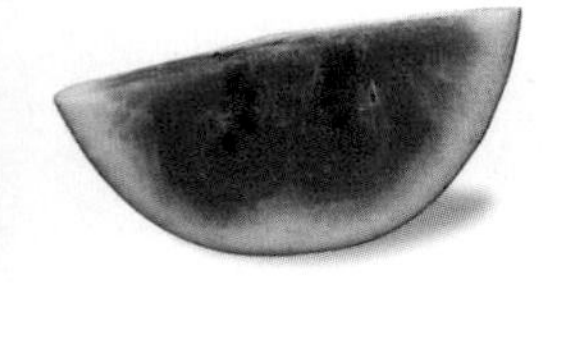

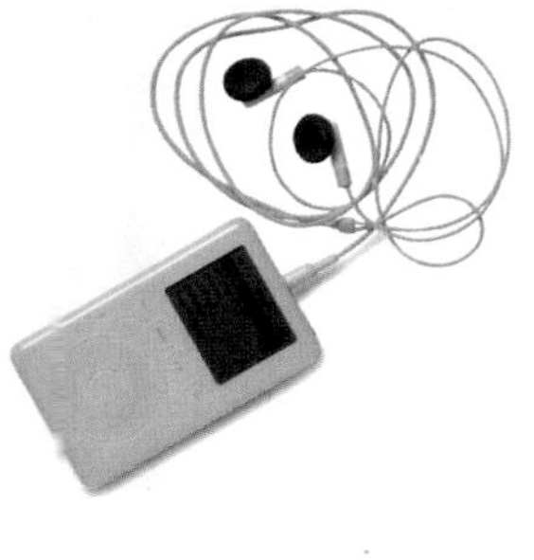

TUTANKHAMUN

ATHLETIC
TRAINING

Activities

Bonjour et au revoir
Hello and goodbye

1

Salut!
Comment ça va?
Hi! How are you?

Ça va bien, merci.
Fine thanks.

Bonjour,
comment vas-tu?
Hello, how are you?

Je vais bien, merci.
Et toi?
I'm fine, thanks.
And you?

Très bien, merci.
Bonne journée!
Very well thanks.
Have a good day!

Toi aussi.
You too.

Puzzle

Look at the greetings on the left. Can you match these greetings to the replies on the right?

Bonne journée!	Bonne nuit!
Bonne nuit!	À plus tard.
Au revoir.	Ça va bien, merci.
Bonjour, comment vas-tu?	Toi aussi.
Salut, ça va?	Je vais bien, merci.

Bonne nuit.
Good night.

Au revoir!
Goodbye!
À plus tard.
See you later.

Top tips

In French, there are two words for "you" – **tu** and **vous**. You say **tu** when speaking to friends and family and **vous** when speaking to people you don't know very well.

★

Similarly, there are two ways of asking people how they are. When you greet your friends, you say

Comment vas-tu? How are you?

When you greet adults and people you don't know very well, you say

Comment allez-vous? How are you?

★

You can also say **Ça va?** or **Comment ça va?** to ask your friends how they are. **Ça va bien** and **Je vais bien** both mean "I'm fine".

★

Salut can mean "Bye" as well as "Hello" or "Hi".

Other words and expressions:

Bon après midi Good afternoon
Bonsoir Good evening
À tout à l'heure See you later
À demain See you tomorrow
À bientôt See you soon

Play the game

1. Play this game with a partner, taking turns to throw a dice.

2. Each circle has a symbol representing a greeting (see the puzzle on the left). When you land on a symbol, say the correct greeting. If you land on a circle showing a moon, for example, you say **Bonne nuit**.

3. Your partner should try to respond to your greeting. If you land on the symbol for **Au revoir**, go back to the beginning. The winner is the first person to reach the end.

Comment tu t'appelles?

What's your name?

Salut! Comment tu t'appelles?
Hello! What's your name?
Je m'appelle Marie.
My name's Marie.
Quel âge as-tu?
How old are you?
J'ai huit ans.
I'm eight.

Count to 12

Listen to the CD to find out how to count up to 12. Point to the numbers as you say them aloud.

Play the game

1. Play this game with a partner using the number flash cards.

2. Spread out the flash cards in numerical order from 1 to 12 with the number facing upwards.

3. Ask your partner to remove one of the cards.

4. Can you say in French which number is missing?

5. To make the game more difficult, remove two or more cards. Take it in turns to say the missing numbers.

1 un	2 deux	3 trois
4 quatre	5 cinq	6 six
7 sept	8 huit	9 neuf
10 dix	11 onze	12 douze

Comment elle s'appelle?
What's she called?
Elle s'appelle Laura.
Elle a huit ans.
She's called Laura.
She's eight.
Comment il s'appelle?
What's he called?
Il s'appelle Eric.
Il a neuf ans.
He's called Eric.
He's nine.

Top tips

In French, verbs (action words) change according to the person doing the action.

You can see how verbs change by looking at the examples shown on page 153.

★

To say how old you are in French, you use the verb **avoir** (to have)

Elle a onze ans She's eleven
J'ai neuf ans I'm nine

If a verb begins with a vowel, **je** becomes **j'** (as in **j'ai**).

★

To say what you are called in French, you use the verb **s'appeler**. In French, verbs that have a pronoun (eg, **me**, **te**, **se**) in front of them are known as reflexive verbs.

Tu t'appelles You are called
Il s'appelle He is called

If the verb begins with a vowel, **me** becomes **m'**, **te** becomes **t'**, and **se** becomes **s'**.

You can find out more about reflexive verbs on page 154.

You can find more numbers on page 116.

Puzzle

Look at the photos of the children on the right, then see if you can answer the following questions:

- Who is the oldest?
- Which two children are the same age?
- Who is ten?
- Who is nine?

Elle s'appelle Laura.
Elle a huit ans.
Elle s'appelle Marie.
Elle a onze ans.
Ben a douze ans.
Eric a neuf ans.
Simone a dix ans.
Paul a huit ans.
Ben
Eric
Marie
Laura
Paul
Simone

Qu'est-ce que c'est?

What is it?

4

C'est quoi ceci?
What's this?
C'est un jeu électronique.
It's a computer game.
C'est quoi cela?
What's that?
C'est un réveil.
It's an alarm clock.
un jeu électronique
une guitare
un réveil

Puzzle

Can you identify the objects in these close-up photos? Look at the labels below and try to match each one to the correct photo. Say **C'est un...** or **C'est une...** (depending on whether the object is masculine or feminine).

1. Une voiture télé-commandée
2. Une fleur
3. Un réveil
4. Un rollerblade
5. Une guitare
6. Un jeu électronique

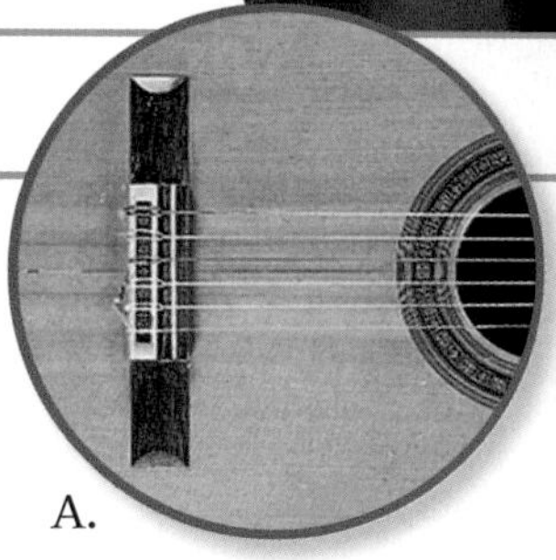

A.

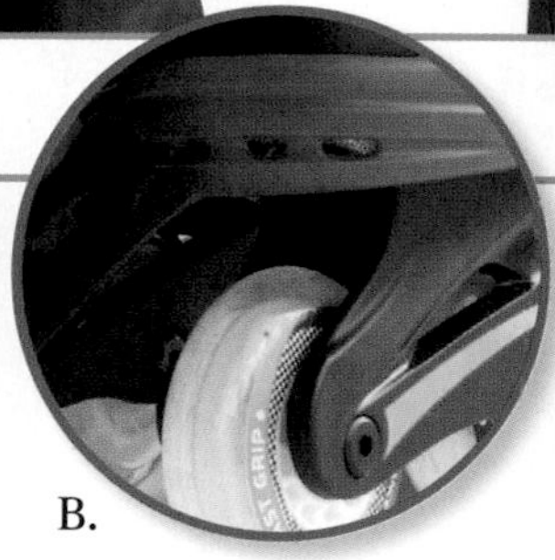

B.

C.

D.

E.

F.

Qu'est-ce que c'est?
What are those?
Ce sont des fleurs.
They're flowers.
une fleur
Qu'est-ce que c'est?
What are these?
Ce sont des rollerblades.
They're rollerblades.
un rollerblade
une voiture télé-commandée

Top tips

To say what something is in French, you use the verb **être**

C'est It is **Ce sont** They are

See how the verb **être** is formed on page 153.

★

All nouns in French are either masculine or feminine. The word for "a" or "an" is either **un** (for masculine nouns) or **une** (for feminine nouns)

Un réveil An alarm clock
Une fleur A flower

★

When you are asking about objects that are close by, you use **ceci**

C'est quoi ceci? What's this?

When you are asking about objects that are further away, you use **cela**

C'est quoi cela? What's that?

★

You can use the question **Qu'est-ce que c'est?** for both singular and plural objects

Qu'est-ce que c'est? What is it?
Qu'est-ce que c'est? What are these? or What are those?

See pages 72–73 for more examples of objects you might find in your bedroom.

Play the game

1. Play this game in pairs, using twelve flashcards (choose either the food or objects flashcards).

2. Place the cards in a pile, with the picture facing upwards.

3. Take turns picking up a card. When it is your turn to pick up a card, ask your partner the question **Qu'est-ce que c'est?**

4. Your partner should answer by saying **C'est un/une...** or **Ce sont des...** (depending on whether the item is masculine/feminine or singular/plural).

5. Turn over the card to check the answer. If your partner is correct, then he/she should keep the card. If not, put the card at the bottom of the pile. The winner is the player with most cards at the end.

Ma famille

My family

5

As-tu des frères ou des sœurs?
Have you got any brothers or sisters?
J'ai un frère et deux sœurs. Et toi?
I've got one brother and two sisters. What about you?
J'ai une sœur. Je n'ai pas de frères.
I've got one sister. I haven't got any brothers.

Top tips

You can use the word **voici** to introduce something or someone

Voici ma famille This is my family

★

There are three ways of saying "my" in French, depending on whether "my" is followed by a feminine, masculine, or plural noun

Ma tante My aunt
Mon oncle My uncle
Mes parents My parents

★

To ask if somebody has "any" brothers or sisters, you use the word **des**

As-tu des frères?
Have you got any brothers?

If your answer is "no", then you change **des** to **de**

Je n'ai pas de frères
I haven't got any brothers

★

To make a sentence negative in French, you put **ne** or **n'** immediately before the verb and **pas** immediately after it.

Je n'ai pas de sœurs
I haven't got a sister

Other words:
Maman Mum **Papa** Dad
Mamie Grandma **Papi** Grandpa

Puzzle

The photographs on the right show Susie, Nina, Antoine, and Michel with their brothers and sisters. Can you say which photograph belongs to each child?

1. Susie a une sœur et deux frères.
2. Nina a un frère et une sœur.
3. Antoine n'a pas de sœurs.
4. Michel a deux frères et une sœur.

A

B

C

D

Voici ma famille.
This is my family.

Mes grands-parents
My grandparents

Mon grand-père
My grandfather

Ma grand-mère
My grandmother

Mes parents
My parents

Mon père
My father

Ma mère
My mother

Mon oncle
My uncle

Ma tante
My aunt

Mon cousin
My cousin

Ma cousine
My cousin

Play the game

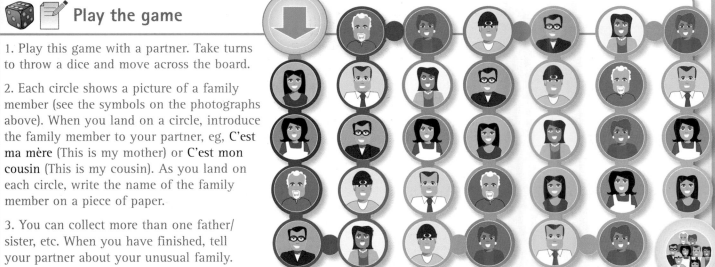

1. Play this game with a partner. Take turns to throw a dice and move across the board.

2. Each circle shows a picture of a family member (see the symbols on the photographs above). When you land on a circle, introduce the family member to your partner, eg, **C'est ma mère** (This is my mother) or **C'est mon cousin** (This is my cousin). As you land on each circle, write the name of the family member on a piece of paper.

3. You can collect more than one father/ sister, etc. When you have finished, tell your partner about your unusual family.

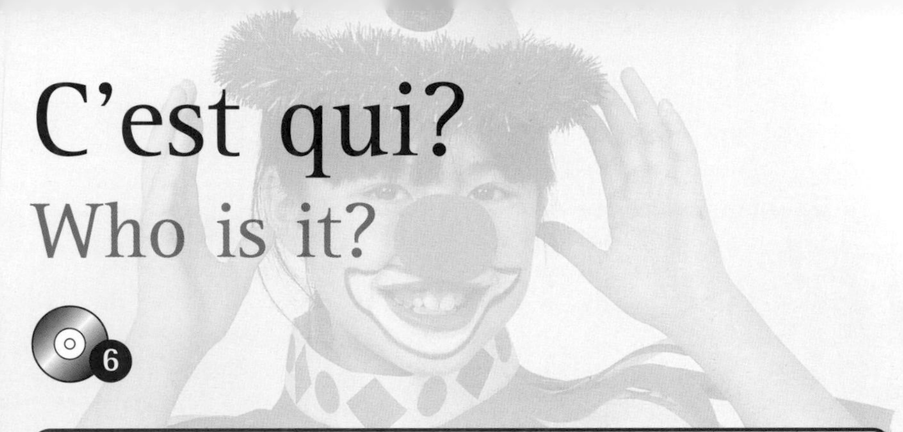

C’est qui?

Who is it?

6

What do they look like?

Il/elle est ...
He’s/She’s ...

Il est grand.
He’s tall.

Elle est petite.
She’s short.

Il est chauve.
He’s bald.

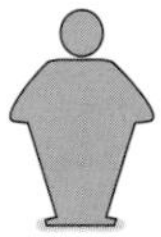

Elle est grosse.
She’s fat.

Il est mince.
He’s thin.

Elle est jeune.
She’s young.

Il est vieux.
He’s old.

Il/elle a ...
He’s/She’s got ...

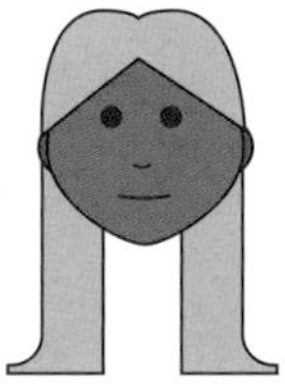

Elle a les cheveux longs.
She’s got long hair.

Elle a les cheveux foncés.
She’s got dark hair.

Il a les cheveux courts.
He’s got short hair.

Elle a les cheveux blonds.
She’s got fair hair.

Il a les yeux bruns.
He’s got brown eyes.

Il a une moustache.
He’s got a moustache.

Elle a les cheveux raides.
She’s got straight hair.

Il a une barbe.
He’s got a beard.

Elle a les cheveux frisés.
She’s got curly hair.

Elle a les cheveux bouclés.
She’s got wavy hair.

Philippe
Daniel
Aimée
Jean-Luc
Sophie

Puzzle

Look at the descriptions of these three children. Can you find them in the picture above?

1. Elle est grande.
   Elle a les cheveux bruns.
   Elle a les yeux bruns.
2. Il a les cheveux courts.
   Il a une moustache.
   Il n’a pas de barbe.
3. Il est chauve.
   Il n’est pas vieux.
   Il est grand.

Olivier
Isabelle
Marc
Marie
Jean
Charlotte
David
Sylvie
Pascale

Play the game

1. Play this game with a partner.

2. Take turns to choose a person in the picture above. Can you describe three things about him/her to your partner? You can use the extra expressions in the top tips as well as the examples on the left.

3. Your partner has to try and guess who you have chosen.

Top tips

In French, adjectives (describing words) change their endings depending on whether the noun they are describing is masculine, feminine, or plural.

You add an "e" to most adjectives when they describe a feminine word (unless they already end in an "e") and an "s" when they describe a plural word

Elle est grande She's tall

Elle a les cheveux blonds
She's got fair hair

★

Some adjectives don't follow this pattern, eg, **vieux** becomes **vieille** in the feminine form.

See page 152 to find out more about adjectives.

★

You use **les** with **cheveux** because "hair" is always plural in French.

★

Remember, to make a verb negative in French, you put **ne** immediately before the verb and **pas** immediately after it

Il n'est pas grand
He isn't tall

★

Your turn!
Can you describe yourself or your friends and family?

Other expressions:

Il a une cicatrice
He's got a scar

Elle a les taches de rousseur
She's got freckles

Il a le nez grand
He's got a big nose

Il porte un chapeau
He's wearing a hat

Elle porte des lunettes
She's wearing glasses

Il a les yeux bleus
He's got blue eyes

Où est le chat?

Where's the cat?

Où est le chat?
Where's the cat?
Je ne sais pas. Il n'est pas dans la cuisine.
I don't know. It's not in the kitchen.
Est-il dans la chambre?
Is it in the bedroom?
Non, il n'y est pas.
No, it isn't.
la souris
Il n'est pas dans la salle de bain.
It isn't in the bathroom.
Est-il dans le salon?
Is it in the living room?
Il est sur le fauteuil.
It's on the armchair.
Ah oui! Le voilà!
Oh yes! There it is!

8 Where are they?

Listen to the CD to find out where the cat (**le chat**) and dog (**le chien**) are. Point to the sentences as you hear them said aloud.

Il est à côté du fauteuil.
It's next to the chair.

Il est sous la table.
It's under the table.

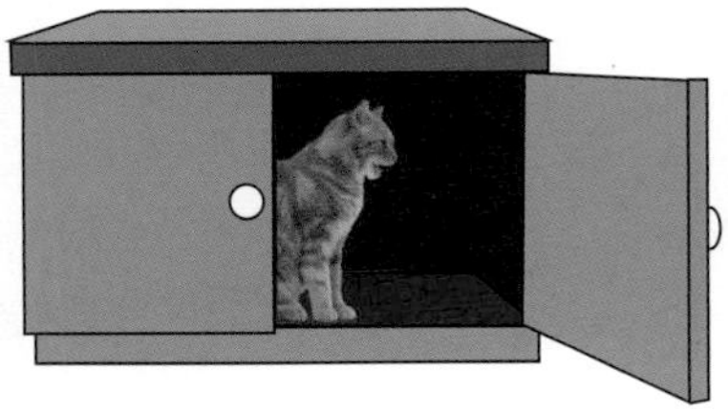

Il est dans l'armoire.
It's in the cupboard.

Il est sur le canapé.
It's on the sofa.

Il est devant la porte.
It's in front of the door.

Il est derrière la télévision.
It's behind the television.

Top tips

In French, there are two words for "it". You use **il** for masculine words and **elle** for feminine words.

★

Prepositions are words that describe where things are

Sous under **Sur** on

À côté de changes to **à côté du** when you use it before a masculine word

À côté du canapé Next to the sofa

★

To ask a question in French, you can often just change the order of the subject and verb and add a hyphen

Il est sur la table It is on the table
Est-il sur la table? Is it on the table?

★

The word **y** is used to mean "there"

Il n'y est pas It isn't there

★

Le voilà! means "There it is!" If you are referring to a feminine word, you say **La voilà!**

Other words:

entre between **au dessus de** above
au dessous de below
près de near to **loin de** far from

Puzzle

Look at the questions below. Can you find where these things are in the picture and match them to the correct answers on the right? The missing objects might be in a room – or they might be near to a piece of furniture, eg, **Où est la souris?** (Where is the mouse?). **Elle est sous la table** (It's under the table).

Où est la souris?	Il est dans la salle de bain.
Où est le chat?	Elle est à côté de l'armoire.
Où est le chien?	Il est dans la chambre.
Où est la télévision?	Elle est derrière le fauteuil.
Où est l'armoire?	Elle est dans la cuisine.
Où est la table?	Elle est sous la table.

À l'école
At school

9

10 Colours

Listen to the CD to hear the names of colours in French.

rouge
red
orange
orange
jaune
yellow
vert
green
bleu
blue
violet
purple
rose
pink
marron
brown
gris
grey
noir
black

le cahier
exercise book
la trousse
pencil case
le stylo
pen
les ciseaux
scissors
les crayons à papier
pencils
la gomme
rubber
la règl
ruler
la calculatrice
calculator
les crayons de couleu
coloured pencils
les livres
books

Combien de crayons à papier y a-t-il?
How many pencils are there?
Il y en a cinq.
There are five.
De quelle couleur sont-ils?
What colour are they?
Ils sont bleus.
They're blue.

Play the game

1. Play this game with a partner.
2. Choose an item from the desk and try to describe it to your partner. For example, you might say **Il/elle est rouge** (It is red) or **Il y en a cinq** (There are five of them).
3. Your partner has to guess what you are describing and say either **C'est un/une...** if there is only one object or **Ce sont des...** if there is more than one object.

es feutres
elt-tips
Combien de stylos y a-t-il?
How many pens are there?
Il y en a un.
There's one.
De quelle couleur est-il?
What colour is it?
Il est rouge.
It's red.

Top tips

You can use **il y a** to mean both "there is" and "there are"

Il y a un sac à dos
There is one rucksack

Il y a cinq stylos
There are five pens

★

To ask the question "How many... are there?", you say **Combien de... y a-t-il...?**

Combien de livres y a-t-il?
How many books are there?

To answer, you can use the word **en** to replace the noun **livres**

Il y en a cinq There are five of them

★

Colours change their endings in the same way as other adjectives

Une gomme verte A green rubber

Les feutres bleus Blue felt-tips

However, not all colours have feminine and masculine endings

marron (brown), **rose** (pink), and **orange** (orange) don't change in the feminine but they do add an "s" in the plural.

★

Your turn!
What objects can you see around you?
Can you say what colour they are?

Puzzle

Can you spot four differences between the two pencil cases below? Describe the differences in French.

photo no. 1

photo no. 2

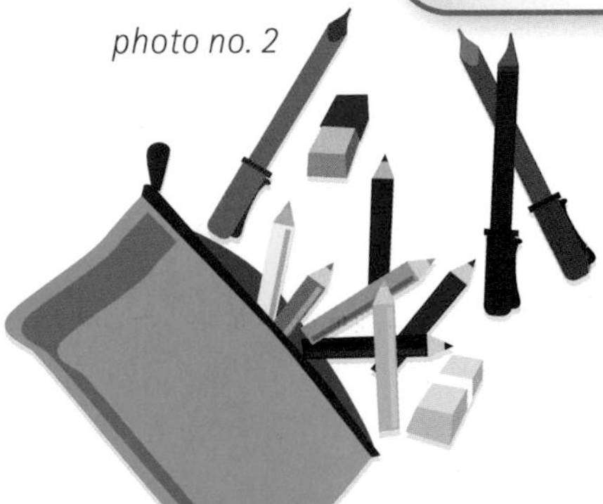

Sur la photo no. 1, il y a deux stylos.
Sur la photo no. 2, il y a trois stylos.

Touche ta tête

Touch your head

Lève-toi
Stand up

Assieds-toi
Sit down

Tourne-toi
Turn round

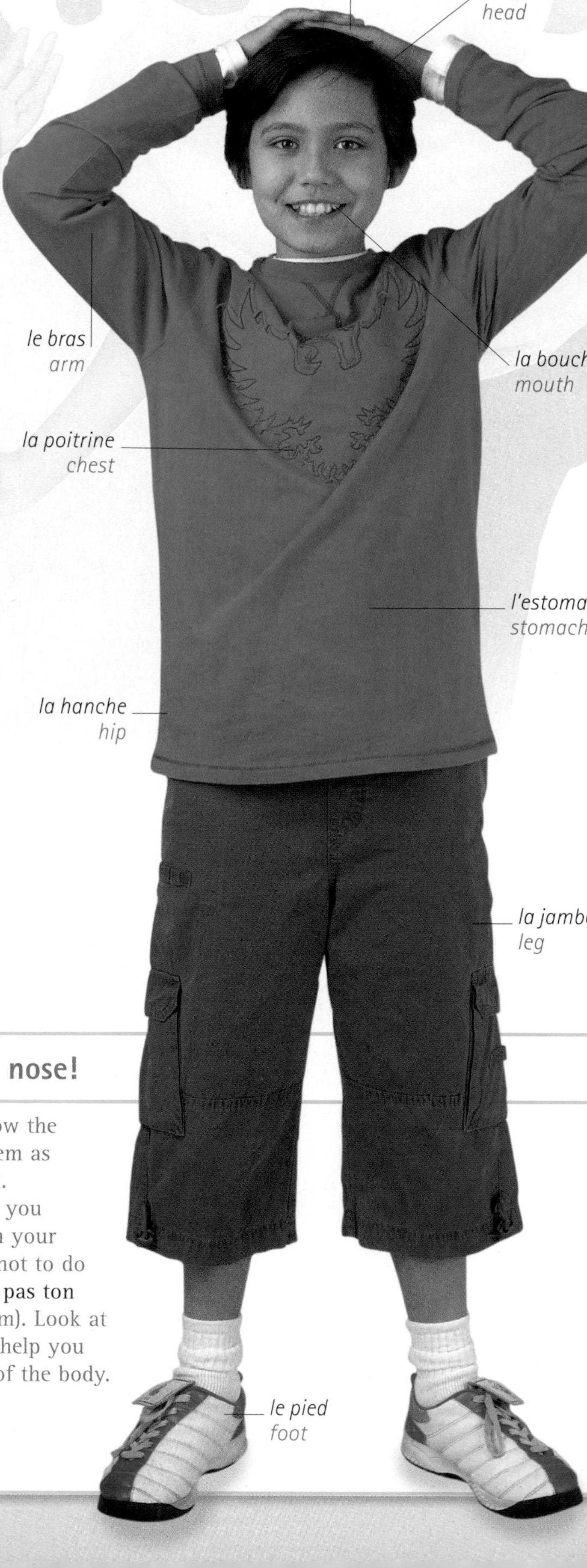
la main
hand
la tête
head
le bras
arm
la bouche
mouth
la poitrine
chest
l'estomac
stomach
la hanche
hip
la jambe
leg
le pied
foot

Montre tes oreilles
Point to your ears

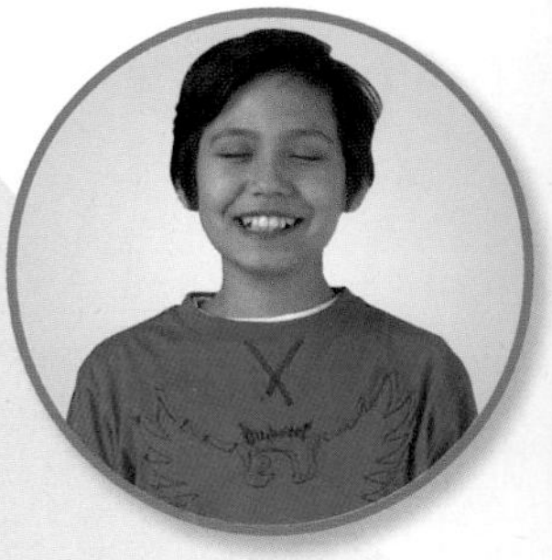

Ferme les yeux
Close your eyes

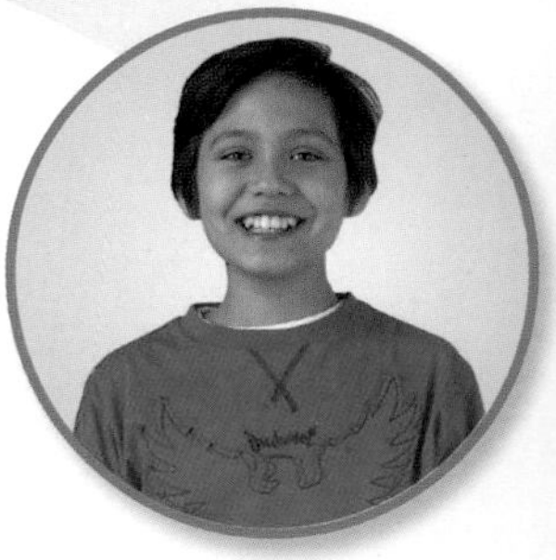

Ouvre les yeux
Open your eyes

Touche ton nez
Touch your nose

Ne touche pas tes pieds
Don't touch your feet

12 Touch your nose!

Listen to the CD and follow the instructions, repeating them as you carry out each action. The instruction might tell you to **Touche ton bras** (Touch your arm) or it might tell you not to do something, eg, **Ne touche pas ton bras** (Don't touch your arm). Look at the photo on the right to help you learn the names of parts of the body.

Play the game

1. Play this game with a partner. Take turns to throw a dice and move your counter.

2. Start at the green traffic light. When you land on an amber (orange) circle, say the instruction out loud and carry out the action shown.

3. If you land on a traffic light, go back to the beginning. The winner is the first person to reach the red traffic light.

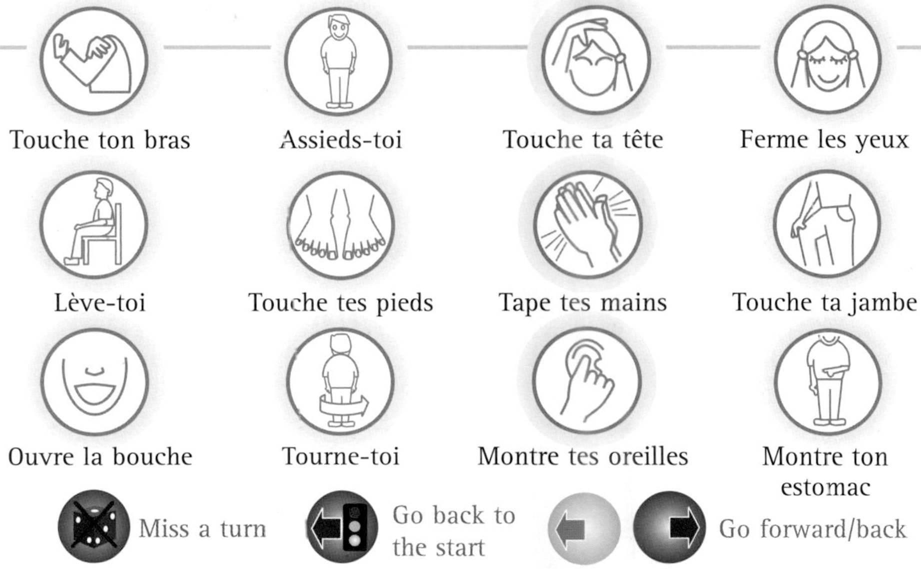

Touche ton bras
Assieds-toi
Touche ta tête
Ferme les yeux
Lève-toi
Touche tes pieds
Tape tes mains
Touche ta jambe
Ouvre la bouche
Tourne-toi
Montre tes oreilles
Montre ton estomac
Miss a turn
Go back to the start
Go forward/back

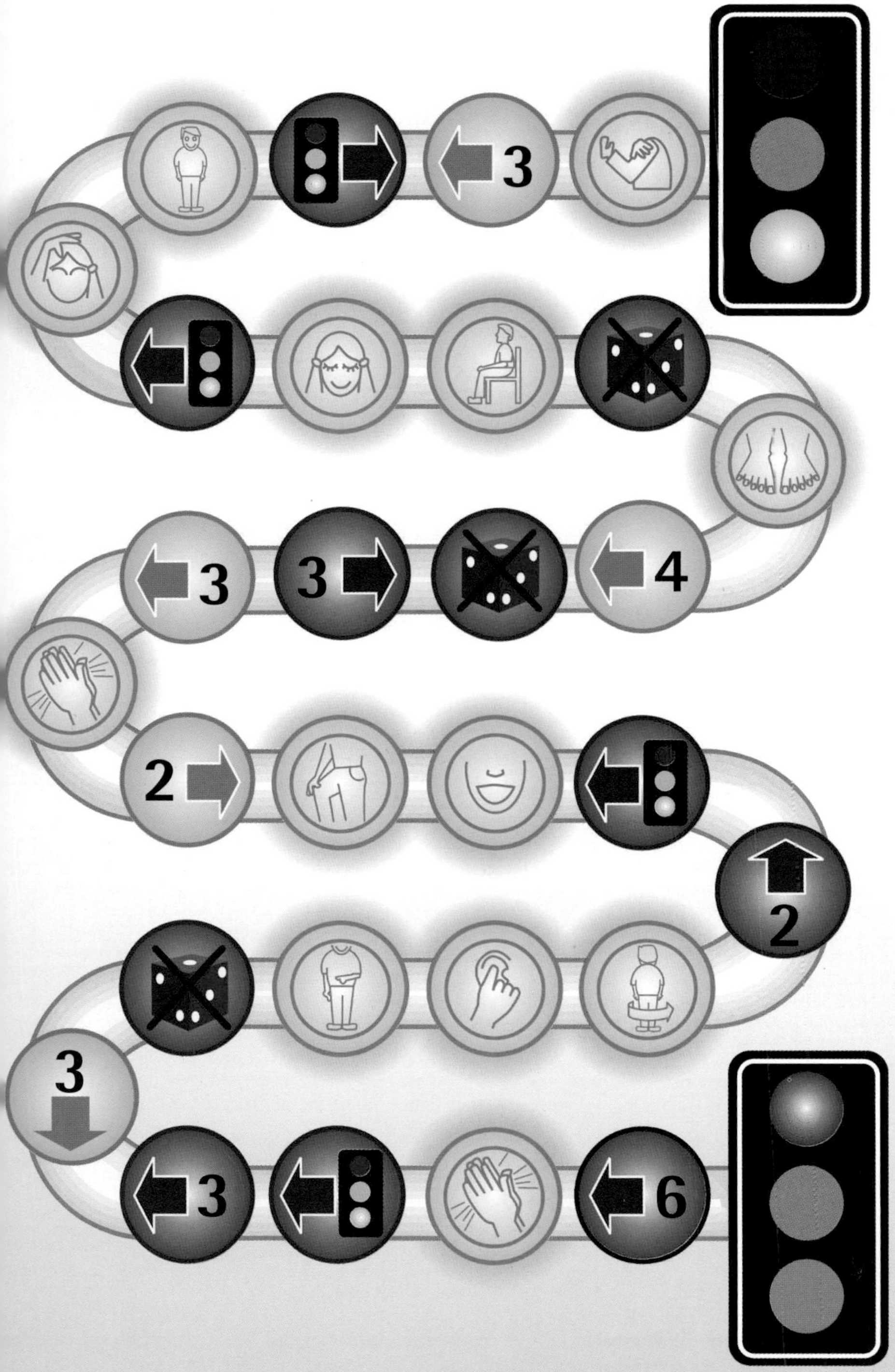

3
3
3
4
2
2
3
3
6

Top tips

To tell somebody to do something in French, you use a part of the verb called the imperative. Verbs that end in **-er** (as well as some verbs such as **ouvrir** and **montrer**), drop the "s" in the **tu** form of the imperative.

Tu fermes la porte You shut the door
Ferme la porte! Shut the door!

See page 155 to find out more about imperatives.

★

The verb **s'asseoir** (to sit down) is an irregular verb (it doesn't follow a regular pattern).

See page 154 to find out how **s'asseoir** is formed.

★

If a verb is reflexive, the pronoun (eg, **toi**) goes at the end and is joined to the verb by a hyphen

Lève-toi Stand up

If a verb is reflexive and you're telling someone not to do something, then the pronoun (**te**) goes before the verb

Ne te lève pas! Don't get up!

See page 65 to find more names of parts of the body.

Other expressions:

Saute à cloche-pied Hop on one leg
Lève la main Put your hand up

Aimes-tu les bananes?

Do you like bananas?

13

Aimes-tu le jus de pomme?
Do you like apple juice?
Oui, je l'aime.
Yes I do.
Aimes-tu les bananes?
Do you like bananas?
Oui, mais je n'aime pas les tomates.
Yes, but I don't like tomatoes.
les chips
les sandwichs
les carottes
le melon
les oranges
les gâteaux
le jus de pomme

Play the game

1. You can play this game with a partner, using the food flash cards. Place the cards in a pile with the picture facing upwards.

2. Pick up a card and ask your partner whether he/she likes the food shown on the card. If you pick up the card showing sweets, for example, you would ask **Aimes-tu les bonbons?** (Do you like sweets?).

3. Your partner should answer **Oui, je les aime** (Yes, I do like them) or **Non, je ne les aime pas** (No, I don't like them).

4. Put the foods your partner likes in one pile and those he/she doesn't like in another pile.

5. Count how many are in each pile, then let your partner ask you the same questions. Who likes the most foods?

Puzzle

These four lunchboxes belong to Tom, Grace, Alice, and Robert. Look at the sentences below and try to match each lunchbox to its correct owner.

1. Alice aime l'eau et les œufs. Elle n'aime pas les bananes.

2. Tom aime le jus d'orange et les sandwichs. Il n'aime pas les tomates.

3. Robert aime les sandwichs et le gâteau. Il n'aime pas les œufs.

4. Grace aime le jus de pomme, les bananes, et le fromage.

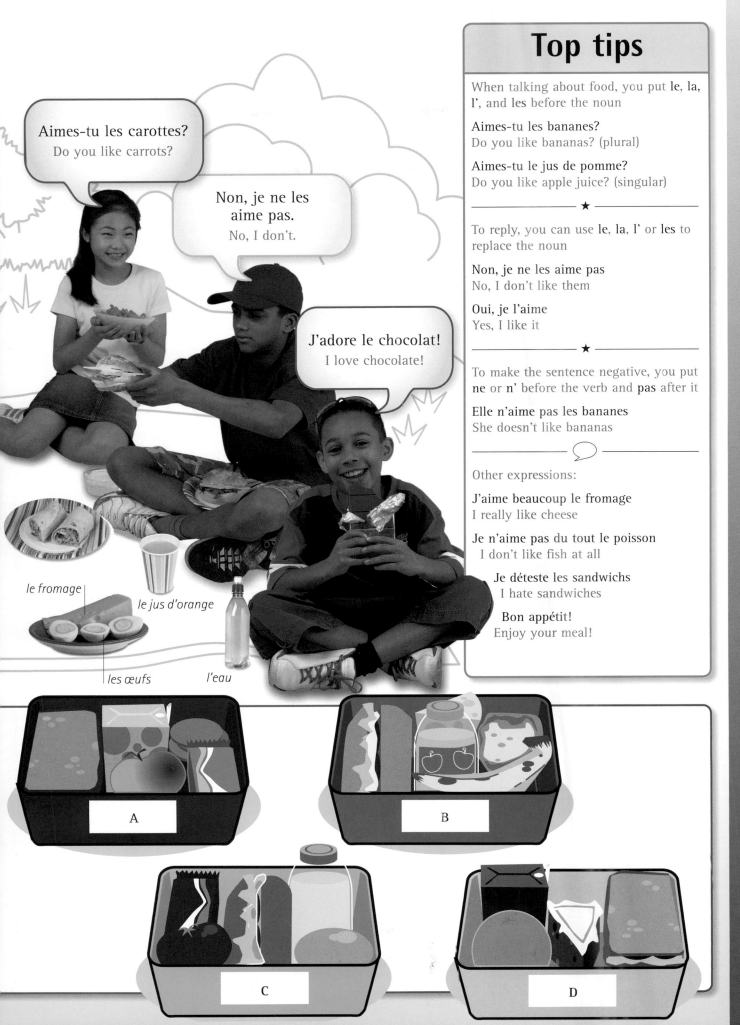

Aimes-tu les carottes?
Do you like carrots?
Non, je ne les aime pas.
No, I don't.
J'adore le chocolat!
I love chocolate!
le fromage
le jus d'orange
les œufs
l'eau

Top tips

When talking about food, you put **le**, **la**, **l'**, and **les** before the noun

Aimes-tu les bananes?
Do you like bananas? (plural)

Aimes-tu le jus de pomme?
Do you like apple juice? (singular)

★

To reply, you can use **le**, **la**, **l'** or **les** to replace the noun

Non, je ne les aime pas
No, I don't like them

Oui, je l'aime
Yes, I like it

★

To make the sentence negative, you put **ne** or **n'** before the verb and **pas** after it

Elle n'aime pas les bananes
She doesn't like bananas

Other expressions:

J'aime beaucoup le fromage
I really like cheese

Je n'aime pas du tout le poisson
I don't like fish at all

Je déteste les sandwichs
I hate sandwiches

Bon appétit!
Enjoy your meal!

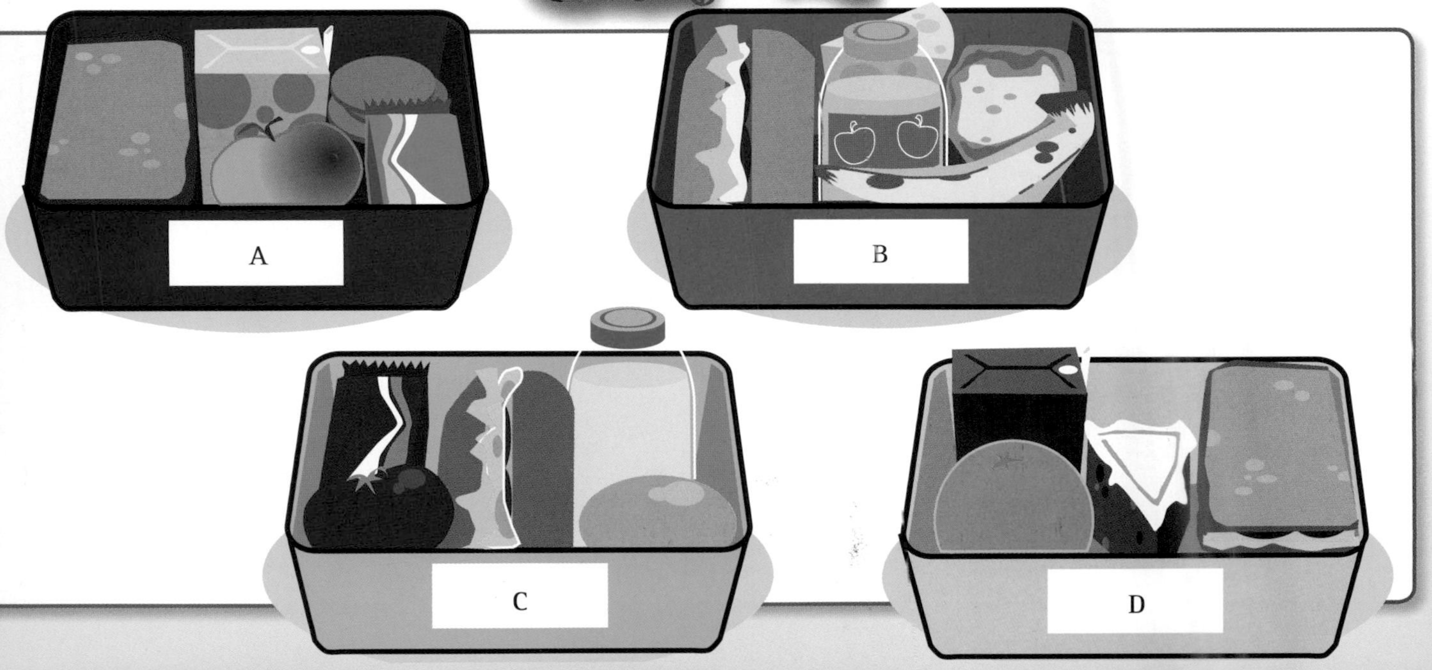
A
B
C
D

Quel temps fait-il?

What's the weather like?

Il fait froid.
It's cold.
Il fait chaud et il fait soleil.
It's hot and sunny.
Il pleut.
It's raining.

Puzzle

The photos below show four different types of weather. Can you match the descriptions of the weather to the correct picture?

Il y a du brouillard.
It's foggy.

Le temps est orageux.
It's stormy.

Le temps est couvert.
It's cloudy.

Il fait beaucoup de vent.
It's very windy.

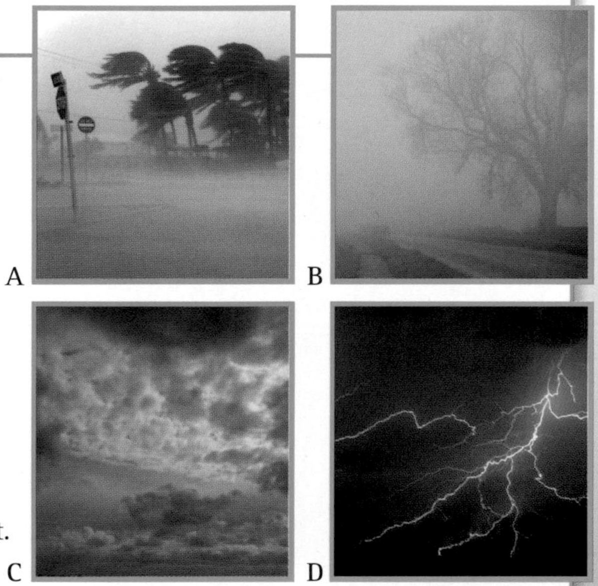

A
B
C
D

Play the game

1. Play this game with a partner. Take turns to throw the dice and move across the board.

2. If you land on a weather symbol, describe the weather in French. The winner is the first person to reach the rainbow.

- Il pleut
- Il neige
- Le temps est couvert
- Il fait chaud
- Il fait soleil
- Il fait froid
- Il fait du vent
- Go back

Il fait du vent.
It's windy.
Il neige.
It's snowing.

Top tips

To talk about the weather in French, you can use **Il fait** followed by an adjective

Il fait froid It's cold
Il fait chaud It's hot

★

You can also use **Il fait** followed by **du**

Il fait du vent It's windy

After the word beaucoup, du becomes de

Il fait beaucoup de vent It's very windy

★

Sometimes, you use a verb

Il pleut It's raining
Il neige It's snowing

Other words and expressions:

Les saisons The seasons
Le printemps spring
L'été summer
L'automne autumn
L'hiver winter
Il fait beau temps The weather's fine
Il fait mauvais temps The weather's bad
Il fait 12°C It's 12 degrees Celsius
un arc-en-ciel rainbow

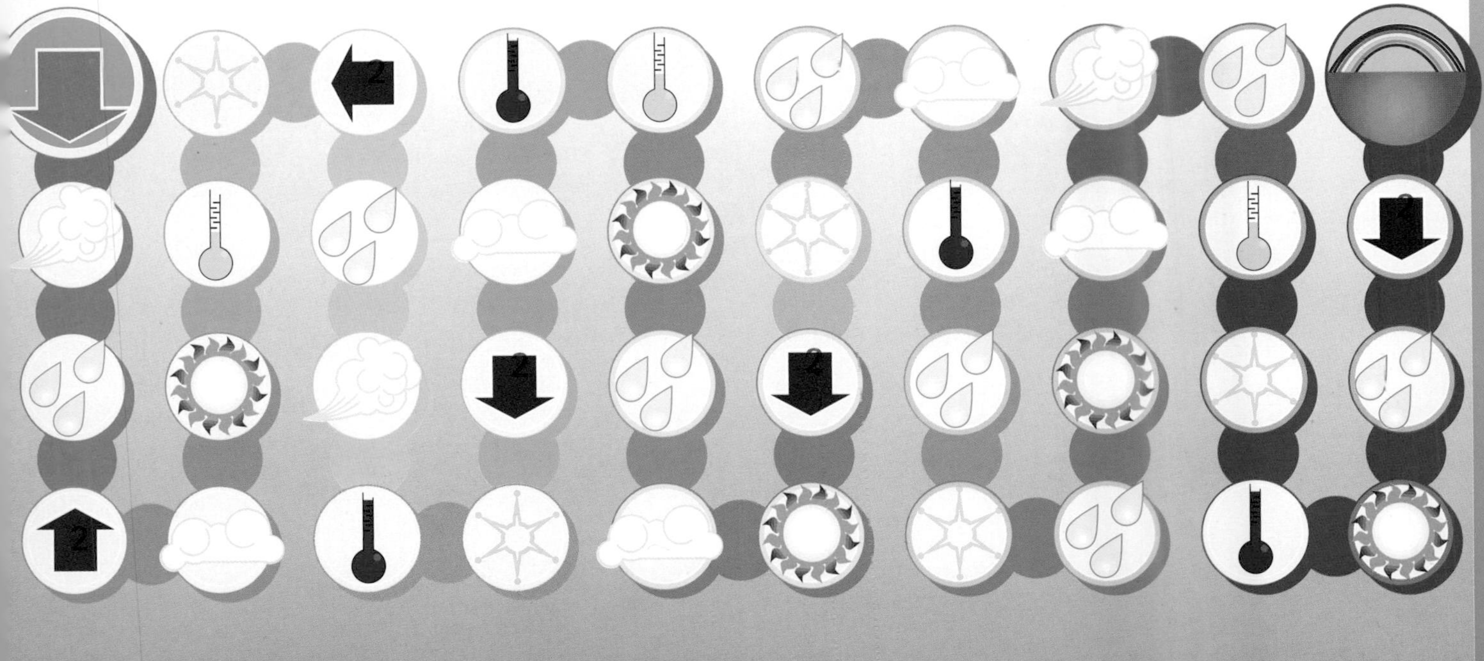

C'est un hippopotame!

It's a hippopotamus!

15

Il est petit. It's small.
Il est noir et blanc. It's black and white.
Il sait nager. It can swim.
Il ne sait pas voler. It can't fly.
C'est un pingouin! It's a penguin!

Elle est grande et mince.
It's tall and thin.
Elle a le cou long.
It's got a long neck.
Elle est marron et jaune.
It's brown and yellow.
Elle sait courir.
It can run.
C'est une giraffe!
It's a giraffe!

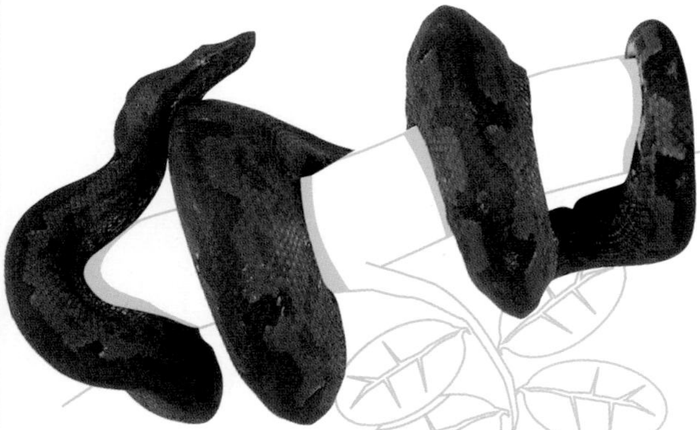

Il est long et mince.
It's long and thin.
Il ne sait pas courir.
It can't run.
Il sait grimper dans les arbres.
It can climb trees.
Il n'a pas de pattes.
It hasn't got legs.
C'est un serpent!
It's a snake!

Play the game

1. Play this game with a partner, using the animal flash cards.

2. Take six cards each and hold them in your hand. Take turns to describe each animal to your partner, using three different sentences, eg, **Il est marron/Il sait sauter/Il ne sait pas voler** (It's brown/It can jump/It can't fly).

3. If your partner guesses your animal correctly, he/she takes the card and puts it in a pile. If not, you take the card and put it in your pile. The winner is the player with the most cards in his/her pile at the end.

Play the game

1. Play this game with a partner, taking turns to throw a dice.

2. When you land on a circle, try to name an animal that fits the description on the board. Use the animal flash cards to help you.

3. Write each animal's name on a piece of paper. You can only say each animal once. If you can't think of an animal, or you repeat one that has already been said, you miss a turn.

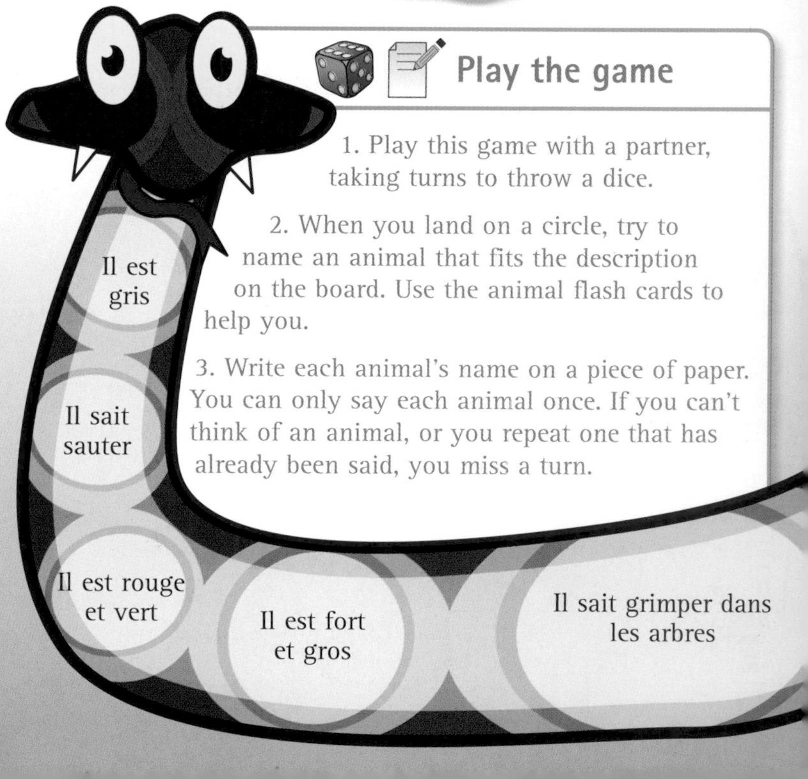
Il est gris
Il sait sauter
Il est rouge et vert
Il est fort et gros
Il sait grimper dans les arbres

Il est marron. It's brown.
Il a la queue longue. It's got a long tail.
Il ne sait pas voler. It can't fly.
Il sait sauter. It can jump.
C'est un kangourou! It's a kangaroo!

Il est rouge et vert.
It's red and green.
Il sait parler.
It can talk.
Il ne sait pas nager.
It can't swim.
Il sait voler.
It can fly.
C'est un perroquet!
It's a parrot!

Il est fort et gros.
It's big and fat.
Il est gris.
It's grey.
Il sait nager.
It can swim.
Il ne sait pas voler.
It can't fly.
C'est un hippopotame!
It's a hippopotamus!

Top tips

To say that an animal (or person) can do something, you use the verb **savoir**. **Savoir** means "to know how to do something"

Il sait voler
It can fly/It knows how to fly

★

You use **il** to refer to an animal if it's masculine and **elle** if it's feminine.

★

Colours change their endings in the same way as other adjectives, depending on whether they are describing a masculine or feminine noun

Il est gris It is grey (masculine)
Elle est grise It is grey (feminine)

★

Some colours, eg, **marron** (brown) and **orange** (orange) don't add an "e" when describing a feminine noun. Others change in a different way, eg, **blanc** (white) becomes **blanche** when describing a feminine noun.

You can find the names of more animals on pages 92–95.

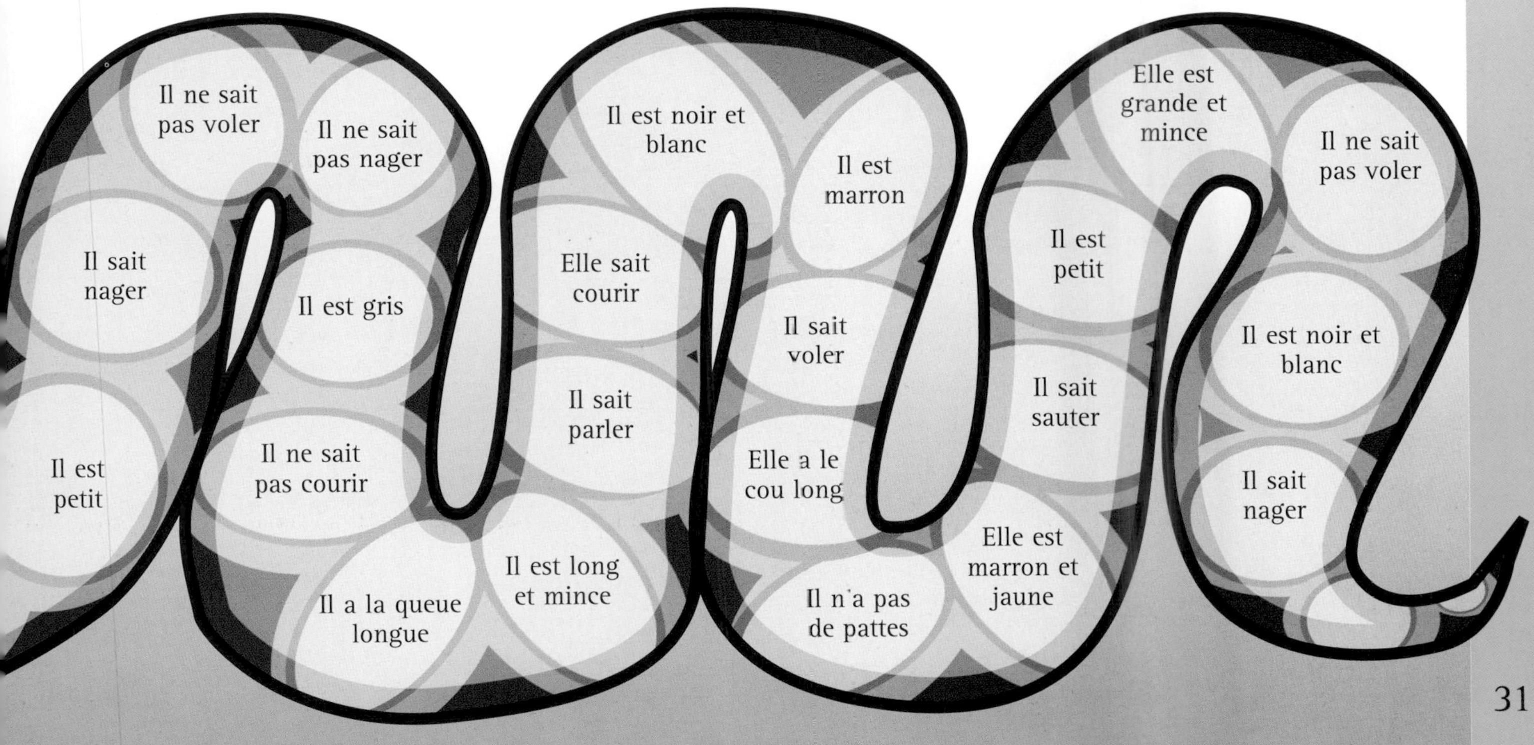

Il ne sait pas voler
Il ne sait pas nager
Il sait nager
Il est gris
Il est petit
Il ne sait pas courir
Il a la queue longue
Il est long et mince
Il sait parler
Elle sait courir
Il est noir et blanc
Il est marron
Il sait voler
Elle a le cou long
Il n'a pas de pattes
Elle est marron et jaune
Il sait sauter
Il est petit
Elle est grande et mince
Il ne sait pas voler
Il est noir et blanc
Il sait nager

Qu'est-ce que tu portes?

What are you wearing?

16

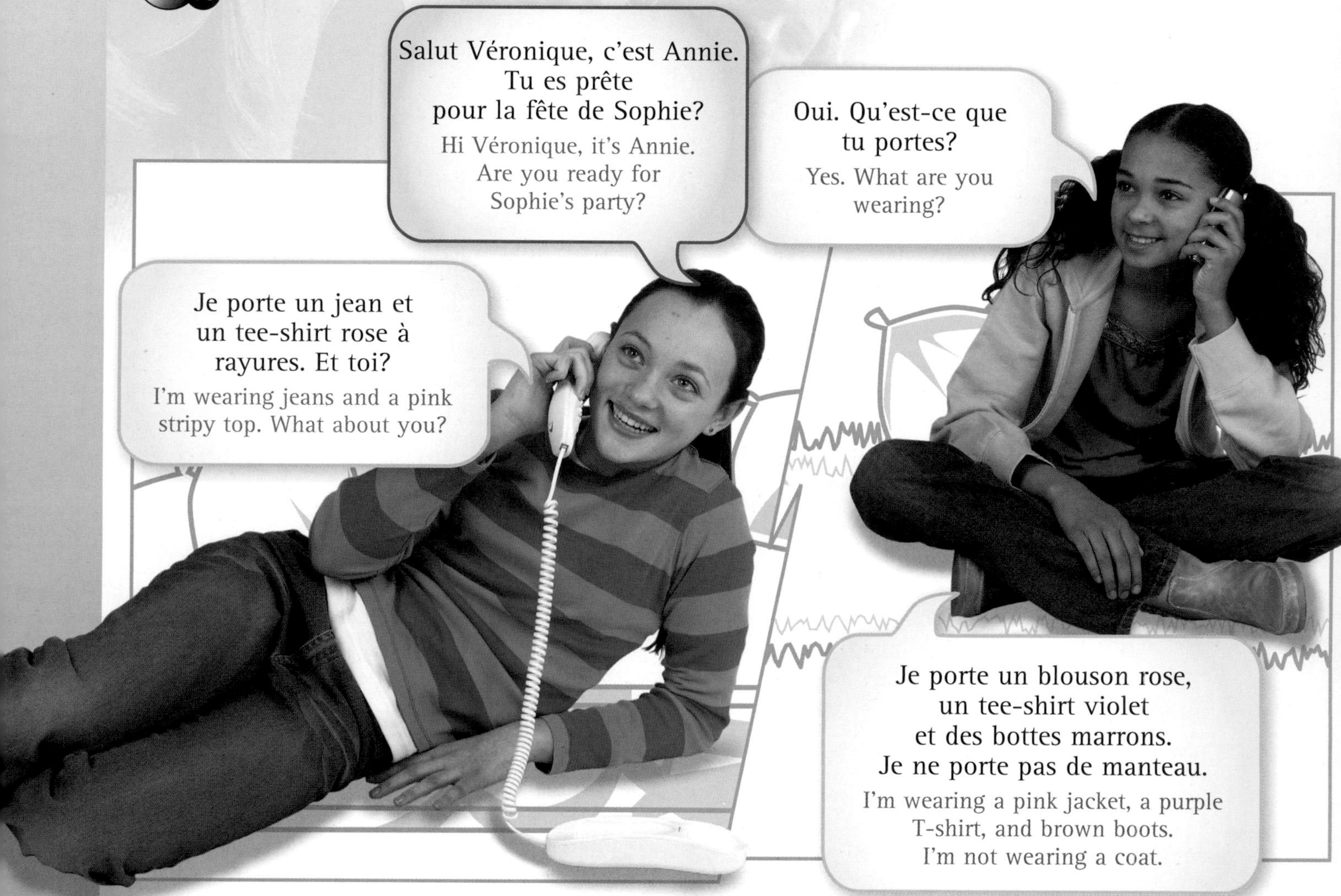
Salut Véronique, c'est Annie. Tu es prête pour la fête de Sophie?
Hi Véronique, it's Annie. Are you ready for Sophie's party?
Oui. Qu'est-ce que tu portes?
Yes. What are you wearing?
Je porte un jean et un tee-shirt rose à rayures. Et toi?
I'm wearing jeans and a pink stripy top. What about you?
Je porte un blouson rose, un tee-shirt violet et des bottes marrons. Je ne porte pas de manteau.
I'm wearing a pink jacket, a purple T-shirt, and brown boots. I'm not wearing a coat.

Play the game

1. Play this game with a partner, using the clothes flash cards. One player should collect the boy's clothes and the other should collect the girl's clothes. Spread out the flash cards with the picture facing upwards.

2. Take turns to throw a dice. If you throw a number one, you collect either the cap or the T-shirt. If you throw a two, you collect the jacket or trousers, and so on. As you pick up each card, say which item of clothing you have collected.

3. If you throw the same number more than once, you miss a turn. The winner is the first player to collect all six items of clothing for his or her character.

Boy's clothes

1. la casquette
   cap
2. le blouson
   jacket
3. le jean
   jeans
4. le pull
   sweater
5. les chaussettes
   socks
6. les baskets
   trainers

Girl's clothes

1. le tee-shirt
   T-shirt
2. le pantalon
   trousers
3. la jupe
   skirt
4. le manteau
   coat
5. la robe
   dress
6. les chaussures
   shoes

Salut Christian! Qu'est-ce que tu portes pour le voyage scolaire?
Hi Christian. What are you wearing for the school trip?
Je porte un jean et une chemise bleue et blanche à carreaux. Et toi?
I'm wearing my jeans and my blue-and-white checked shirt. What about you?
Je porte un jean et un sweat-shirt bleu.
I'm wearing jeans and my blue sweatshirt.

Puzzle

Look at the descriptions on the right and see if you can find out which three children are wearing the clothes described. Then see if you can say what the other children are wearing in French.

1. Il porte un pantalon bleu, des chaussures vertes et un tee-shirt jaune et gris.
2. Elle porte une jupe bleue et un tee-shirt rose.
3. Il porte un jean, un tee-shirt blanc et un blouson vert.

Corinne
Giles
Danielle
Christophe
David
Fabienne

Top tips

When you are talking on the telephone in French, you begin by saying **Salut, c'est...** followed by your name

Salut, c'est Annie Hello, it's Annie

★

To describe what you are wearing, you use the verb **porter** (to wear).

For more information on verbs that end in **–er**, see page 153.

★

All items of clothing are masculine or feminine

Une jupe verte A green skirt
Un tee-shirt violet A purple T-shirt

Remember, adjectives go after the noun in French.

★

Some nouns that are plural in English are singular in French, eg, **le jean** (jeans) and **le pantalon** (trousers)

Je porte un jean
I'm wearing jeans
Il porte un pantalon bleu
He's wearing blue trousers

★

If a noun is plural, you use **des** before it

Il porte des baskets
He's wearing trainers

Elle porte des bottes
She's wearing boots

See pages 66–67 to find more items of clothing.

Other words and expressions:

La mode
Fashion
C'est à la mode
It's fashionable
Le manteau te va bien
The coat suits you

Chez le médecin

At the doctor's

17
Qu'est-ce que tu as?
What's the matter?
J'ai mal au pied.
I've got a sore foot.
Je tousse.
I've got a cough.
Elle a mal à la gorge.
She's got a sore throat.

Play the game

1. Play this game with a partner. Take turns to throw a dice and move across the board.

2. Each circle shows a symbol representing an illness. When you land on a symbol, your partner should ask **Qu'est-ce que tu as?** (What's the matter?) Try to describe your illness to your partner, eg, **J'ai mal à la gorge** (I've got a sore throat).

3. Your partner should then advise you to **Vas te coucher** (Go to bed) or **Vas chez le médecin** (Go to the doctor's).

4. Each time you land on a symbol, write the illness down on a piece of paper. When you have had five different illnesses, your partner should say **Vas à l'hôpital** (Go to hospital) and you are out of the game!

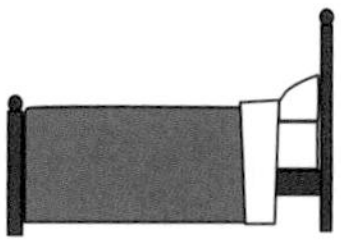

Vas te coucher!
Go to bed!

Vas chez le médecin!
Go to the doctor's!

Vas à l'hôpital!
Go to hospital!

J'ai un rhume.
I've got a cold.
J'ai le bras cassé.
I've got a broken arm.
J'ai mal à l'estomac.
I've got a stomach ache.

Top tips

Chez le médecin means "At the doctor's". You can also use the word **chez** in the phrases **Chez David** (At David's house) or **Chez moi** (At my house).

★

To describe some illnesses in French, you use a verb

Je tousse I've got a cough

You can also use the expression **J'ai mal à...** The **à** in **J'ai mal à** becomes **au** before masculine nouns and **aux** before plural nouns

J'ai mal aux oreilles I've got earache

Find more names for parts of the body on page 65.

Other expressions:

Où est-ce que tu as mal?
Where does it hurt?
Il me fait mal It hurts
Il me fait très mal It really hurts
J'ai de la fièvre I've got a temperature
Guerris vite! Get well soon!

Que font-ils?
What are they doing?

Ils jouent au foot.
They're playing football.

Ils nagent.
They're swimming.

Elle joue au tennis.
She's playing tennis.

Elle court.
She's running.

Elles dansent.
They're dancing.

Ils jouent au basket.
They're playing basketball.

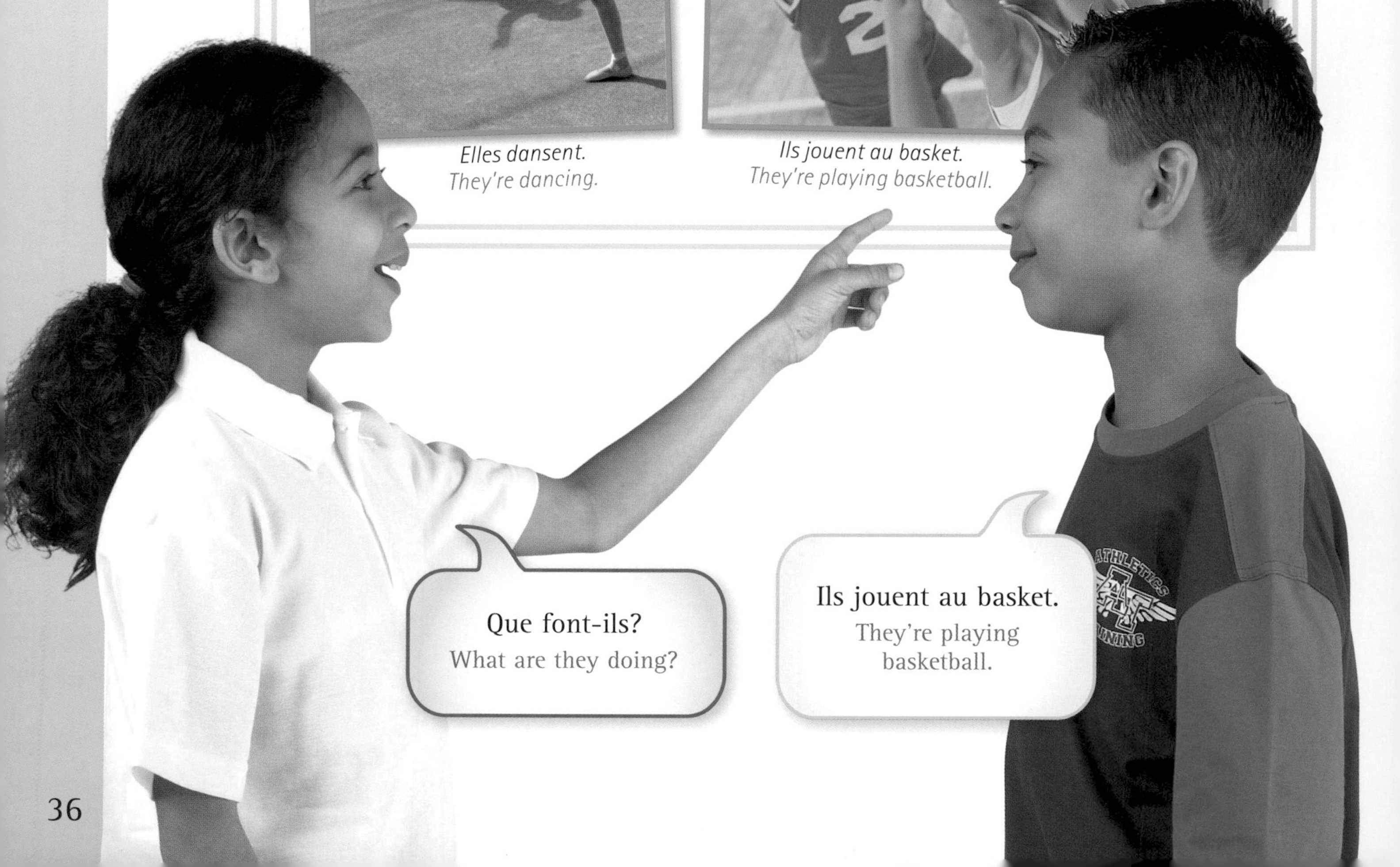
Que font-ils?
What are they doing?
Ils jouent au basket.
They're playing basketball.

Top tips

In French, you use **ils** (they) if there is more than one person (or a mixture of boys and girls). You use **elles** if you are talking about girls only.

★

In French, verb endings change to show that there is more than one person

Ils nagent They're swimming (boys and girls, or all boys)

Elles dansent They're dancing (all girls)

★

When you are talking about sports and hobbies, you use the verb **jouer** (to play) followed by the preposition **à**. If the sport is masculine, **à** becomes **au**

Je joue au rugby I'm playing rugby
Je joue au tennis I'm playing tennis

★

You sometimes use the verb **faire** (to do) followed by **de** and the sport

Elle fait de la gymnastique
She's doing gymnastics

Il fait du vélo He's cycling

See pages 80–81 for more sports and hobbies.

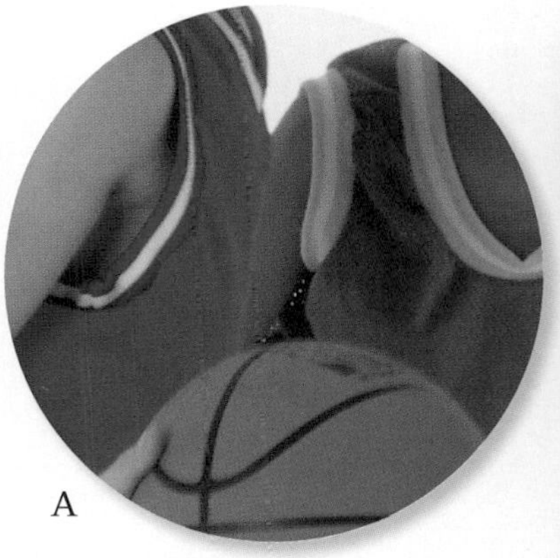

A

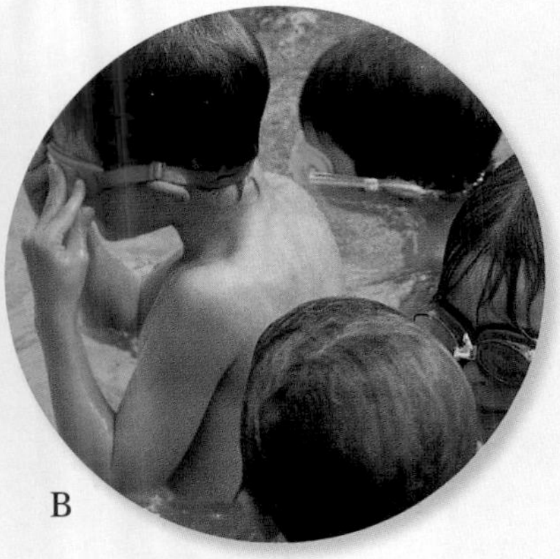

B

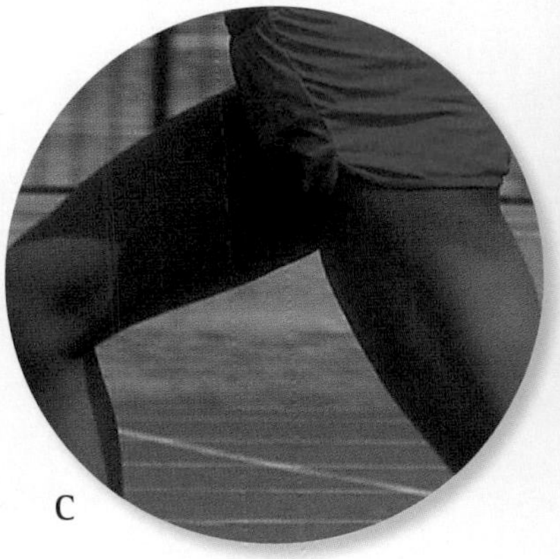

C

Giro
AIR ATTACK

D

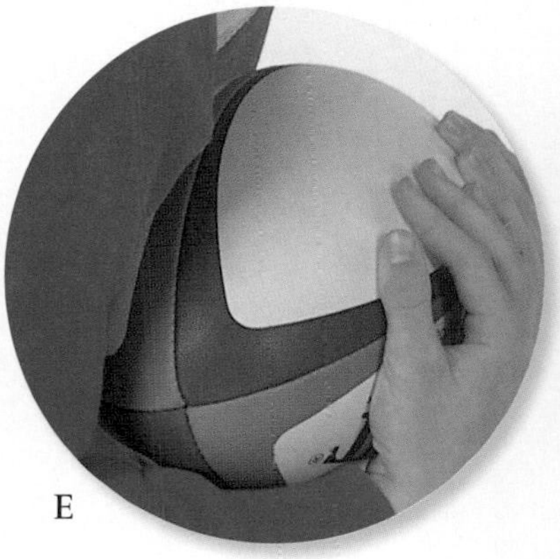

E

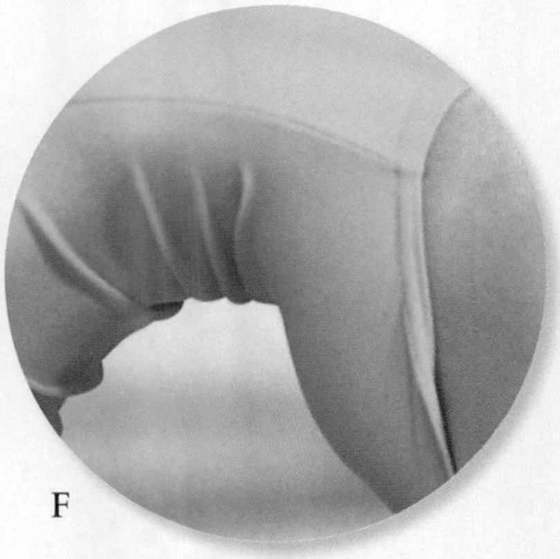

F

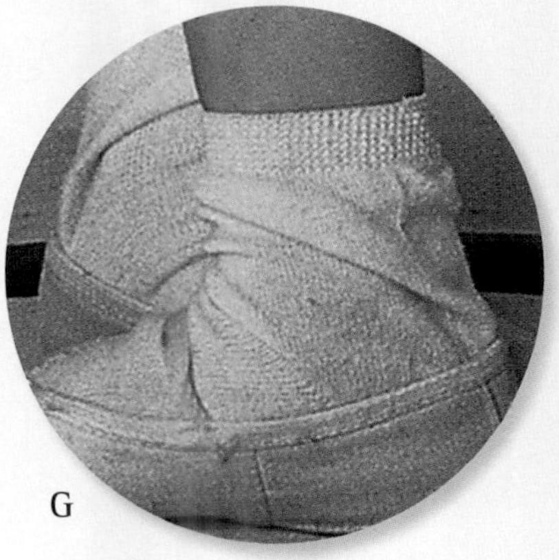

G

Play the game

1. Play this game with a partner. Write the following sentences down on six pieces of paper.

Je joue au tennis.
Je nage.
Je cours.
Je joue au basket.
Je joue au foot.
Je danse.

2. Fold up the bits of paper, then mix them up and put them in a pile. Take turns to pick up a piece of paper.

3. Try to guess what sport is on your partner's piece of paper by asking questions such as **Tu nages?** (Are you swimming?).

4. Each player has three guesses. If you guess correctly and your partner answers **Oui, je nage** (Yes, I'm swimming), you keep the piece of paper. If your partner answers **Non, je ne nage pas** (No, I'm not swimming), the piece of paper goes back on the pile.

5. The winner is the player who has the most pieces of paper at the end.

Puzzle

Can you identify what the children are doing in these close-up photos? Say your answers out loud in French. Look at the examples in the Top tips box to find some of the answers.

Comment est-il?
What does it look like?

une coccinelle
a ladybird

De quelle couleur est-elle?
What colour is it?
A-t'elle des rayures?
Has it got stripes?
Combien de pattes a-t'elle?
How many legs has it got?

Il a des ailes.
It's got wings.
Il n'a pas de rayures.
It hasn't got stripes.
Il a six pattes.
It's got six legs.

un scarabée
a beetle

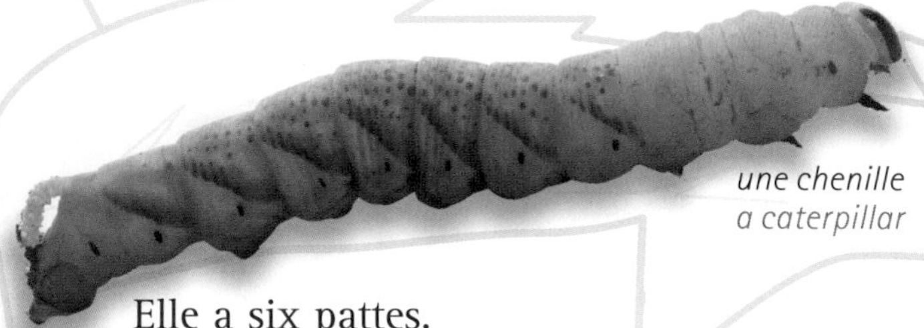

une chenille
a caterpillar

Elle a six pattes.
It's got six legs.
Elle n'a pas d'ailes.
It hasn't got wings.
Elle a des rayures.
It's got stripes.

une araignée
a spider

Combien de pattes a-t'elle?
How many legs has it got?
A-t'elle des ailes?
Has it got wings?
A-t'elle des taches?
Has it got spots?

Play the game

1. Play this game in pairs or in a small group. Each player should take a piece of paper and fold it into six sections.

2. Take turns to throw a dice. Each number on the dice corresponds to a part of the beetle's body.

3. If you throw the number one, then draw the top left part of the beetle's body on the piece of paper. If you throw the number six, draw the bottom right part of the beetle, etc.

4. If you throw the same number more than once, you miss a turn.

5. The winner is the first player to draw a complete beetle and shout Scarabée! (Beetle!).

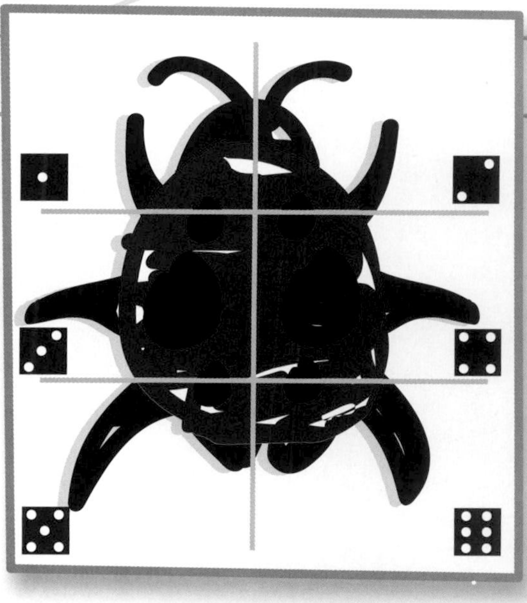

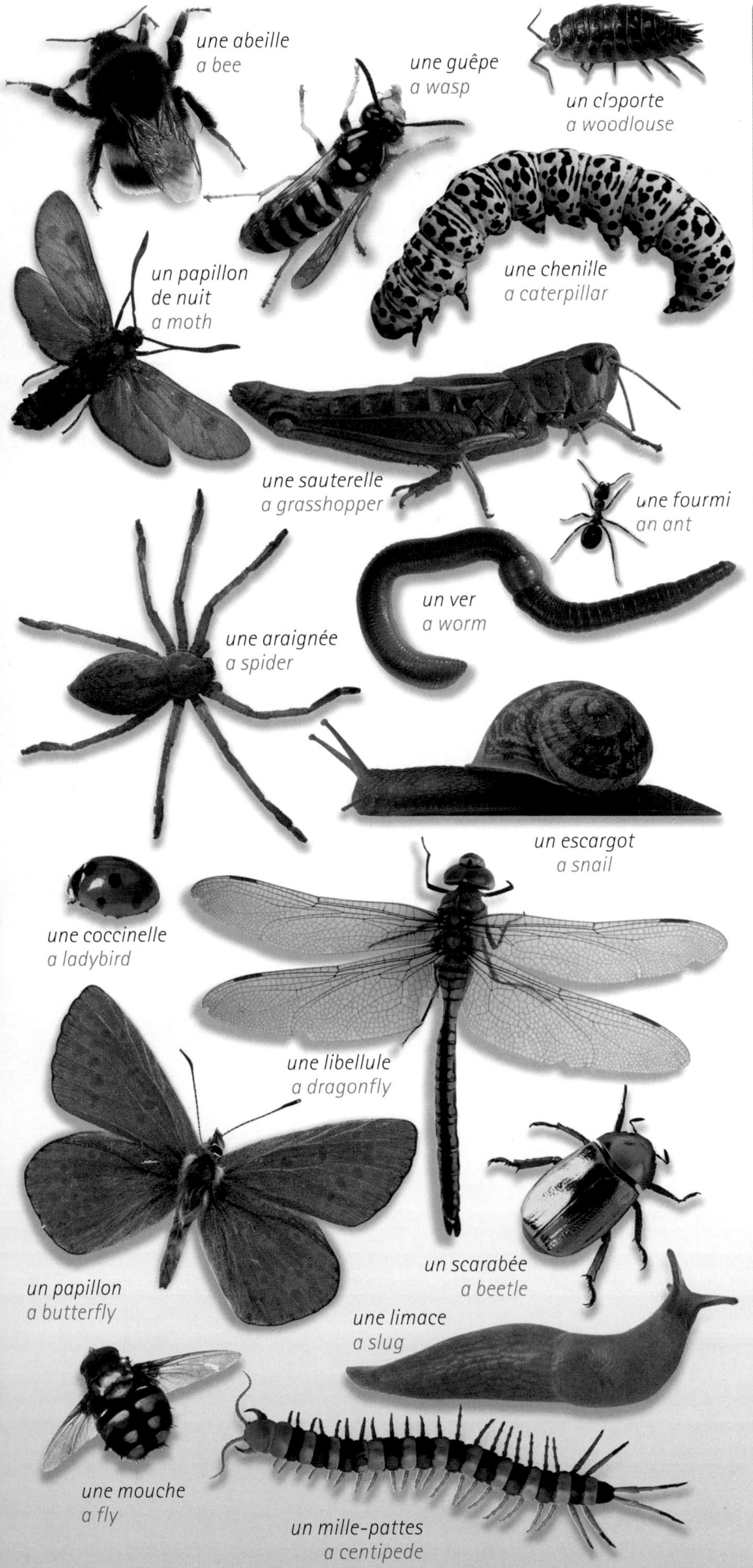
une abeille
a bee
une guêpe
a wasp
un cloporte
a woodlouse
un papillon de nuit
a moth
une chenille
a caterpillar
une sauterelle
a grasshopper
une fourmi
an ant
un ver
a worm
une araignée
a spider
un escargot
a snail
une coccinelle
a ladybird
une libellule
a dragonfly
un scarabée
a beetle
un papillon
a butterfly
une limace
a slug
une mouche
a fly
un mille-pattes
a centipede

Top tips

All animals are either masculine or feminine in French

C'est une coccinelle It's a ladybird
C'est un scarabée It's a beetle

★

If you don't know whether a noun is feminine or masculine in French, you use **il**

Comment est-il? What's it like?

However, if you know that the noun is feminine, you use **elle**

Comment est-elle? What's it like?

★

In French, you use **des** to mean "some" or "any"

Il a des taches
It's got (some) spots

A-t'il des taches?
Has it got (any) spots?

★

Remember that **des** becomes **de** or **d'** after a negative

Il n'a pas d'ailes It hasn't got wings

Elle n'a pas de rayures It hasn't got stripes

See pages 92–95 to find more animals and insects.

Puzzle

1. Ask a partner to choose a creature from the photographs on the left. Then try to guess which creature your partner has chosen by asking questions such as **De quelle couleur est-il?** (What colour is it?) or **A-t'il des rayures?** (Has it got stripes?).

2. Your partner should answer **C'est un...** or **C'est une...** (depending on whether the creature is masculine or feminine). Take turns to ask each other questions.

Quel jour sommes-nous aujourd'hui?

What day is it?

20

Quel jour sommes-nous aujourd'hui?
What day is it?
Nous sommes lundi.
It's Monday.
Nous avons maths aujourd'hui.
We've got Maths today.
Oh non!
Oh no!

21 Days of the week

Listen to the CD to find how to say the days of the week. Then listen to the names of the subjects you learn at school.

lundi
mardi
mercredi
jeudi
vendredi
samedi
dimanche

géographie
Geography

histoire
History

maths
Maths

éducation physique
PE

Play the game

1. Play this game with a partner. Choose your four favourite subjects from the eight subjects shown in the box above and list them on a piece of paper under the heading **Hourra!** (Hooray!). Then list your four least favourite subjects under the heading **Oh, non!** (Oh no!).

2. Start on Monday. Take it in turns to throw a dice and move down the board.

3. If you land on a subject you like, say **Hourra! Nous avons histoire aujourd'hui** (Hooray! We've got History today). If you land on a subject you don't like, say **Oh, non! Nous avons dessin aujourd'hui** (Oh no! We've got art today).

4. Every time you say **Hourra!** move forward one space. Every time you say **Oh, non!** go back one space. The winner is the first person to get to the weekend.

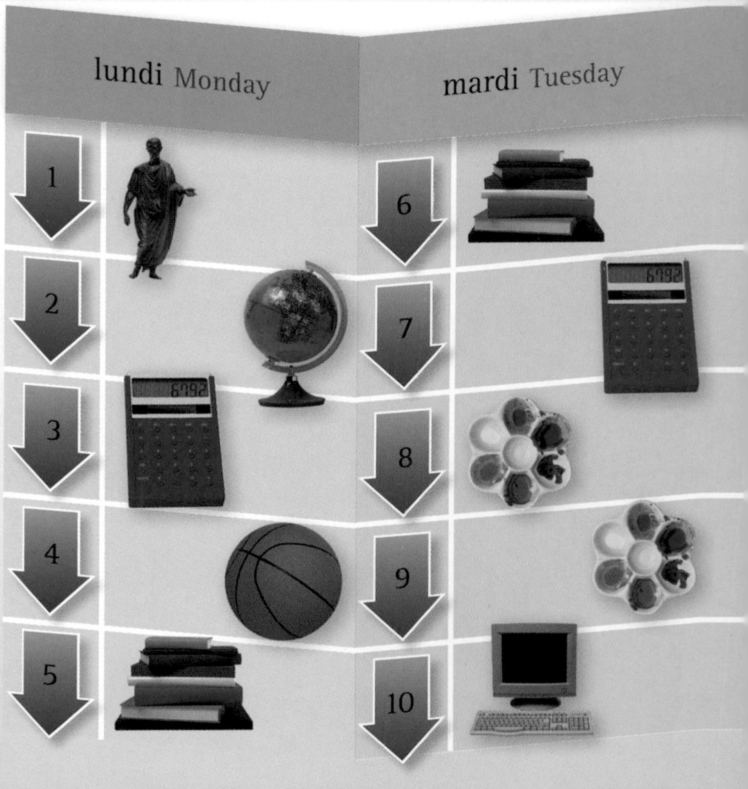
lundi Monday
mardi Tuesday
1
2
3
4
5
6
7
8
9
10

Nous avons éducation physique aujourd'hui.
We've got PE today.
Hourra!
Hooray!

anglais English	informatique IT	dessin Art	sciences naturelles Science

Top tips

There are two ways of saying "it's Monday" in French

Nous sommes lundi It's Monday
Aujourd'hui, c'est lundi
It's Monday today

Demain c'est mardi
Tomorrow is Tuesday

★

Days of the week are not written with capital letters in French.

★

Le lundi means "On Mondays" in general. If you are talking about a specific Monday, you just say lundi

Le lundi nous avons histoire
We have history on Mondays

Lundi je vais chez le docteur
On Monday, I'm going to the doctor

★

Your turn!
Can you say what day it is today?

Other words and expressions:
Demain Tomorrow
Hier Yesterday
C'est le weekend It's the weekend
Le weekend At the weekend

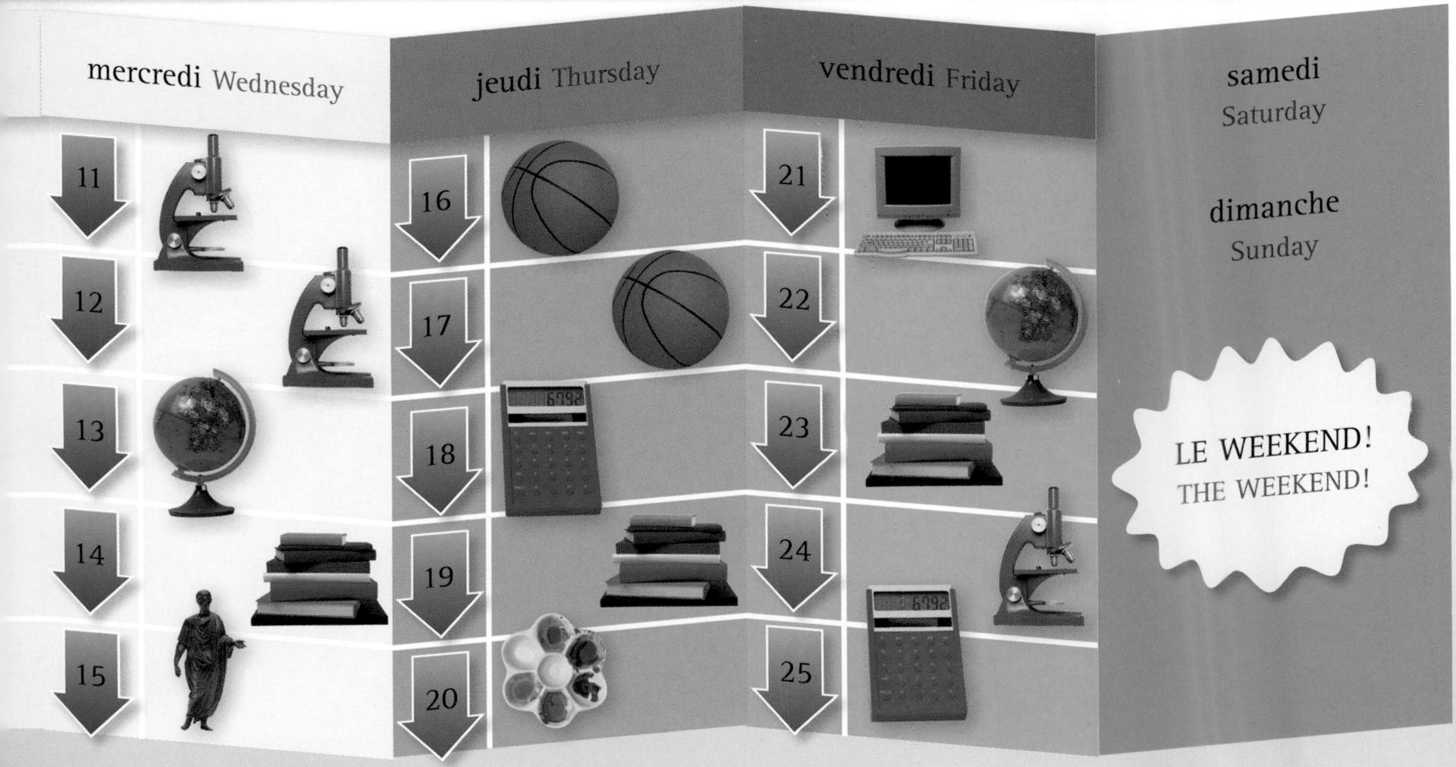
mercredi Wednesday
jeudi Thursday
vendredi Friday
samedi
Saturday
dimanche
Sunday
11
12
13
14
15
16
17
18
19
20
21
22
23
24
25
LE WEEKEND!
THE WEEKEND!

C'est quand ton anniversaire?

When's your birthday?

22

C'est quand ton anniversaire?
When's your birthday?
C'est le quatre avril.
It's on the fourth of April.

janvier January	février February	mars March
avril April	mai May	juin June
juillet July	août August	septembre September
octobre October	novembre November	décembre December

23 What's the date?

Listen to the CD to find out how to say the date. Point to each date as you hear it said aloud.

				1st le premier	2nd le deux	3rd le trois
4th le quatre	5th le cinq	6th le six	7th le sept	8th le huit	9th le neuf	10th le dix
11th le onze	12th le douze	13th le treize	14th le quatorze	15th le quinze	16th le seize	17th le dix-sept
18th le dix-huit	19th le dix-neuf	20th le vingt	21st le vingt et un	22nd le vingt-deux	23rd le vingt-trois	24th le vingt-quatre
25th le vingt-cinq	26th le vingt-six	27th le vingt-sept	28th le vingt-huit	29th le vingt-neuf	30th le trente	31st le trente et un

Top tips

For dates, you use **le premier** for the first day of each month

le premier mai May 1st

For all other dates, you use **le** followed by the number

le seize juillet July 16th

★

Months are not written with a capital letter in French.

★

Your turn!
Can you say what the date is today?

Other expressions:

Joyeux Noël Happy Christmas!
Joyeuses Pâques Happy Easter!
Bonne année! Happy New Year!
Bonnes vacances! Happy Holidays!

Play the game

1. Play this game with a partner or in a small group. Take it in turns to throw a dice and move round the board.

2. When you land on a strawberry, say the date you have landed on, eg, **C'est le douze novembre** (It's the twelfth of November). If you land on your birthday (or the birthday of someone you know) say **C'est mon anniversaire** or **C'est l'anniversaire à papa**, etc.

3. The winner is the first player to reach the kiwi in the centre of the birthday cake.

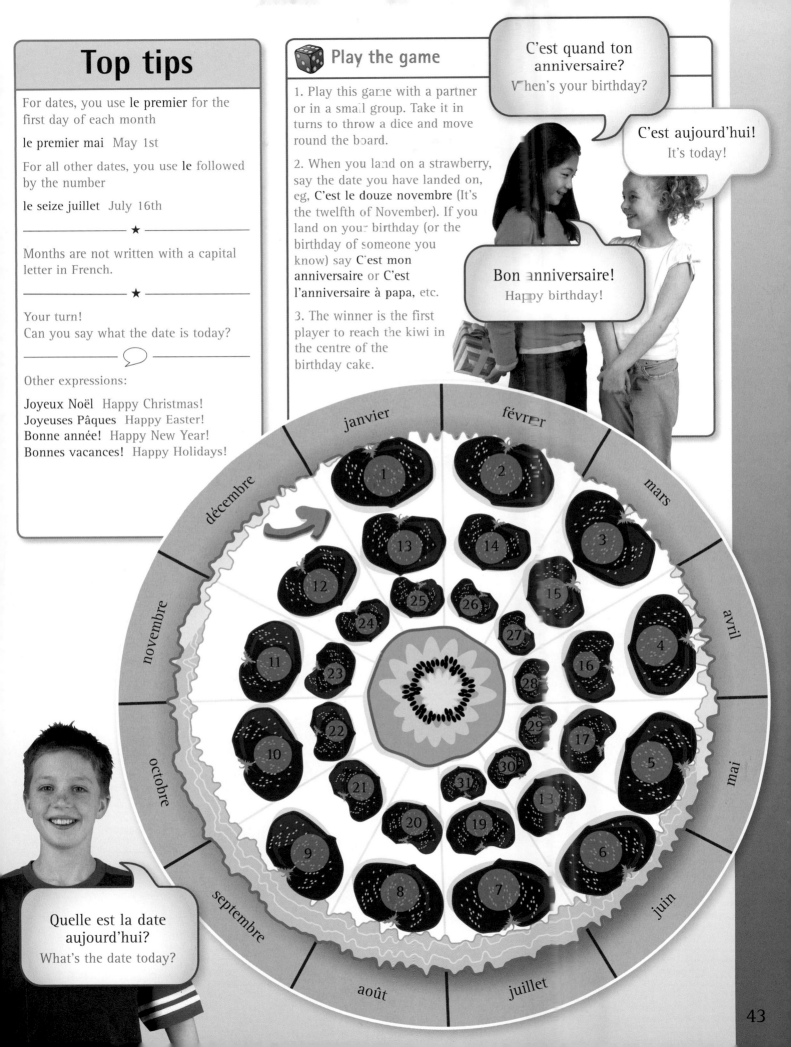

C'est quand ton anniversaire?
When's your birthday?
C'est aujourd'hui!
It's today!
Bon anniversaire!
Happy birthday!

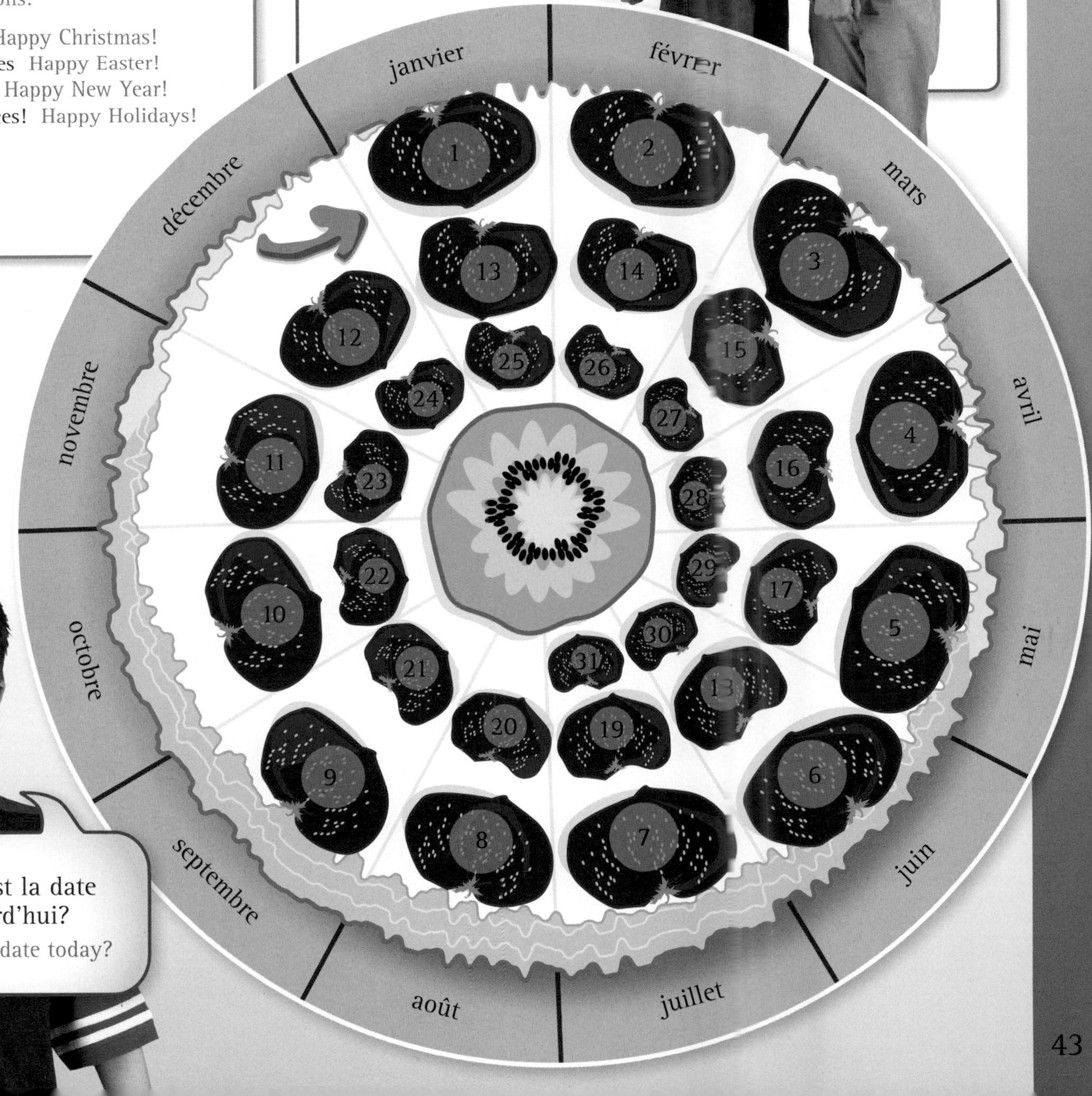
janvier
février
mars
avril
mai
juin
juillet
août
septembre
octobre
novembre
décembre

Quelle est la date aujourd'hui?
What's the date today?

Quelle heure est-il?

What's the time?

Il est quatre heures.
It's four o'clock.

Il est quatre heures cinq.
It's five past four.

Il est quatre heures dix.
It's ten past four.

Il est quatre heures et quart.
It's a quarter past four.

Il est quatre heures vingt.
It's twenty past four.

Il est quatre heures vingt-cinq.
It's twenty-five past four.

Il est quatre heures et demie.
It's half past four.

Il est cinq heures moins vingt-cinq.
It's twenty-five to five.

Il est cinq heures moins vingt.
It's twenty to five.

Il est cinq heures moins le quart.
It's a quarter to five.

Il est cinq heures moins dix.
It's ten to five.

Il est cinq heures moins cinq.
It's five to five.

Quelle heure est-il?
What time is it?
Il est neuf heures du matin.
It's nine o'clock in the morning.

Play the game

1. Play this game in a group. Choose one person to be Mr Wolf.

2. Mr Wolf should stand with his back to the group. Everyone else should line up about 10 metres behind him and say in a chorus **Qu'elle heure est-il, Monsieur Loup?** (What time is it Mr Wolf?).

3. If Mr Wolf replies **Il est trois heures**, everyone should take three steps forward. If he says **Il est six heures**, everyone should take six steps forward, etc.

4. Mr Wolf can say **C'est l'heure du dîner!** (It's dinner time!) at any time. When he says this, he should run after the others and try to catch one of them. The person he catches becomes Mr Wolf, and the game begins again.

5. If somebody reaches Mr Wolf before he says **C'est l'heure du dîner**, that person can choose the next Mr Wolf.

Puzzle

Can you match the times listed below with the correct clock? Say the time in French as you point to each clock.

1. Il est midi et demie.
2. Il est trois heures moins le quart.
3. Il est cinq heures vingt.
4. Il est cinq heures moins dix.
5. Il est onze heures et quart.
6. Il est une heure moins dix.

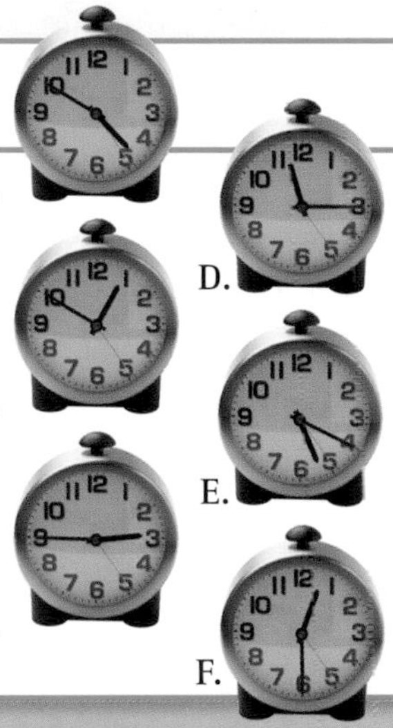

A. B. C. D. E. F.

Top tips

To say the time in French, you always begin with **Il est...** followed by the hour. You use **heure** (singular) for one o'clock and **heures** (plural) for all other times

Il est une heure It's one o'clock
Il est six heures It's six o'clock

★

There is no word for "past" in French. You add the number of minutes past the hour

Il est quatre heures dix
It's ten past four

★

To say "It's ten to" or "It's twenty-five to" you use **moins** (less) and the number of minutes to the hour

Il est six heures moins cinq
It's five to six

★

Du matin and **du soir** mean "in the morning" and "in the evening". You can also say **de l'après-midi** (in the afternoon).

★

Your turn!
Can you say what time it is now in French?

Other words and expressions:
Une seconde A second
Une minute A minute
Une heure An hour
Un jour A day
Une semaine A week
Un mois A month
Un an/une année A year
Il est quatre heures pile
It's exactly four o'clock
Il est environ cinq heures
It's about five o'clock
Il est presque six heures
It's nearly six o'clock
Il est midi
It's midday
Il est minuit
It's midnight

À quelle heure tu te lèves?

What time do you get up?

25

Je me lève à sept heures et demie.
I get up at half past seven.

Je prends le petit déjeuner à huit heures.
I have breakfast at eight o'clock.

À quelle heure tu te lèves?
What time do you get up?
Je me lève à sept heures.
I get up at seven o'clock.

26

Isabelle's day

Listen to the CD to hear about Isabelle's day. Point to each each activity as you hear it said aloud.

Play the game

1. Play the game on the right with a partner. Take turns to throw a dice.

2. If you land on a square showing an activity, say what time you usually do that activity, eg, **Je déjeune à midi** (I have lunch at midday).

3. The winner is the first player to get to bed-time!

Je me lève à six heures et demie.
Je m'habille à sept heures.
Je prends le petit déjeuner à sept heures et demie.
Je me brosse les dents à huit heures.
Je vais à l'école à huit heures et demie.
Je déjeune à midi.
Je rentre à quatre heures.
Je dîne à six heures.
Je fais mes devoirs à six heures et demie.
Je regarde la télé à sept heures.
Je prends une douche à sept heures et demie.
Je vais au lit à huit heures et demie.

Je vais à l'école à huit heures et demie.
I go to school at half past eight.

Je déjeune à midi.
I have lunch at midday.

Je rentre à quatre heures moins le quart.
I go home at a quarter to four.

Je dîne à six heures.
I have dinner at six o'clock.

Je vais au lit à huit heures.
I go to bed at eight o'clock.

Top tips

To talk about your daily routine, you use verbs in the present tense

Je regarde, je mange, je vais, je fais
I watch, I eat, I go, I do

See pages 153–154 to see how the present tense is formed.

★

Some verbs are known as reflexive verbs. They have an extra pronoun (eg, **me, te, se**)

Je me lève I get myself up
Je m'habille I dress myself
Je me brosse les dents I clean my teeth

See page 154 for more information on reflexive verbs.

★

To talk about a specific time in French, you use **à**

À dix heures At ten o'clock

★

Your turn!
Can you talk about your day in French?

Other expressions:

Chaque jour Every day
Chaque matin Every morning
Chaque après-midi Every afternoon
Chaque soir Every evening
D'habitude je vais au lit à neuf heures
I usually go to bed at nine o'clock
Je ne vais jamais au lit de bonne heure
I never go to bed early

Que veux-tu être?

What do you want to be?

Je veux être...
I want to be...

artiste
an artist

maître d'école
a teacher

femme médecin
a doctor

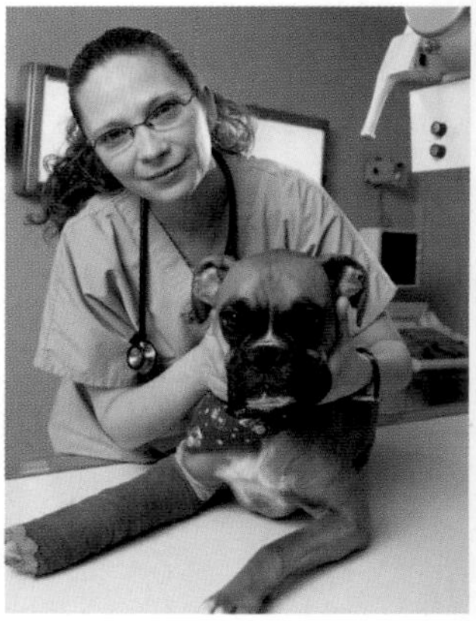

vétérinaire
a vet

femme policier
a police officer

employée de bureau
an office worker

écrivain
a writer

Play the game

1. Play this game to help you find out what you would like to be.

2. Follow the red or blue arrows depending on whether you answer **Oui** (Yes) or **Non** (No) to the questions below. Follow the blue arrows if you answer **Oui** and the red arrows if you answer **Non**.

Veux-tu travailler à l'intérieur?
Do you want to work inside?
Non
No
Oui
Yes
Veux-tu travailler avec des animaux?
Do you want to work with animals?
Non
No
Oui
Yes
Veux-tu travailler avec des enfants?
Do you want to work with children?
Non
No
Oui
Yes
Je veux être...
I want to be...

fermier
a farmer

acteur
an actor

ouvrier
a builder

pompier
a firefighter

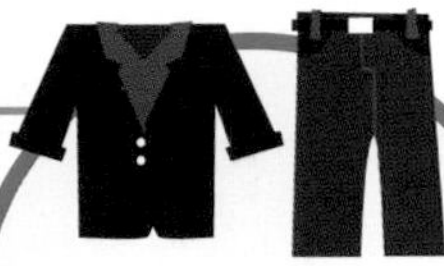

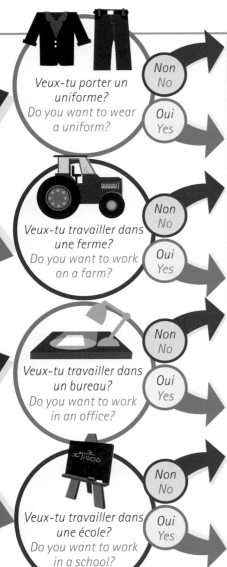

Veux-tu porter un uniforme?
Do you want to wear a uniform?

Non / *No* → *Veux-tu être ouvrier (m) ouvrière (f)?* *Do you want to be a builder?*

Oui / *Yes* → *Veux-tu être policier (m) femme policier (f)?* *Do you want to be a police officer?*

Veux-tu travailler dans une ferme?
Do you want to work on a farm?

Non / *No* → *Veux-tu être vétérinaire (m/f)?* *Do you want to be a vet?*

Oui / *Yes* → *Veux-tu être fermier (m) fermière (f)?* *Do you want to be a farmer?*

Veux-tu travailler dans un bureau?
Do you want to work in an office?

Non / *No* → *Veux-tu être artiste (m/f)?* *Do you want to be an artist?*

Oui / *Yes* → *Veux-tu être employé de bureau (m) employée de bureau (f)?* *Do you want to be an office worker?*

Veux-tu travailler dans une école?
Do you want to work in a school?

Non / *No* → *Veux-tu être médecin (m) femme médecin (f)?* *Do you want to be a doctor?*

Oui / *Yes* → *Veux-tu être maître d'école (m) maîtresse d'école (f)?* *Do you want to be a teacher?*

Top tips

When you talk about what you want to be in French, you say **Je veux être** (I want to be) followed by the job title. In French, you don't use "a" or "an" before the name of the profession

Je veux être artiste
I want to be an artist

★

In French, some jobs have a feminine and a masculine form

maître d'école teacher (male)
maîtresse d'école teacher (female)

★

Some jobs add the word **femme** in the feminine form

policier (m) **femme policier** (f)

★

Other jobs use the same word for both the masculine and the feminine form

artiste artist **écrivain** writer

★

Your turn!
Can you say what you want to be when you grow up?

Dans les magasins

At the shops

28

Bonjour madame, avez-vous des crayons de papier?
Hello, have you got any pencils?

Je suis désolée. Je n'en ai pas, mais j'ai des feutres.
No, I'm sorry, I haven't got any, but I've got some felt-tips.

les carottes 1,50
les œufs 1,10
le jus de pomme 1,05
l'eau 1,00
le pain 2,00
les sandwichs 2,30
les fraises 2,10/kg

Combien coûtent ces crayons de couleur?
How much are these crayons?

Ils coûtent trois euros.
They're three euros.

Puzzle

These four shopping baskets belong to Marc, Natalie, Guy, and Charlotte. Can you match each child with the right shopping basket?

1. Charlotte a des fraises et des pâtes. Elle n'a pas de sandwichs.
2. Marc a du jus de pomme et du pain. Il n'a pas d'eau.
3. Natalie a des sandwichs et des oranges. Elle n'a pas de pâtes.
4. Guy a des bonbons et des carottes. Il n'a pas d'œufs.

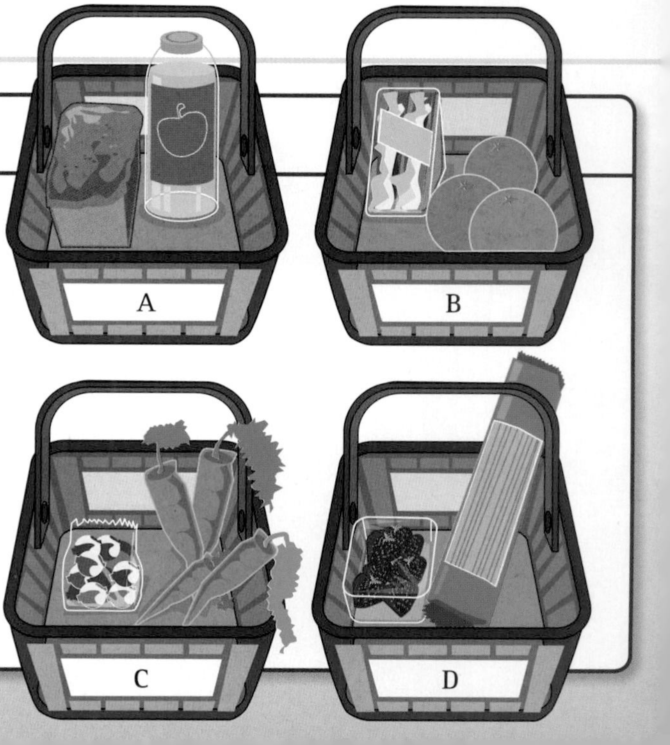

A
B
C
D

Combien coûte ce carnet?
How much is this notebook?
Il coûte un euro quarante.
It's one euro forty.
Voilà!
Here you are.
Merci.
Thank you.
les crayons de couleur 3,00
les pâtes 1,25
les bonbons 0,75
les oranges 1,00/kg
les carnets 1,40

Play the game

1. Play this game with a partner, using the food flash cards. Spread out the cards, with the picture facing upwards.

2. Look at the cards and try to remember which items of food are on each card. Then shuffle the cards and take six cards each. Take turns to ask your partner questions, such as **Avez-vous des pommes, s'il vous plaît?** (Have you got any apples, please?).

3. Your partner should reply **Oui, voici** (Yes, here you are) and hand the card over, or **Non, je n'en ai pas** (No, I haven't got any). When your partner hands you a card, put it in a pile in front of you. The winner is the first person to win all the cards.

Top tips

To ask someone for something in a shop, you use **vous** (the polite form of **tu**)

Avez-vous des pâtes?
Have you got any pasta?

See page 152 to find out more about **tu** and **vous**.

★

In French, you use **de** to mean "some" or "any". You use **du** before masculine nouns, **de la** before feminine nouns, **de l'** before nouns starting with a vowel and **des** before plural nouns

Avez-vous du pain?
Do you have any bread?

Avez-vous de la confiture?
Do you have any jam?

Avez-vous de l'argent?
Do you have any money?

Avez-vous des tomates?
Do you have any tomatoes?

★

In French, you can use the word **en** to replace a noun

Avez-vous des pommes?
Do you have any apples?

Je n'en ai pas I haven't got any

★

In France, people use euros and centimes. There are 100 centimes in a euro. To ask how much something is you say

Combien coûte...? How much is...?

Combien coûtent...? How much are...?

Most fruit and vegetables are priced per kilo. For example, if oranges are priced at 1 euro per kilogram you say

Les oranges coûtent un euro le kilo
The oranges cost one euro a kilo

See page 116 to learn more numbers, and pages 82–85 to find more words to do with food and shopping.

Qu'est-ce que tu aimes faire?

What do you like doing?

29

Qu'est-ce que tu aimes faire?
What do you like doing?
J'aime jouer aux jeux électroniques et écouter de la musique.
I like playing computer games and listening to music.
Aimes-tu lire?
Do you like reading?
Oui, j'adore lire. Je n'aime pas nager.
Yes, I love reading. I don't like swimming.
Nous aimons jouer aux échecs.
We like playing chess.

30 Whose hobbies?

Listen to Lucie, Pascal, and Étienne talking about their hobbies on the CD. The boxes on the right show what each child likes doing (and doesn't like doing). Can you match each child to the correct box?

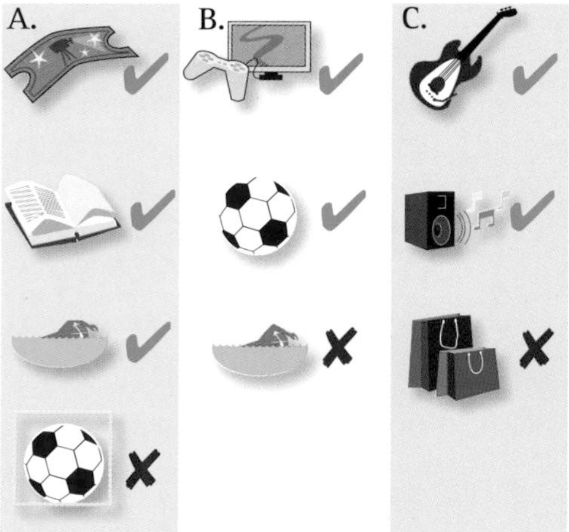
A.
B.
C.

Play the game

1. Play this game with a partner. Take turns to throw a dice and move across the board.

2. If you land on an activity, ask your partner if he/she likes that activity. For example, if you land on the symbol for swimming, ask your partner **Aimes-tu nager?** (Do you like swimming?). Your partner should reply **Oui, j'aime nager** (Yes, I like swimming) or **Non, je n'aime pas nager** (No, I don't like swimming).

3. The winner is the first person to get to the end.

Qu'est-ce que tu aimes faire?
What do you like doing?
J'aime aller au cinéma et jouer de la guitare.
I like going to the cinema and playing the guitar.
Aimes-tu faire les courses?
Do you like shopping?
Non, je déteste faire les courses, mais j'adore jouer au foot.
No, I hate shopping, but I love playing football.

Top tips

To talk about what you like (or don't like) doing, you use the verbs **aimer** (like), **adorer** (love), or **détester** (hate) followed by another action verb

J'aime nager
I like swimming
Je déteste chanter
I hate singing

★

To talk about playing a musical instrument, you say **jouer de**. Remember that **de** becomes **du** before a masculine **noun** and **de la** before a feminine noun

Je joue de la guitare
I play the guitar
Je joue du piano
I play the piano

★

Your turn!
Can you say what your hobbies are?

See pages 88–89 for more hobbies.

Other expressions:

J'aime beaucoup danser
I really like dancing
Je n'aime pas du tout nager
I don't like swimming at all
J'aime tout!
I like everything!

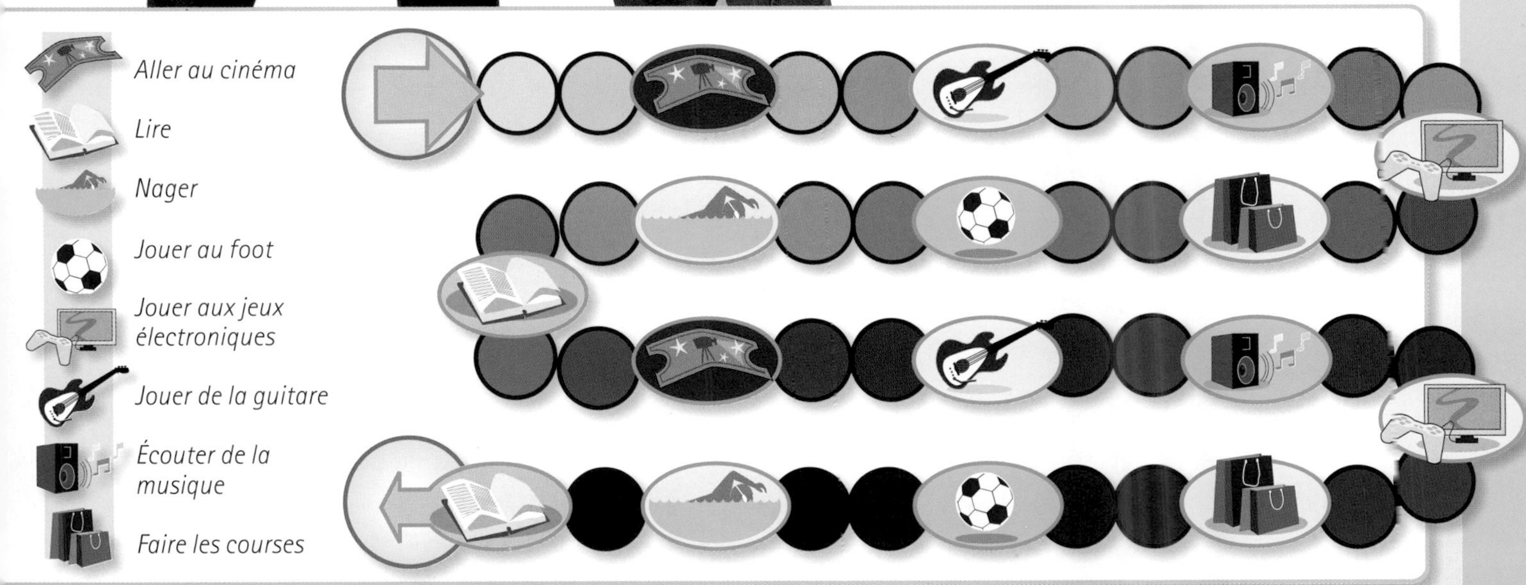
Aller au cinéma
Lire
Nager
Jouer au foot
Jouer aux jeux électroniques
Jouer de la guitare
Écouter de la musique
Faire les courses

Au restaurant

At the restaurant

31

Vous désirez?
What would you like?
Je voudrais du poulet avec des frites et de l'eau, s'il vous plaît.
I'd like chicken with chips and some water, please.
Je voudrais des pâtes et du jus d'orange, s'il vous plaît.
I'd like pasta and an orange juice, please.
Je voudrais un sandwich s'il vous plaît.
I'd like a sandwich, please.
La Carte

32 Whose dinner?

Listen to the CD to find out what Elisabeth, Antoine, and Eric are having for dinner. Can you match each child to their correct plate?

1.
2.
3.

La Carte

menu

le poulet
chicken

le steak
steak

l'omelette
omelette

le riz
rice

les frites
chips

les pommes de terre
potatoes

les pâtes
pasta

les carottes
carrots

les petits pois
peas

les haricots verts
green beans

le fromage
cheese

le jus d'orange
orange juice

le jus de pomme
apple juice

l'eau
water

la salade de fruits
fruit salad

la glace
ice cream

Top tips

To ask for things in a restaurant, you say **Je voudrais...** (I would like...).

When speaking to customers, the waiter would use **vous** (the polite form of **tu**)

Vous désirez?
What would you like?

See page 152 to find out more about **tu** and **vous**.

★

In French, you use **de** to mean "some". Remember that **de** becomes **du** before masculine nouns, **de la** before feminine nouns, **de l'** before nouns starting with a vowel, and **des** before plural nouns

Je voudrais du pain
I would like some bread

Je voudrais de l'eau
I would like some water

Je voudrais des carottes
I would like some carrots

★

Your turn!
Look at the menu. What would you order if you were in the café?

See pages 82–83 for more vocabulary to do with food.

Play the game

1. Play this game with a partner. Take turns to throw a dice.

2. If you throw a number from one to five, choose an item from the list on the right and write it down. For example, if you throw a five, you chose an item from Group 5. If you throw a six, you can choose any item you like.

3. If you throw the same number more than once, you miss a turn.

4. The winner is the first person to collect all five parts of the meal.

Group 1
le jus d'orange
le jus de pomme
l'eau

Group 2
le poulet
l'omelette
le steak

Group 3
les frites
le riz
les pommes de terre

Group 4
les petits pois
les haricots verts
les carottes

Group 5
la glace
la salade de fruits
le fromage

Bon appétit!

Où est le cinéma?

Where's the cinema?

23

Excusez-moi, où est le cinéma, s'il vous plaît?
Excuse me, where's the cinema, please?
Allez tout droit, puis tournez à droite. Il est à gauche, à côté du parc.
Go straight on, then turn right. It's on the left, next to the park.
Excusez-moi, il y a une poste près d'ici?
Excuse me, is there a post office near here?
Oui, allez tout droit puis tournez à gauche. Elle est à droite, en face de l'école.
Yes, go straight on, then turn left. It's on the right, opposite the school.

Puzzle

Look at the map below. Start at the school and follow the directions given. Where are you?

1. Allez tout droit, puis tournez à droite. Il est à côté de la banque et en face du parc.
2. Allez tout droit, puis tournez à gauche. Il est à gauche, en face de la gare.
3. Tournez à droite. Il est à droite, en face du cinéma.
4. Allez tout droit, puis traversez le pont. Il est à gauche.

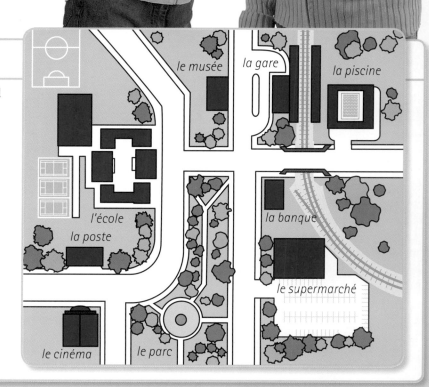

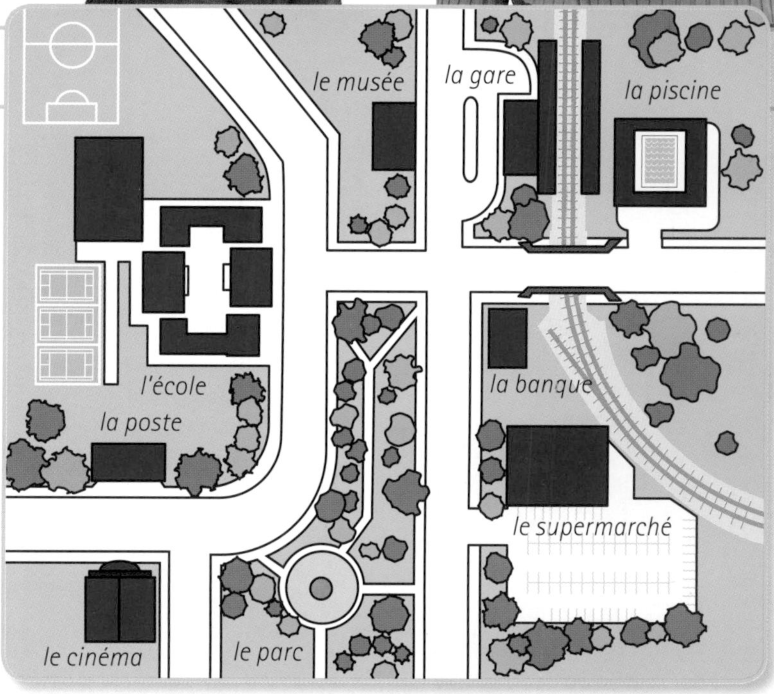
le musée
la gare
la piscine
l'école
la poste
la banque
le supermarché
le cinéma
le parc

Excusez-moi, où est la piscine s'il vous plaît?
Excuse me, where's the swimming pool, please?
Traversez le pont et tournez à droite. Elle est juste à côté de la gare.
Go over the bridge and turn right. It's just next to the station.

Top tips

When asking for directions, it is polite to say **Excusez-moi** (excuse me). **S'il vous plaît** is the polite way to say "please".

★

If you want to give someone directions in French, you use the polite form of the verb:

Tournez à droite Turn right
Traversez le pont Go over the bridge

For more information on how to use the polite form see page 152.

Other words and expressions:

la bibliothèque library
le centre commercial shopping centre
le marché market

Pour allez à? How do I get to?
Prenez la première rue à droite
Take the first road on the right
Prenez la deuxième rue à gauche
Take the second road on the left
C'est près de la place
It's near the square
Ce n'est pas loin It's not far

Play the game

1. Play in pairs or small groups. The object of the game is to get back to your house in the middle of the board.

2. Start from one of the four buildings in the corners. Throw a dice and move towards the centre of the board.

3. If you land on an arrow say **Tournez à gauche**, **Tournez à droite** or **Allez tout droit** and follow the directions. The first player to arrive back home is the winner.

Allez tout droit
Tournez à gauche
Tournez à droite

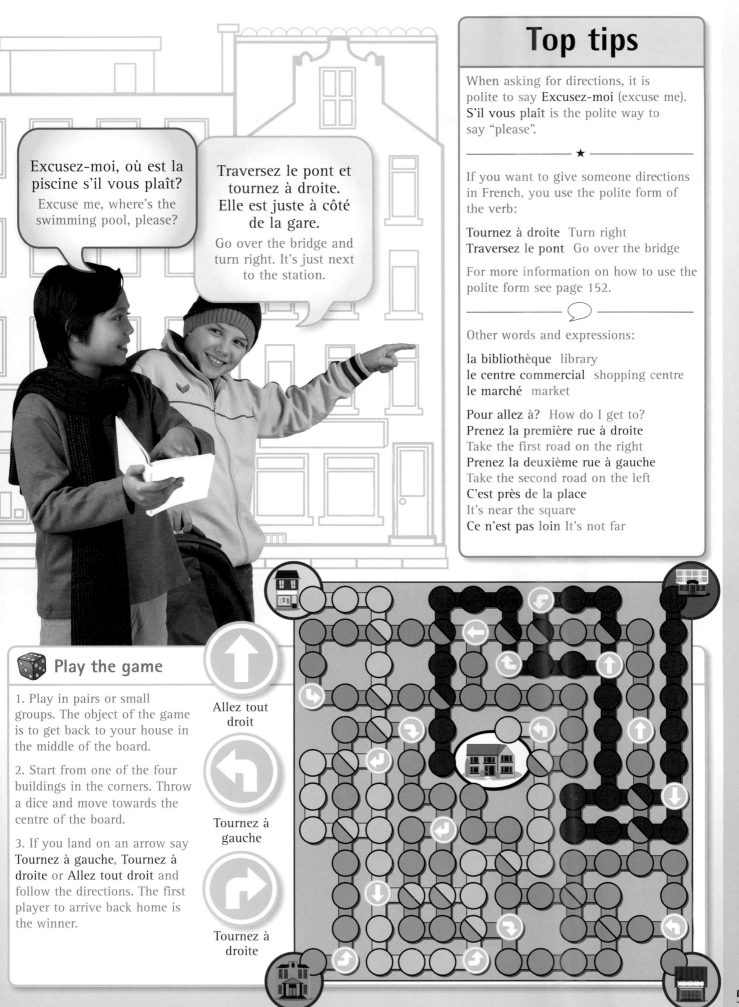

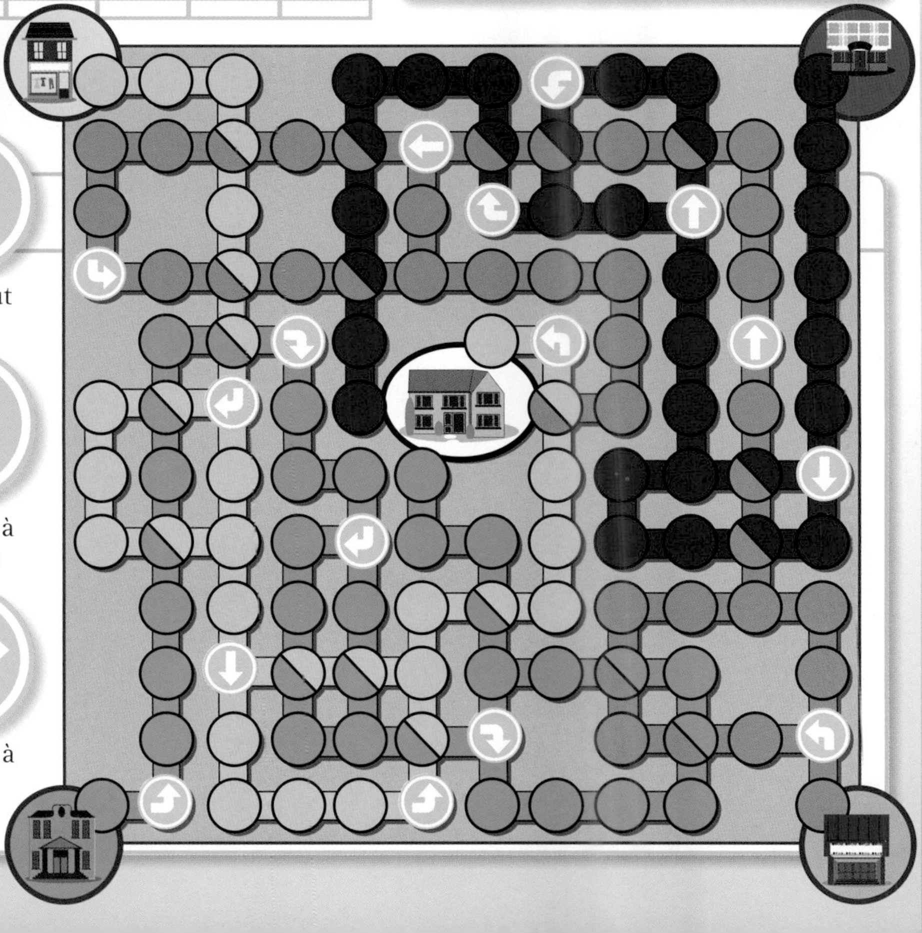

Qu'est-ce que tu as fait ce weekend?

What did you do at the weekend?

34

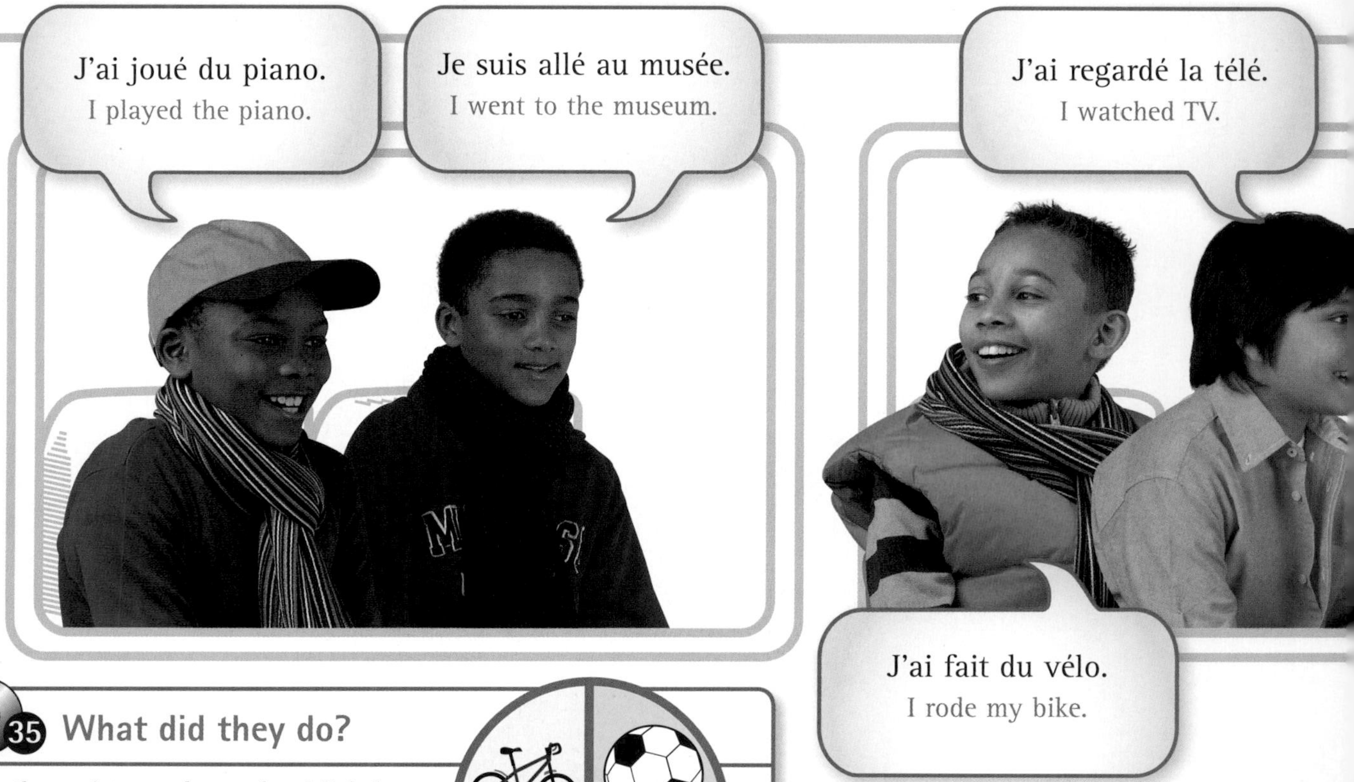
J'ai joué du piano.
I played the piano.
Je suis allé au musée.
I went to the museum.
J'ai regardé la télé.
I watched TV.
J'ai fait du vélo.
I rode my bike.

35 What did they do?

These three pictures show what Michel, Sophie, and Pierre did at the weekend. Look at the sentences below and try to match the activities to each child.

1. Je n'ai pas écouté de la musique.
   Je suis allée au musée.
   J'ai joué du piano.
   J'ai joué au tennis.
2. Je suis allé nager.
   J'ai écouté de la musique.
   Je n'ai pas regardé la télé.
   J'ai fait du camping.
3. J'ai fait du vélo.
   Je n'ai pas joué du piano.
   J'ai regardé la télé.
   J'ai joué au foot.

Play the game

1. Play this game with a partner. Take turns to throw a dice and move across the board.

2. If you land on an activity, eg, playing the piano, you say, **Le weekend, j'ai joué du piano** (At the weekend, I played the piano).

3. The winner is the first person to reach the end. When you have finished, tell your partner which activities you didn't do, eg, **Je ne suis pas allé(e) nager** (I didn't go swimming).

Je n'ai pas fait mes devoirs!
I didn't do my homework!

J'ai fait du camping.
I went camping.

J'ai écouté de la musique.
I listened to music.

Top tips

To talk about something that happened in the past, you use the present tense of avoir (eg, **j'ai**) with the past participle of the verb (eg, **joué**, **fait**)

J'ai joué de la guitare
I played the guitar

J'ai fait mes devoirs
I did my homework

See page 154 to find more about the past tense.

★

Not all verbs use **avoir** to form the past tense. Some verbs, eg, **aller** (to go), use **être** plus the past participle

Je suis allé au cinéma
I went to the cinema

If you are female, you must add another "e" to the past participle

Je suis allée au cinéma

See page 154 to find out more about verbs that use **être** in the past tense.

★

To make a sentence negative, you put **ne** and **pas** around **avoir** or **être**

Je n'ai pas joué au foot
I didn't play football

Je ne suis pas allé au cinéma
I didn't go to the cinema (male)

J'ai écouté de la musique.

Je suis allé(e) au musée.

J'ai joué du piano.

J'ai joué au tennis.

Je suis allé(e) nager.

J'ai regardé la télé.

J'ai fait du vélo.

J'ai fait du camping.

J'ai joué au foot.

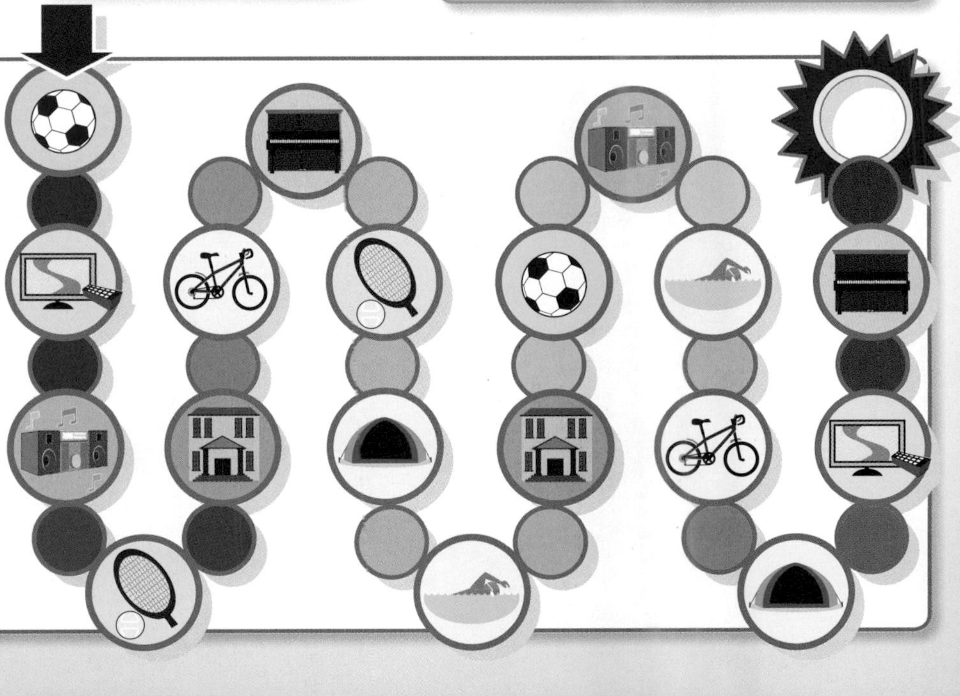

Les vacances
The holidays

36

Je vais passer les vacances à Paris. Je vais emporter mon appareil photo et un guide.
I'm going to spend the holidays in Paris. I'm going to take my camera and a guide book.

Je vais passer les vacances à la campagne.
Je vais voyager en train.
Je vais emporter mon vélo.
I'm going to spend the holidays in the country.
I'm going to travel by train.
I'm going to take my bicycle.

37 Whose holiday?

Listen to the CD to hear Monique, Christian, and Charlotte describing their holiday plans. Can you match each child to the correct sentences below?

Je vais passer les vacances à l'hôtel à Madrid. Je vais prendre des photos et je vais lire.

Je vais passer les vacances dans un camping. Je vais faire du vélo et je vais emporter mon sac de couchage.

Je vais passer les vacances près de la plage. Je vais voyager en avion. Je vais jouer au tennis.

A

B

C

Bon voyage!
Have a good journey!

Je vais passer les vacances près de la plage. Je vais emporter mes lunettes de soleil et mon maillot de bain.

I'm going to spend the holidays by the beach. I'm going to take my sunglasses and my swimsuit.

Je vais passer les vacances dans un camping. Je vais emporter ma tente et mon sac de couchage.

I'm going to spend the holidays on a campsite. I'm going to take my tent and my sleeping bag.

Top tips

To talk about what you are going to do in the future, you say **Je vais...** (I am going to...) followed by another verb

Je vais emporter mes lunettes de soleil
I'm going to take my sunglasses

See pages 154–155 for more information on how to use this form of the verb.

★

When you are talking about different ways of travelling, you use either **en** or **à**

en avion by plane
en bus by bus
en train by train
en voiture by car
en bateau by boat
à pied on foot

★

Your turn!
Can you say how you are going to spend the holidays?

See pages 90–91 and 102–103 for more words to do with travel and holidays.

Je vais passer les vacances à Rome. Je vais voyager à pied. Je vais emporter une tente. Je vais faire du vélo. Je vais manger des bananes!

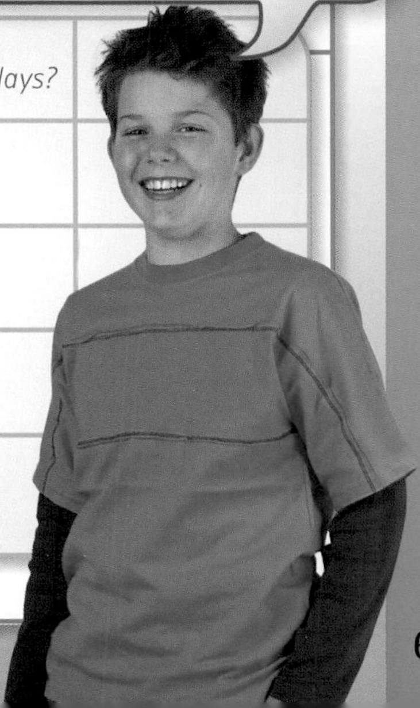

Play the game

1. Play this game in a small group. Choose one person to ask the questions. The other players should each take a piece of paper and write down an answer to the first question **Où vas-tu passer les vacances?** (Where are you going to spend the holidays?) You might answer, for example, **Je vais passer les vacances à la campagne** (I'm going to spend the holidays in the country).

2. Fold over the top of the paper and pass it to the next person. Write an answer to the second question, fold the paper again and pass it on. When you have written the answer to the final question, open your paper and tell the others what you are going to do on your holidays!

Où vas-tu passer les vacances? *Where are you going to spend the holidays?*	
Comment vas-tu voyager? *How are you going to travel?*	
Que vas-tu emporter? *What are you going to take?*	
Que vas-tu faire? *What are you going to do?*	
Que vas-tu manger? *What are you going to eat?*	

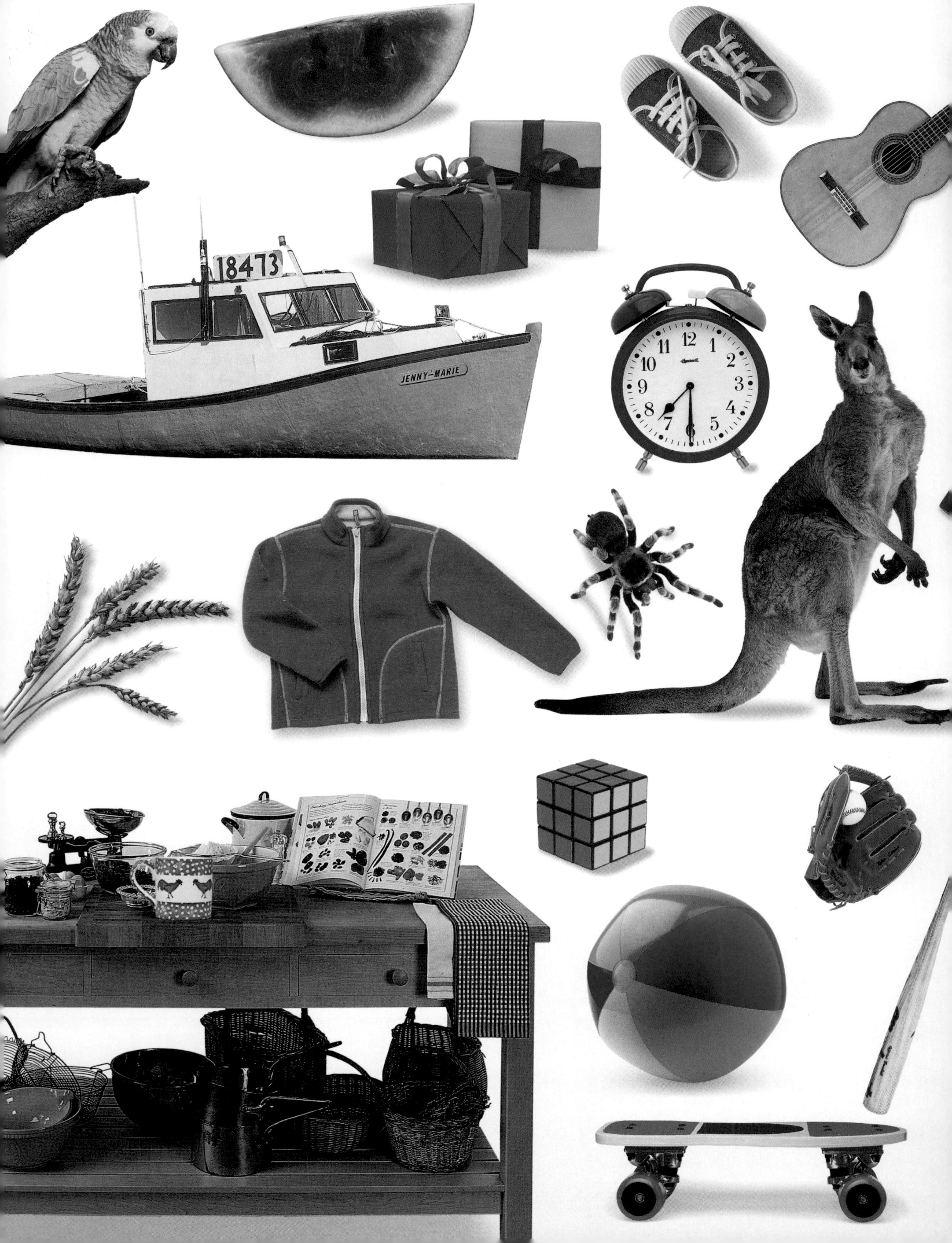
18473
JENNY-MARIE

Picture dictionary

Tout à mon sujet

All about me

Je suis **grande**.
I'm tall.

la sœur
suhr
sister

le frère
frair
brother

le grand-père
grandfather

la grand-mère
grandmother

les grands-parents
grah(n)-par-ah(n)
grandparents

le père
pair
father

la mère
mair
mother

Voici ma **famille**.
This is my family.

le bébé
bay-bay
baby

l'enfant
lahn-fah(n)
child

la tante
tahnt
aunt

l'oncle
lonk-luh
uncle

Nous sommes **contentes**!
We're happy!

contente
kon-tahnt
happy

Thomas est **en colère.**
Thomas is angry.

en colère
ah(n) ko-lehr
angry

Extra words to learn

les cheveux
shuh-vuh
hair

le cou
koo
neck

le coude
kood
elbow

la dent
dah(n)
tooth

le dos
do
back

la famille
fa-mee-ye
family

le genou
zhuh-noo
knee

le sourcil
soor-seel
eyebrow

le visage
vee-zazh
face

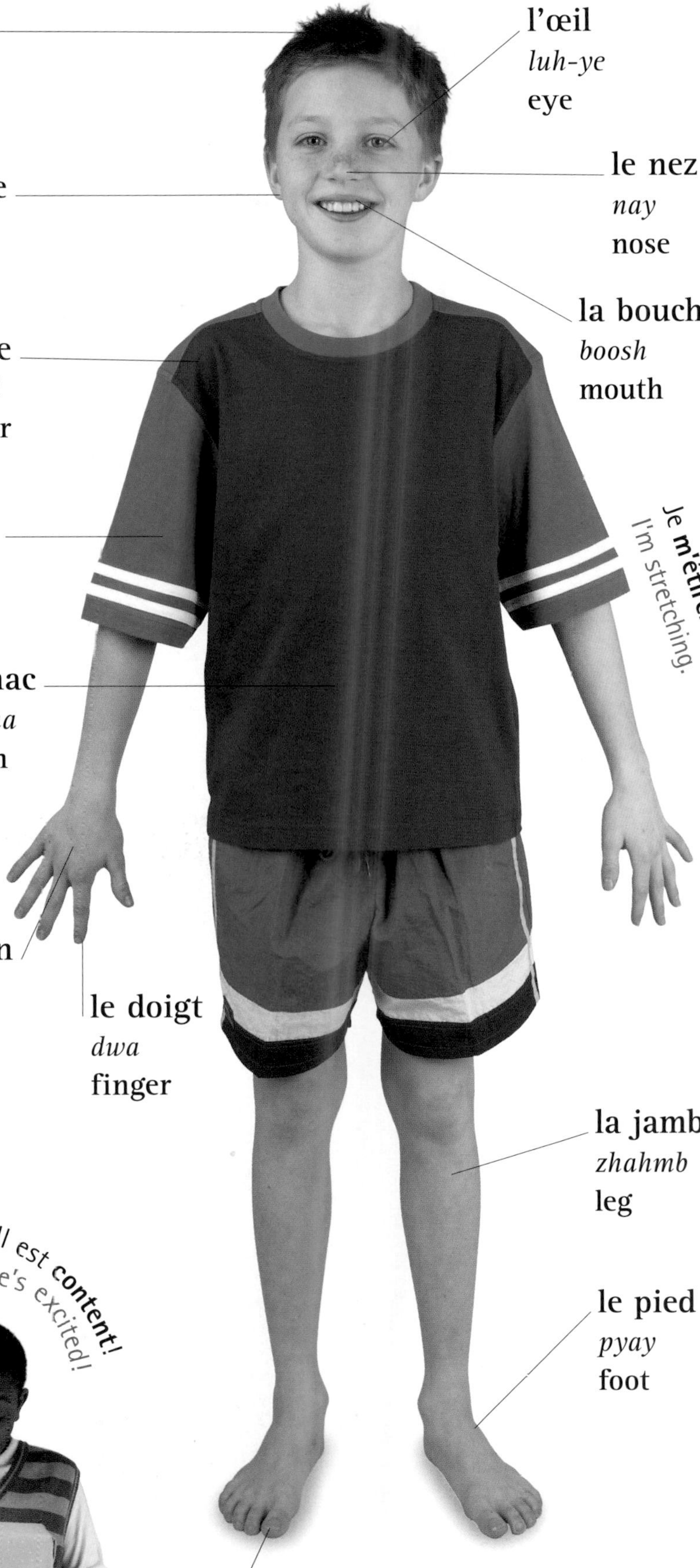

la tête
teht
head
l'œil
luh-ye
eye
le nez
nay
nose
l'oreille
lo-raye
ear
la bouche
boosh
mouth
l'épaule
lay-pohl
shoulder
le bras
bra
arm
l'estomac
les-to-ma
stomach
la main
ma(n)
hand
le doigt
dwa
finger
la jambe
zhahmb
leg
le pied
pyay
foot
l'orteil
lor-teye
toe

Je **m'étire.**
I'm stretching.

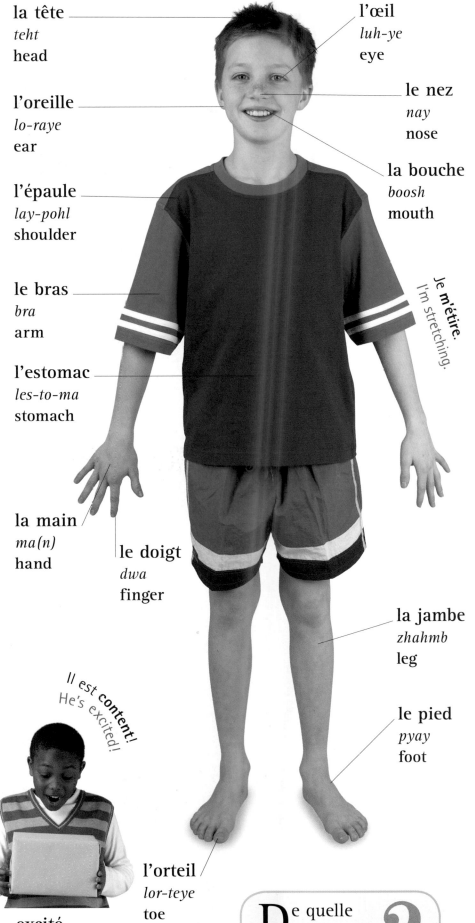

Je **pleure** quand je suis **triste.**
I cry when I'm sad.

triste
treest
sad

Il est **content!**
He's excited!

excité
ek-see-tay
excited

De quelle couleur sont tes yeux ?

Les vêtements

Clothes

les chaussettes
shoh-sets
socks

le bouton
button

la chemise
shuh-meez
shirt

le jean
jeen
jeans

Extra words to learn

la chaussure
shoh-soor
shoe

le gant
gah(n)
glove

les lunettes
lew-net
glasses

la pantoufle
pahn-too-fluh
slipper

le pull
pewl
jumper

le pyjama
pee-zha-ma
pyjamas

la robe
rob
dress

les sous-vêtements
soo-veht-mah(n)
underwear

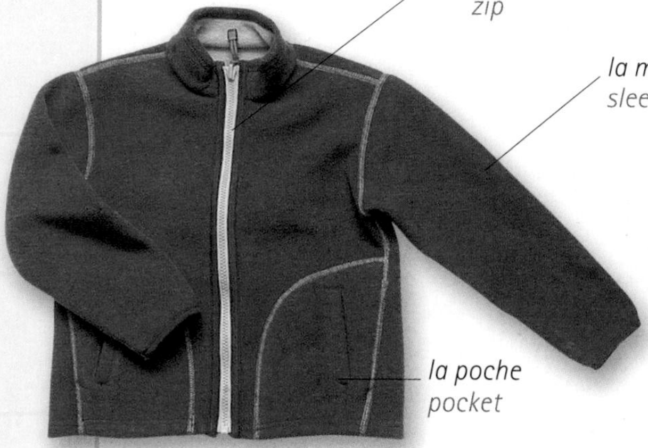
la fermeture
éclair
zip
la manche
sleeve
la poche
pocket

la polaire
po-lair
fleece

les baskets
bas-ket
trainers

Mon **manteau** me tient **chaud**.
My coat keeps me warm.

le gant
glove

l'écharpe
lay-sharp
scarf

le manteau
mahn-toh
coat

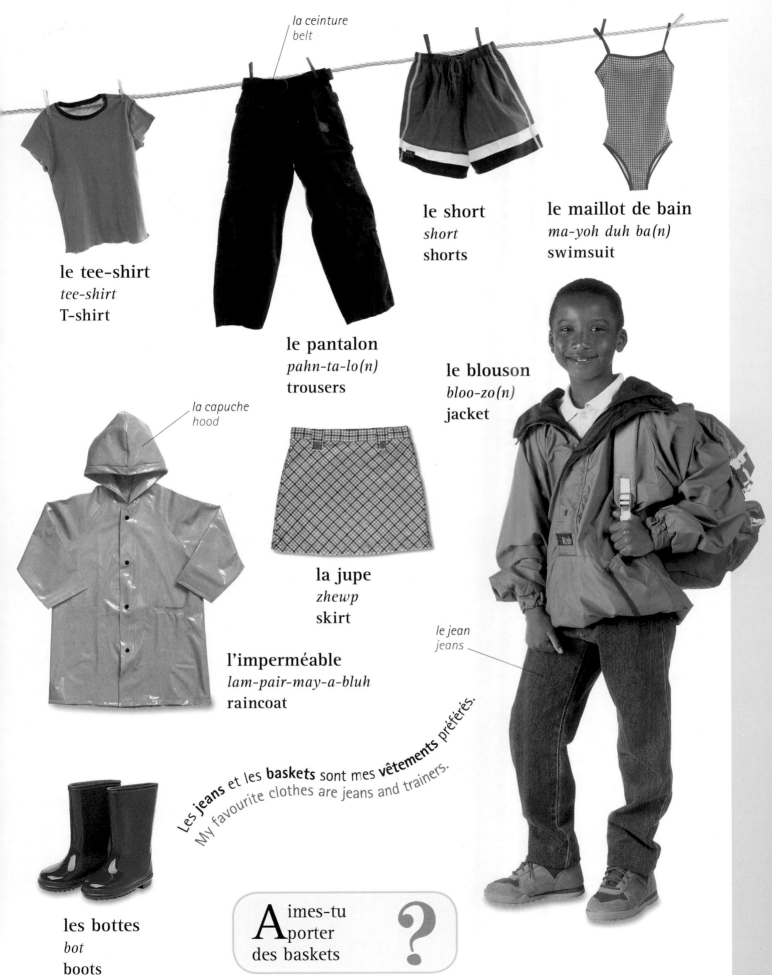

la ceinture
belt

le tee-shirt
tee-shirt
T-shirt

le pantalon
pahn-ta-lo(n)
trousers

le short
short
shorts

le maillot de bain
ma-yoh duh ba(n)
swimsuit

le jean
jeans

le blouson
bloo-zo(n)
jacket

la capuche
hood

la jupe
zhewp
skirt

l'imperméable
lam-pair-may-a-bluh
raincoat

les bottes
bot
boots

Les **jeans** et les **baskets** sont mes **vêtements** préférés.
My favourite clothes are jeans and trainers.

Aimes-tu porter des baskets ?

La cuisine
Kitchen

la poêle
pwal
frying pan

l'assiette
la-syet
plate

la casserole
saucepan
le four
oven

la cuisinière
kwee-zeen-yair
cooker

la cuillère
kwee-yehr
spoon

la tasse
tahss
mug

le torchon
tor-sho(n)
tea towel

le livre
book

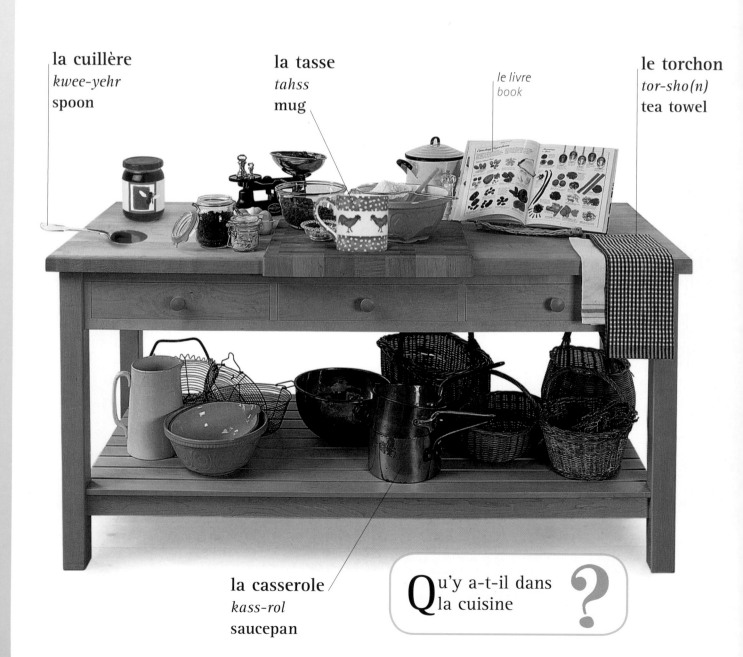

la casserole
kass-rol
saucepan

Qu'y a-t-il dans la cuisine ?

Merci de **faire la vaisselle**.
Thank you for washing the dishes.

le placard
cupboard

l'évier
layv-yay
sink

le congélateur
freezer

le réfrigérateur
ray-free-zhair-a-tuhr
fridge

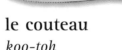

le couteau
koo-toh
knife

la fourchette
foor-shet
fork

Aimes-tu **faire de la pâtisserie**?
Do you like baking?

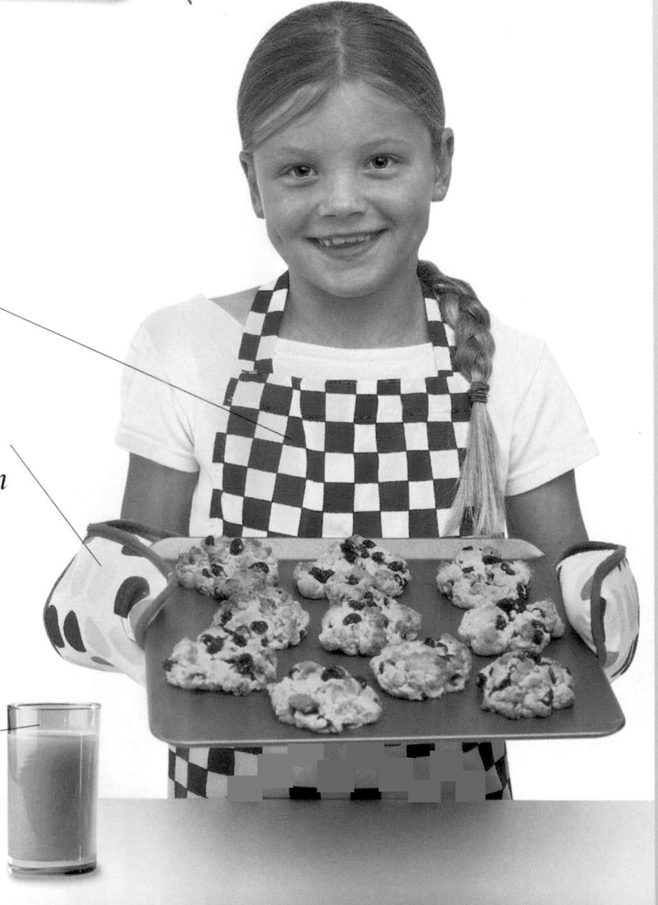

le tablier
tab-lee-yay
apron

le gant de cuisine
gah(n) duh kwee-zeen
oven glove

le verre
vair
glass

Extra words to learn

la bouilloire
booy-wahr
kettle

la cruche
krewsh
jug

le fer à repasser
fair ah ruh-pah-say
iron

le grille-pain
gree-ye-pa(n)
toaster

la machine à laver
ma-sheen ah la-vay
washing machine

le plateau
pla-toh
tray

la poubelle
poo-bell
bin

la tasse
tahss
cup

La salle de bain

Bathroom

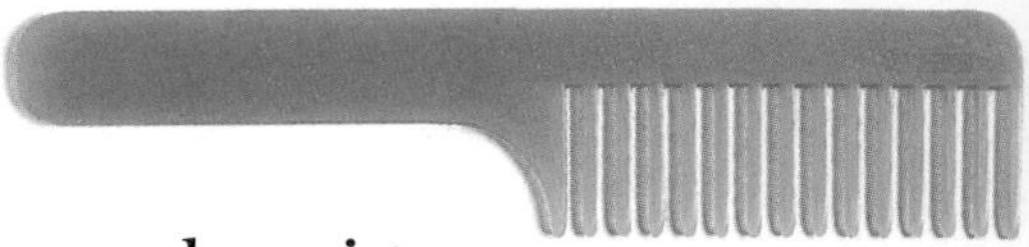

le peigne
pain-ye
comb

la baignoire
bayn-wahr
bath

C'est rigolo de faire des **bulles**.
It's fun making bubbles.

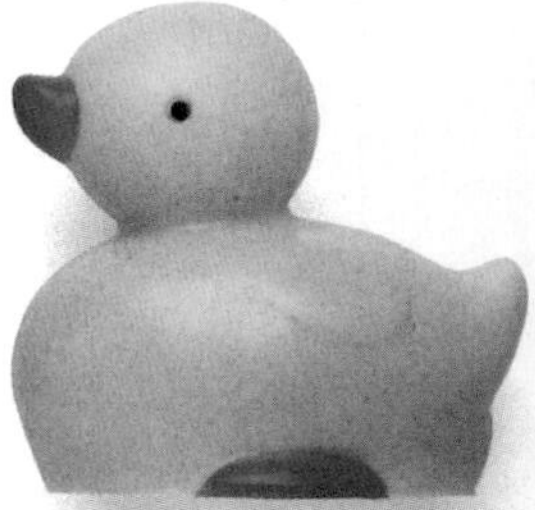

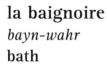

le jouet
zhoo-way
toy

l'eau
loh
water

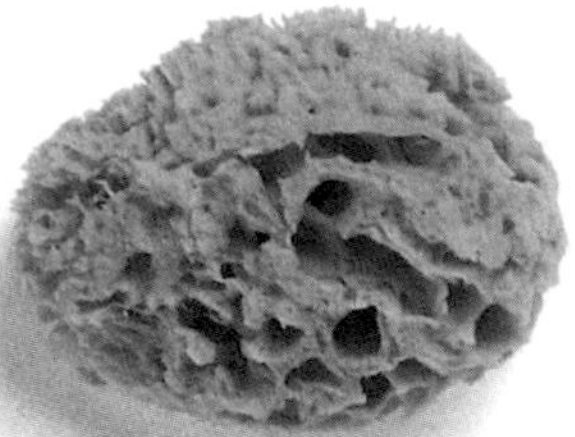

l'éponge
lay-ponzh
sponge

les serviettes
sair-vee-et
towels

Je mets du **dentifrice** sur ma **brosse à dents**.
I put toothpaste on my toothbrush.

le tube
tube

le dentifrice
dahn-tee-freess
toothpaste

la brosse à dents
bros ah dah(n)
toothbrush

Combien d'objets jaunes y a-t-il sur cette page ?

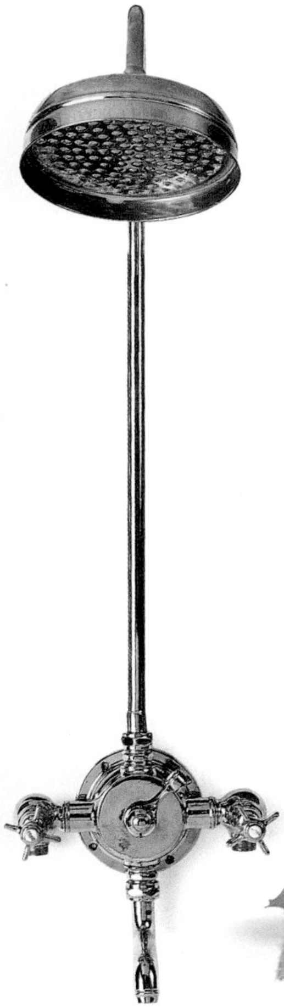

le shampooing
shahm-pwa(n)
shampoo

le miroir
meer-wahr
mirror

Extra words to learn

la brosse à cheveux
bros ah shuh-vuh
hairbrush

la buée
bway
steam

le maquillage
ma-kee-yazh
make-up

les mouchoirs en papier
moosh-wahrs ah(n) pap-yay
tissues

se laver
suh la-vay
washing

la serviette de toilette
sair-vee-et duh twa-let
flannel

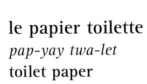

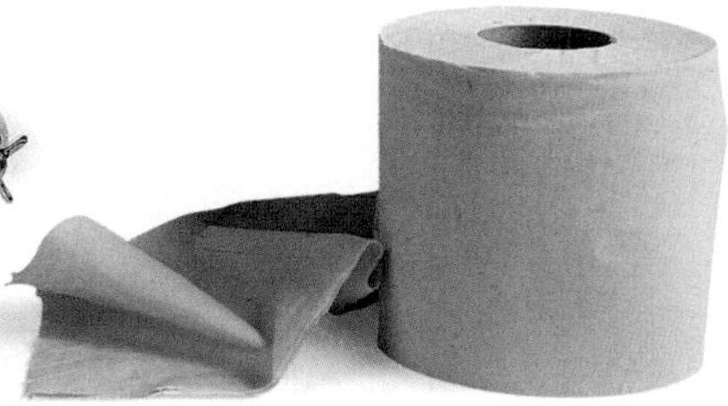

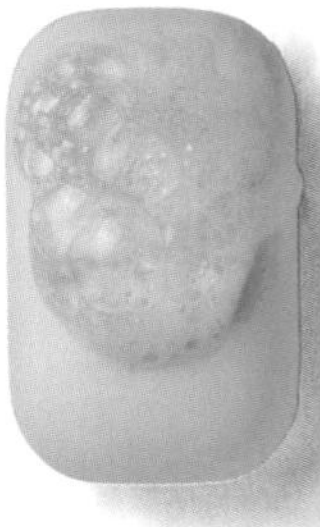

la douche
doosh
shower

le papier toilette
pap-yay twa-let
toilet paper

le savon
sa-vo(n)
soap

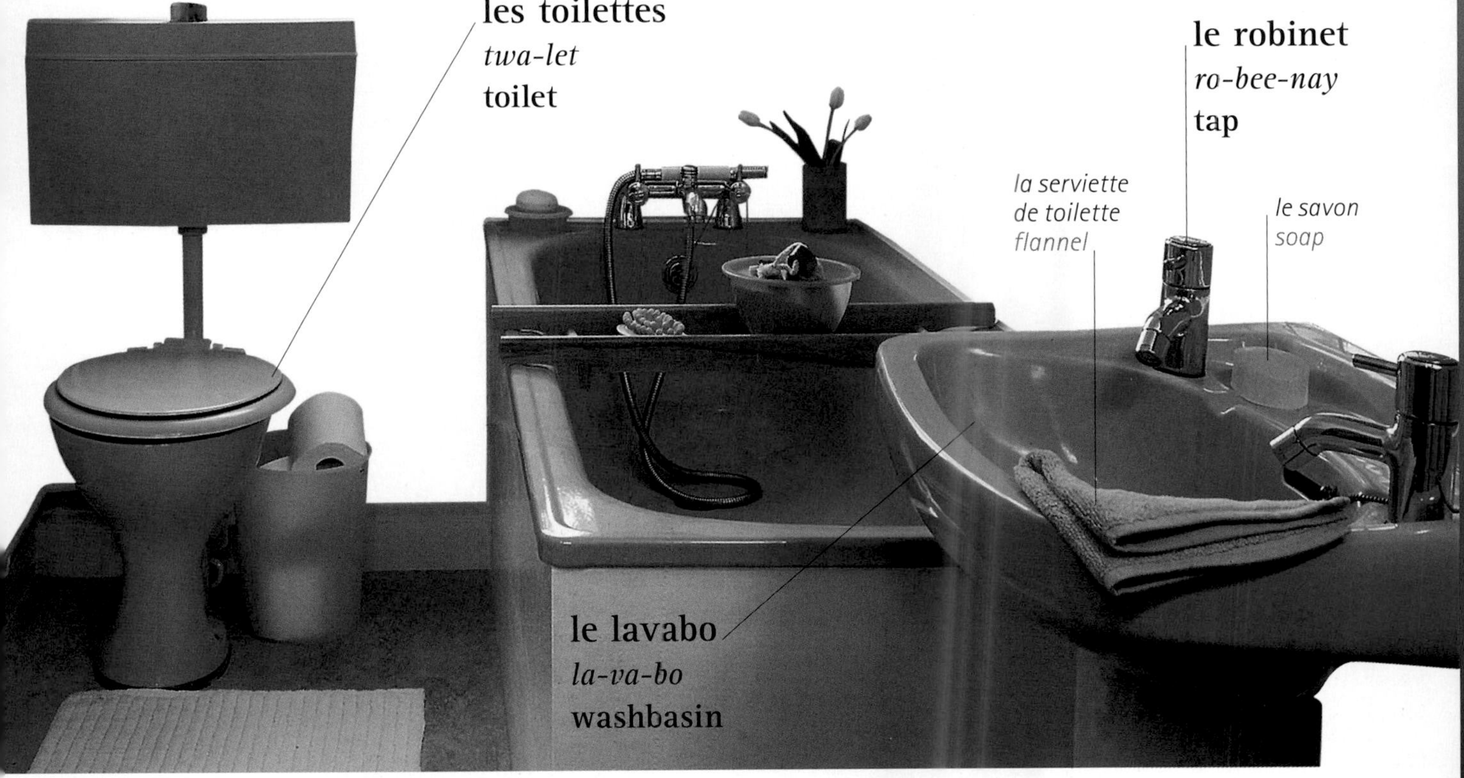
la serviette de toilette flannel
le savon soap

les toilettes
twa-let
toilet

le robinet
ro-bee-nay
tap

le lavabo
la-va-bo
washbasin

Ma chambre

My bedroom

le réveil
ray-vaye
alarm clock

le lit
lee
bed

l'oreiller
lo-ray-yay
pillow

la couette
koo-et
duvet

la chaise
shehz
chair

la commode
kom-mod
chest of drawers

Je **dors** dans mon **lit.**
I sleep in my bed.

le jeu électronique
zhuh ay-lek-tro-neek
computer game

Nous **jouons** à un **jeu de plateau.**
We're playing a board game.

Mon **chat dort** sous mon **lit.**
My cat sleeps under my bed.

la moquette
moh-ket
carpet

Qu'y a-t-il dans **l'armoire**?
What's in the wardrobe?

les livres
leev-ruh
books

les échecs
chess

e tapis
a-pee
ug

La **moquette** est bleue.
The carpet is blue.

Je sais jouer de la **guitare**.
I can play the guitar.

l'armoire
larm-wahr
wardrobe

la guitare
ghee-tar
guitar

le cintre
san-truh
coat hanger

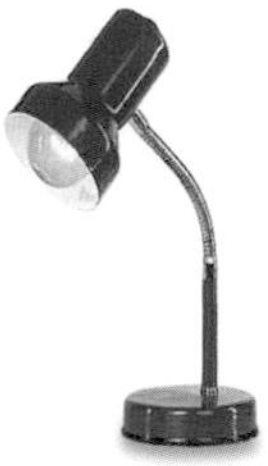

la lampe
lahmp
lamp

le miroir
meer-wahr
mirror

Le jardin
Garden

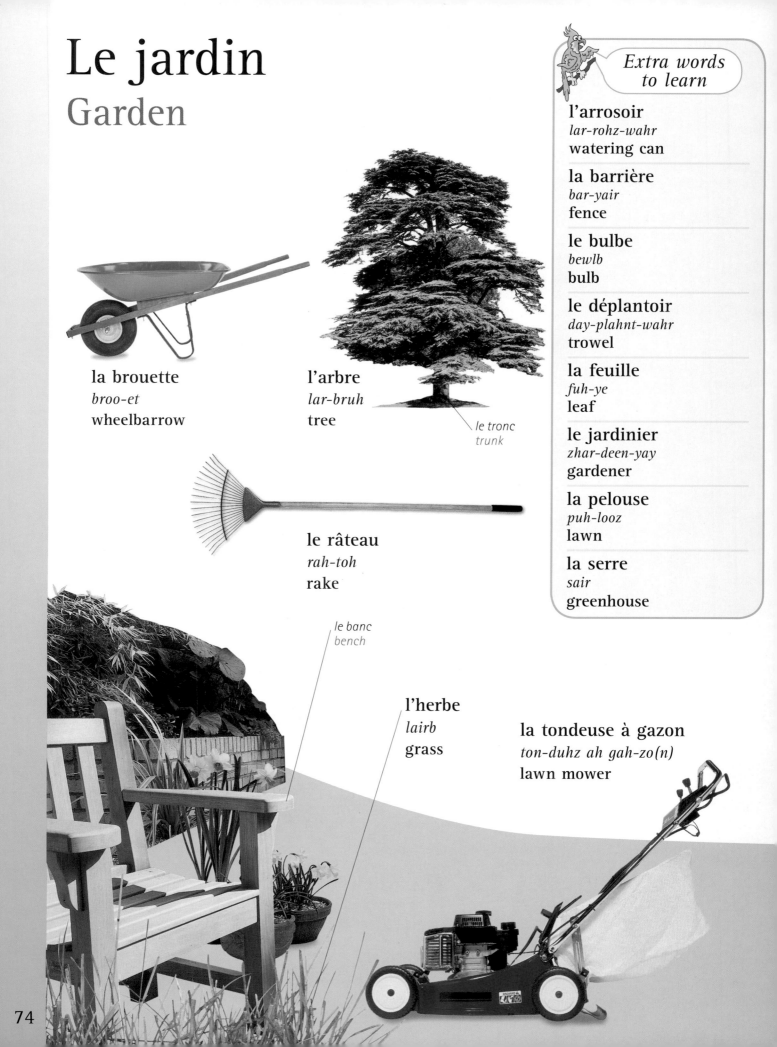

la brouette
broo-et
wheelbarrow

le tronc
trunk

l'arbre
lar-bruh
tree

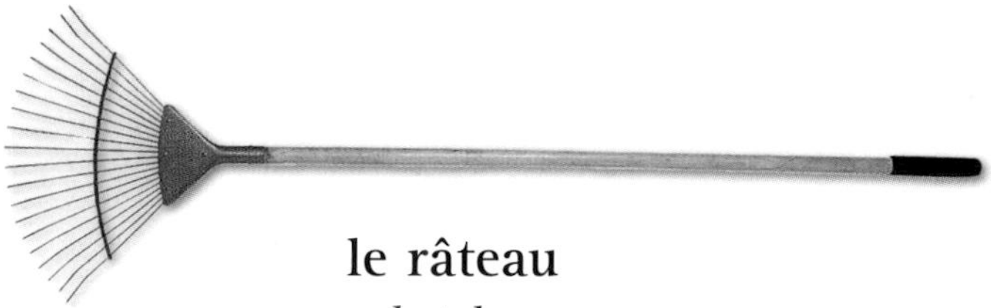

le râteau
rah-toh
rake

le banc
bench

l'herbe
lairb
grass

la tondeuse à gazon
ton-duhz ah gah-zo(n)
lawn mower

Extra words to learn

l'arrosoir
lar-rohz-wahr
watering can

la barrière
bar-yair
fence

le bulbe
bewlb
bulb

le déplantoir
day-plahnt-wahr
trowel

la feuille
fuh-ye
leaf

le jardinier
zhar-deen-yay
gardener

la pelouse
puh-looz
lawn

la serre
sair
greenhouse

De quelle couleur est la coccinelle sur cette page ?

l'aile
wing

le papillon
pa-pee-yo(n)
butterfly

l'escargot
les-kar-goh
snail

le ver
vair
worm

l'abeille
la-baye
bee

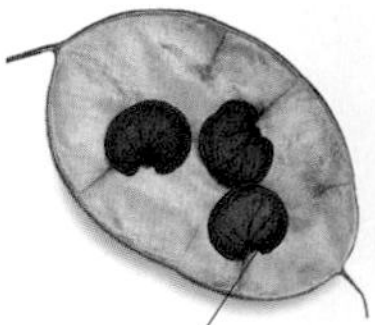

la graine
grehn
seed

la coccinelle
kok-see-nel
ladybird

Les **fleurs poussent** dans le **jardin**.
Flowers are growing in the garden.

Marie **creuse** dans le **jardin**.
Marie is digging in the garden.

la fleur
fluhr
flower

la chenille
shuh-nee-ye
caterpillar

la terre
tair
soil

la pelle
pel
spade

La vie en ville

City life

DB

l'autobus
lohto-bews
bus

la maison
may-zo(n)
house

Quelle heure est-il sur l'horloge bleue ?

le gratte-ciel
grat-syel
skyscraper

Les **villes** ont des **hauts bâtiments** appelés **gratte-ciels**.
Cities have tall buildings called skyscrapers.

l'horloge
lor-lozh
clock

les appartements
ap-par-tuh-mah(n)
flats

la rue
rew
street

le magasin
ma-ga-za(n)
shop

Extra words to learn

l'arrêt de bus
lar-reh duh bews
bus stop

l'autoroute
loh-toh-root
motorway

la banque
bahnk
bank

le café
ka-fay
café

la gare
gar
station

la route
root
road

le trottoir
trot-wahr
pavement

l'usine
lew-zeen
factory

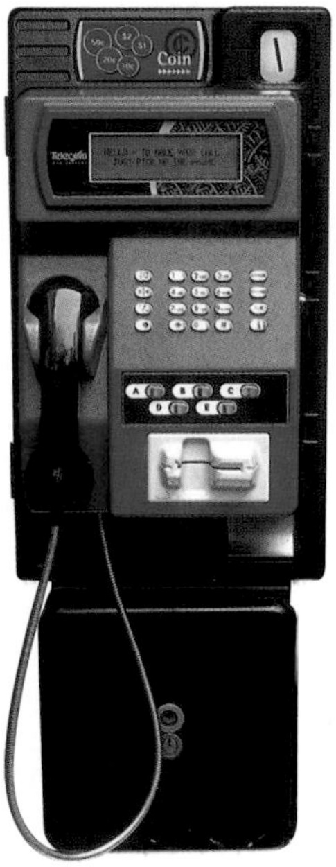
Coin

le téléphone
tay-lay-fon
phone

le panneau
pan-noh
sign

les feux de signalisation
fuh duh seen-ya-lee-za-syo(n)
traffic lights

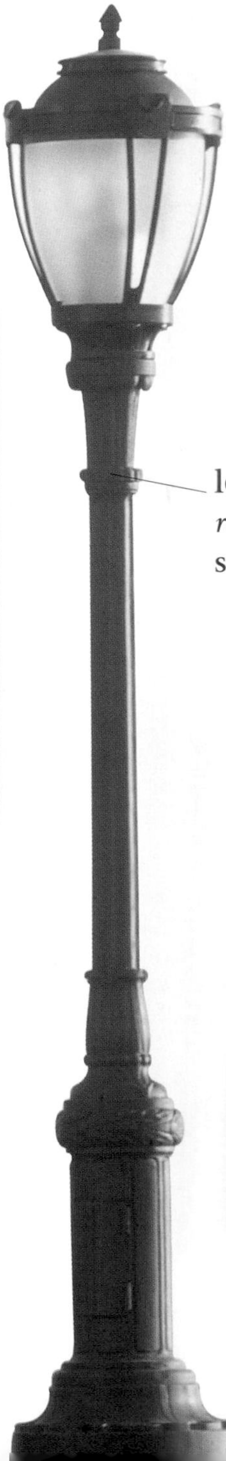

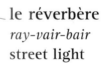

le réverbère
ray-vair-bair
street light

METRO
THEATRE
FEARLESS

le cinéma
see-nay-ma
cinema

le carrefour
kar-foor
crossing

le taxi
tak-see
taxi

ALBERT

l'hôtel
lo-tel
hotel

Au parc

In the park

le cerf-volant
sair-vo-lah(n)
kite

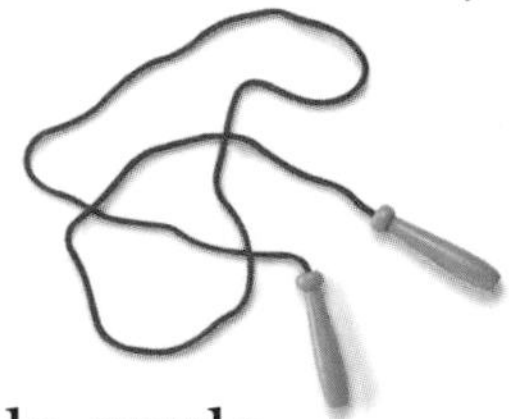

la corde à sauter
kord ah soh-tay
skipping rope

le skate-board
skate-board
skateboard

les fleurs
fluhr
flowers

le tourniquet
toor-nee-kay
roundabout

J'adore **sauter à la corde!**
I love skipping.
As-tu un **cerf-volant?**
Have you got a kite?

une fille
fee-ye
girl

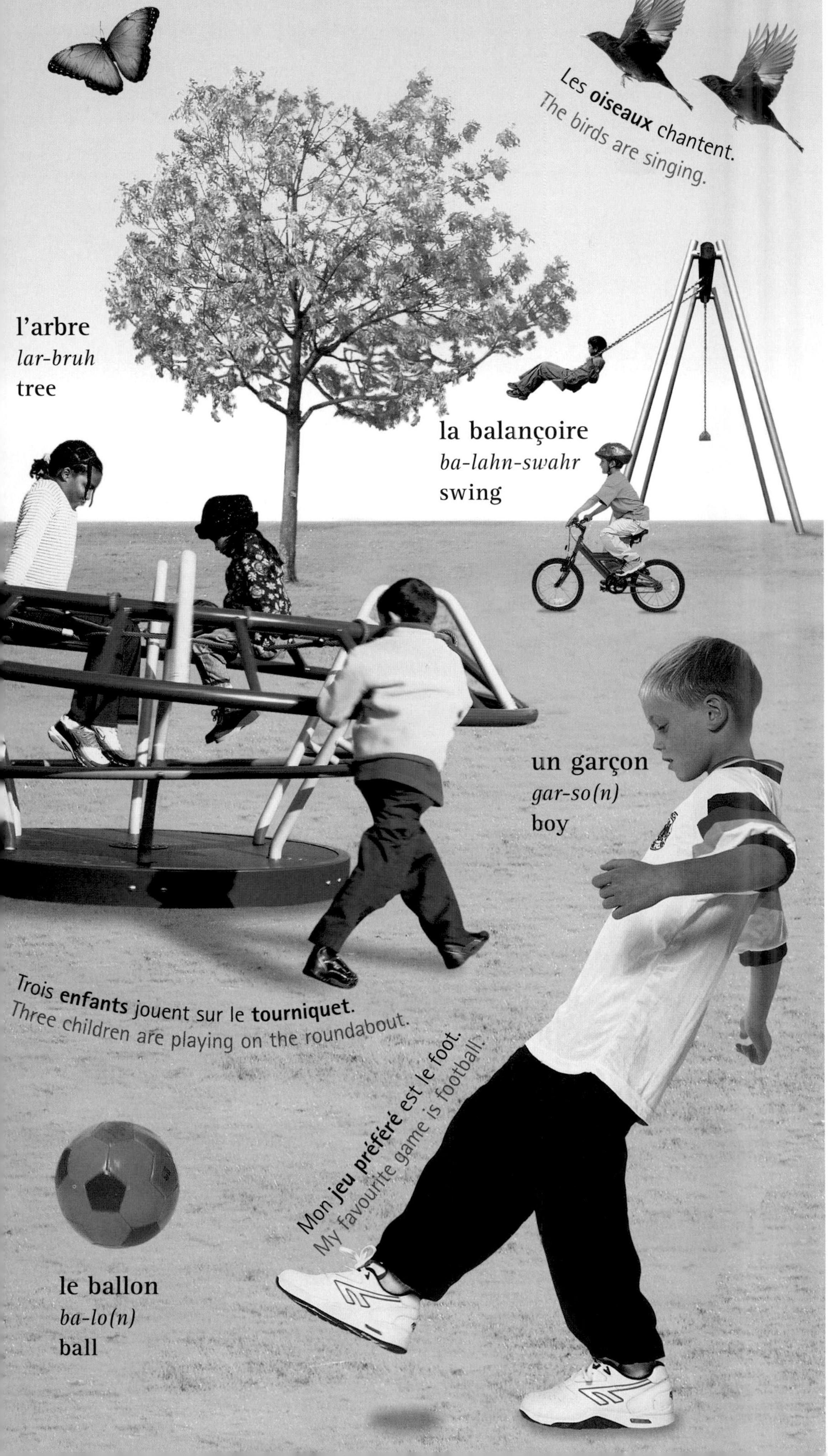

Les **oiseaux** chantent.
The birds are singing.

l'arbre
lar-bruh
tree

la balançoire
ba-lahn-swahr
swing

un garçon
gar-so(n)
boy

Trois **enfants** jouent sur le **tourniquet**.
Three children are playing on the roundabout.

Mon **jeu préféré** est le foot.
My favourite game is football.

le ballon
ba-lo(n)
ball

le papillon
pa-pee-yo(n)
butterfly

l'oiseau
lwa-zoh
bird

le vélo
vay-lo
bike

la feuille
fuh-ye
leaf

l'herbe
lairb
grass

Les loisirs

Hobbies

Mes **fleurs** poussent.
My flowers are growing.

le jardinage
zhar-dee-nazh
gardening

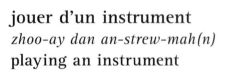

faire du camping
fair dew kahm-peeng
camping

Je suis **prête** à **aller** nager.
I'm ready to go swimming.

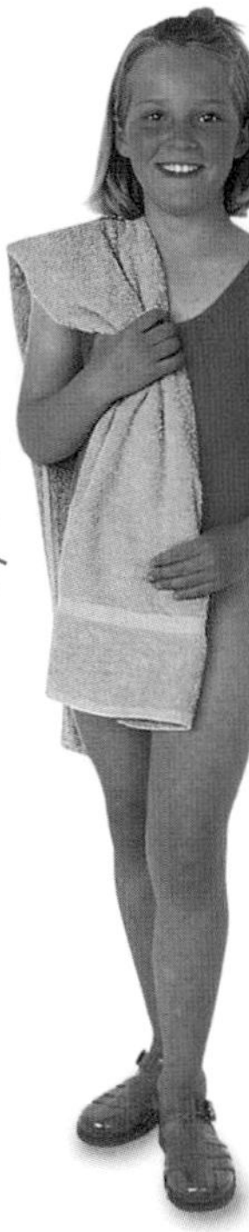

la natation
na-ta-syo(n)
swimming

Mathilde **s'entraîne** tous les jours.
Mathilde trains every day.

jouer d'un instrument
zhoo-ay dan an-strew-mah(n)
playing an instrument

observer les oiseaux
ob-zair-vay layz wa-zoh
bird-watching

faire de la danse
fair duh la dahnss
dancing

Extra words to learn

le chant
shah(n)
singing

collectionner
kol-lek-syo-nay
collecting

le dessin
de-sa(n)
drawing

faire la cuisine
fair la kwee-zeen
cooking

faire du roller
fair dew ro-lair
rollerblading

faire du théâtre
fair dew tay-a-truh
acting

faire du vélo
fair dew vay-lo
cycling

la lecture
lek-tewr
reading

Quel est ton loisir préféré ?

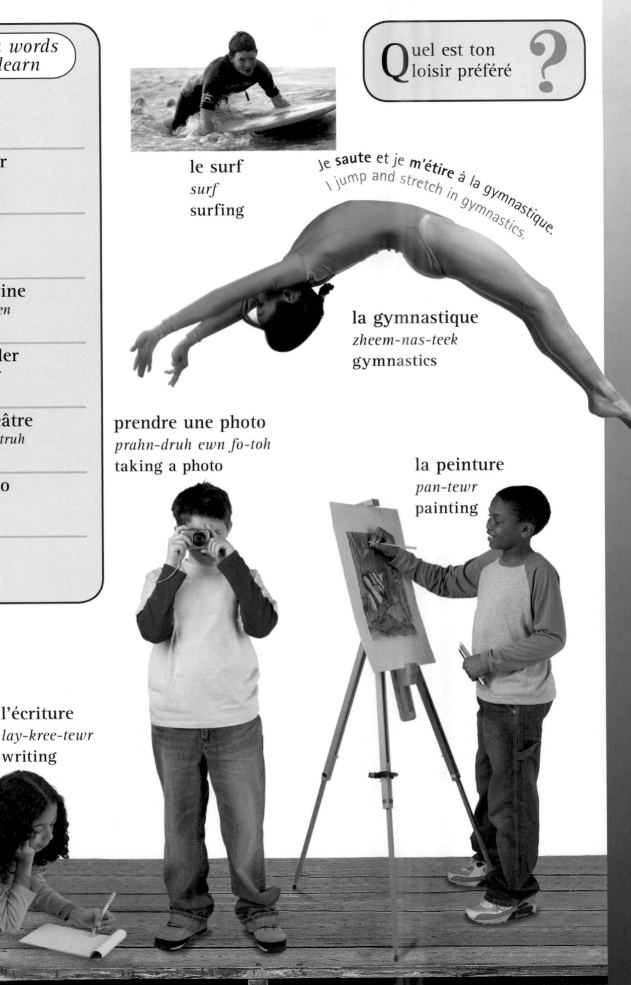

le surf
surf
surfing

Je **saute** et je **m'étire** à la gymnastique.
I jump and stretch in gymnastics.

la gymnastique
zheem-nas-teek
gymnastics

prendre une photo
prahn-druh ewn fo-toh
taking a photo

la peinture
pan-tewr
painting

l'écriture
lay-kree-tewr
writing

La nourriture

Food

l'orange
lor-ahnzh
orange

la pomme
pom
apple

la graine
seed

la pastèque
pas-tehk
watermelon

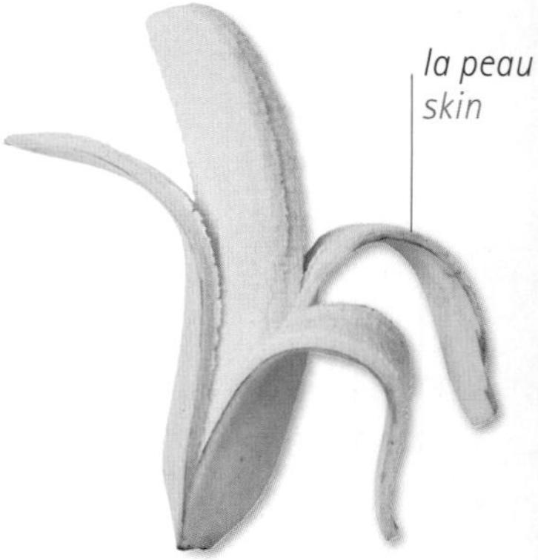
la peau
skin

la banane
ba-nan
banana

la tomate
tom-at
tomato

la carotte
ka-rot
carrot

la laitue
lay-tew
lettuce

le chou
shoo
cabbage

Nous **mangeons** des **pâtes**!
We're eating pasta!

l'assiette
plate
le verre
glass
le couteau
knife
la fourchette
fork
la chaise
chair
la table
table

Un ananas est un **fruit.**
A pineapple is a fruit.

l'ananas
lan-an-ass
pineapple

la pomme de terre
pom duh tair
potato

l'œuf
luhf
egg

le yaourt
ya-oort
yoghurt

le lait
lay
milk

la confiture
kon-fee-tewr
jam

Que manges-tu au petit-déjeuner ?

J'aime le **pain** avec du **miel**.
I like bread with honey.

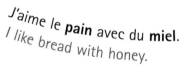

le pain
pa(n)
bread

le beurre
buhr
butter

le miel
myel
honey

les pâtes
paht
pasta

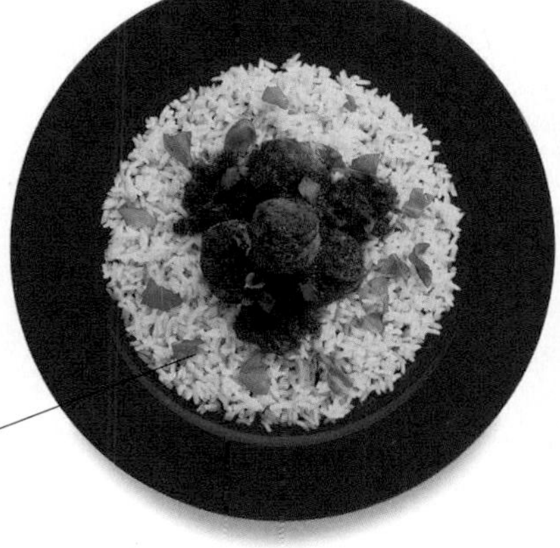
le riz
rice

la viande
vyanhnd
meat

Extra words to learn

le biscuit
bee-skwee
biscuit

la farine
far-een
flour

le fruit
frwee
fruit

le légume
lay-gewm
vegetable

l'oignon
lohn-yo(n)
onion

le poulet
poo-lay
chicken

la salade
sal-ad
salad

les spaghettis
spa-get-ee
spaghetti

le sucre
soo-kruh
sugar

Les courses
Shopping

Aimes-tu faire les courses ?

le prix
price

le marché
mar-shay
market

l'argent
lar-zhahn
money

le sac
sak
shopping bag

Je **dois acheter** des **œufs.**
I've got to buy some eggs.

Nous **attendons** dans la **queue.**
We're waiting in the queue.

le panier
pan-yay
basket

le caddie
ka-dee
trolley

la serveuse
sair-vuhz
waitress

le café
ka-fay
café

pain
oeufs
lait
beurre
sucre
farine

la liste de courses
leest duh koorss
shopping list

2/89¢
$1.49

le supermarché
soo-pair-mar-shay
supermarket

Elle a beaucoup de **sacs**!
She's got lots of bags!

l'acheteuse
lash-tuhz
shopper

160 · BAKERY · 160
ITALIAN BREAD & BISCUITS
VESUVIO BAKERY

la boulangerie
boo-lahn-zhree
bakery

BOOKSHOP

la librairie
leeb-rair-ee
bookshop

Extra words to learn

l'addition
lad-dee-syo(n)
bill

la caisse
kehss
checkout

en espèces
ah(n) es-pehss
(in) cash

faire les courses
fair lay koorss
to go shopping

le magasin
ma-ga-za(n)
shop

le prix
pree
price

le ticket de caisse
tee-kay duh kehss
receipt

le vendeur
vahn-duhr
shop assistant

À la fête
At the party

la boisson
bwa-so(n)
drink

les sandwichs
sahnd-weetsh
sandwiches

les cartes d'anniversaire
kart dan-ee-vair-sair
birthday cards

les bougies
boo-zhee
candles

le gâteau d'anniversaire
gah-toh dan-ee-vair-sair
birthday cake

Nous aimons **danser.**
We like dancing.
le magicien
ma-zhee-sya(n)
magician
le lecteur de CD
lek-tuhr duh say-day
CD player
Vois-tu le gâteau d'anniversaire?
Can you see the birthday cake?

Bon anniversaire!
Happy birthday!
Je veux **ouvrir** les **cadeaux.**
I want to open the presents.
Vois-tu les cartes d'anniversaire?
Can you see the birthday cards?

les décorations
day-ko-ra-syo(n)
decorations

les cadeaux
ka-doh
presents

les ballons
bal-o(n)
balloons

l'appareil photo
lap-pa-ray fo-toh
camera

les biscuits
bee-skwee
biscuits

la glace
glass
ice cream

les bonbons
bo(n)-bo(n)
sweets

Temps libre

Free time

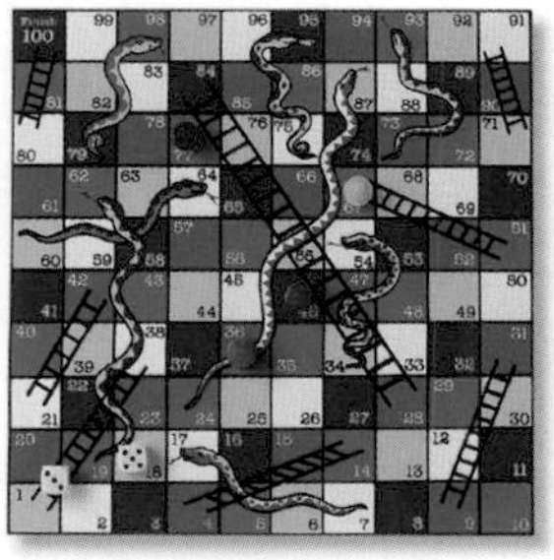

le jeu de société
zhuh duh so-see-eh-tay
board game

le ballon
bal-o(n)
ball

le robot
ro-boh
robot

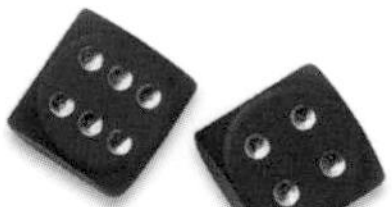

les dés
day
dice

l'ordinateur portable
lor-dee-na-tuhr por-ta-bluh
laptop

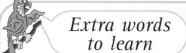

Extra words to learn

cache-cache
kash-kash
hide-and-seek

les cubes
kewb
toy blocks

le jeu
zhuh
game

le jouet
zhoo-way
toy

la marionnette
mar-yon-net
puppet

le masque
mask
mask

partir en vacances
par-teer ah(n) vak-ahns
going on holiday

la poupée
poo-pay
doll

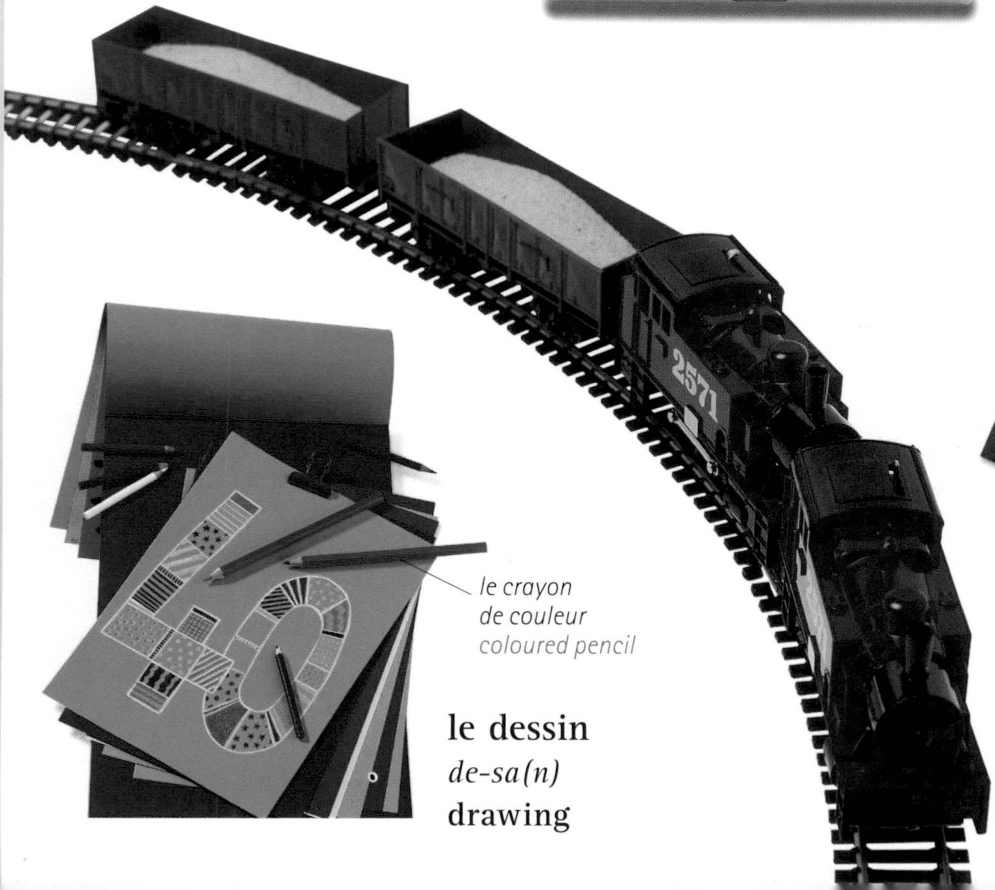
2571
le crayon
de couleur
coloured pencil

le puzzle
puh-zluh
puzzle

le dessin
de-sa(n)
drawing

le train
tra(n)
train

les cartes
kart
cards

les CD
say-day
CDs

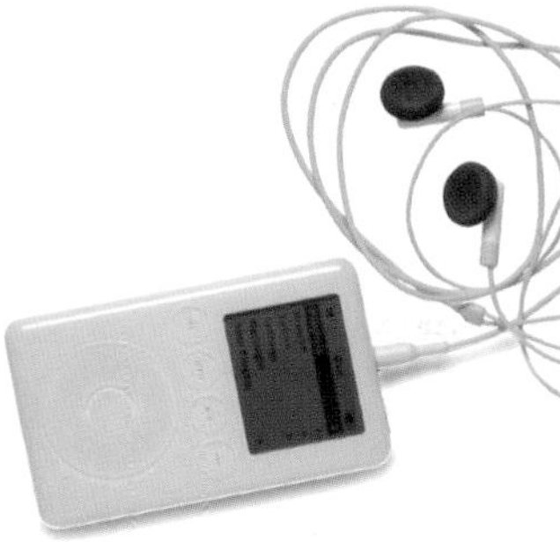

le lecteur MP3
lek-tuhr em-pay-trwa
MP3 player

le jeu électronique
zhuh ay-lek-tro-neek
computer game

le casque
helmet

Il **bouge** très vite!
He moves really fast!

Nous adorons les **toboggans aquatiques.**
We love water slides.

faire du roller
fair dew roh-lehr
rollerblading

Aimes-tu les jeux électroniques?

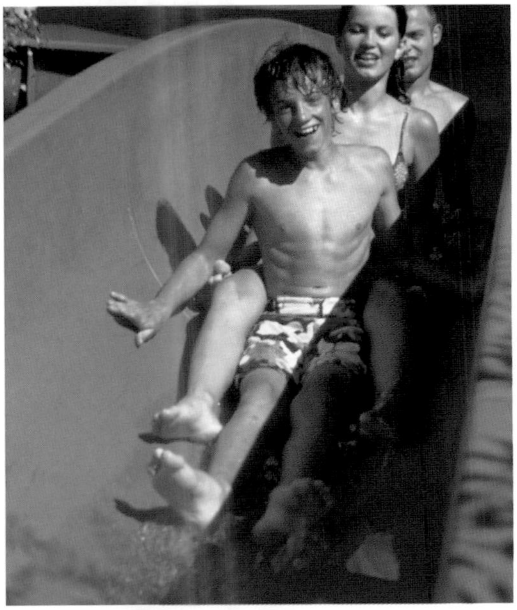

le toboggan aquatique
to-bog-ah(n) a-kwa-teek
water slide

aller au cinéma
ah-lay oh see-nay-ma
going to the cinema

la fête foraine
feht fo-rehn
fairground

Les moyens de transport

Transport

l'avion
lav-yo(n)
plane

le ferry-boat
fay-ree boht
ferry

le bateau à voiles
ba-toh ah vwal
sailing boat

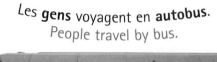

le taxi
tak-see
taxi

le camion
kam-yo(n)
lorry

le vélo
vay-lo
bike

Les **gens** voyagent en **autobus**.
People travel by bus.

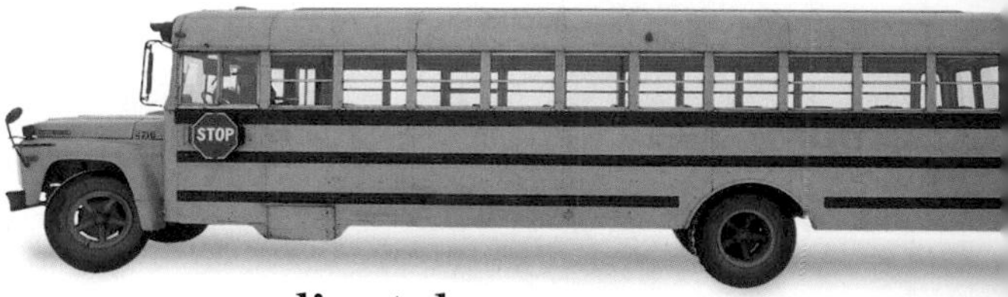
STOP

l'autobus
lohto-bews
bus

Pour les secours

To the rescue

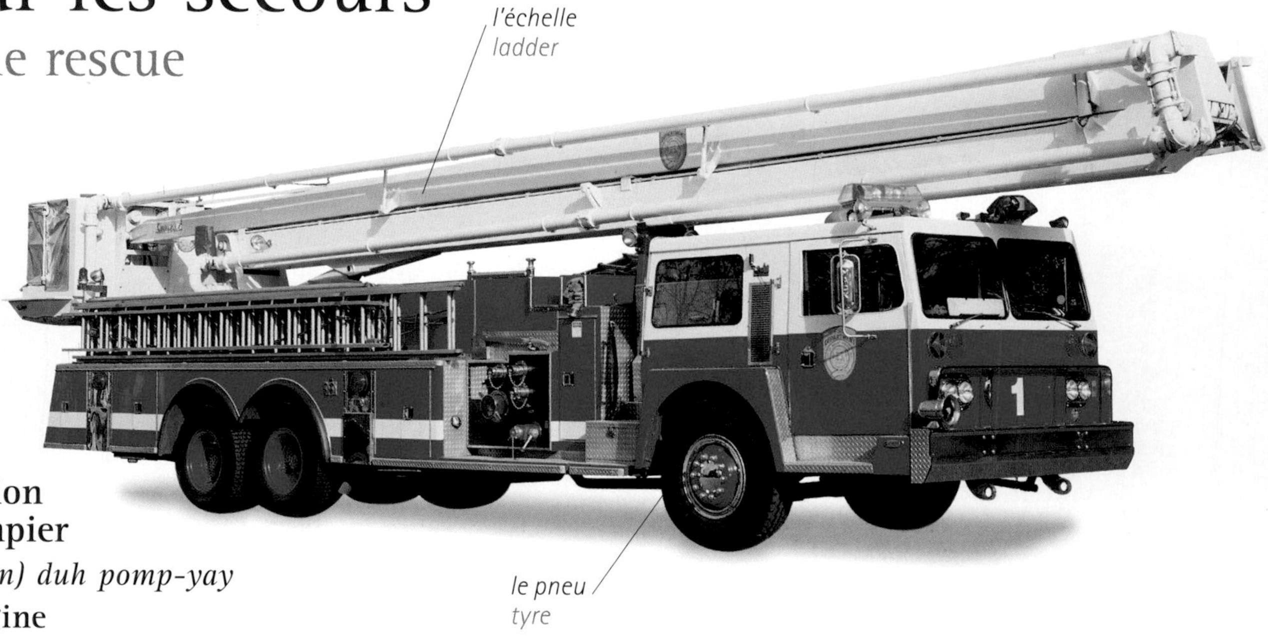
l'échelle
ladder
le pneu
tyre

le camion
de pompier
kam-yo(n) duh pomp-yay
fire engine

le panier
basket

Une **montgolfière vole** dans le ciel.
A hot-air balloon is flying in the sky.

la montgolfière
mohn-golf-yair
hot-air balloon

le train
tra(n)
train

les bagages
luggage

la voiture
vwah-tewr
car

la roue
wheel

la moto
moh-toh
motorbike

Extra words to learn

l'autocar
lohto-kar
coach

le billet
bee-yay
ticket

la camionnette
kam-yon-net
van

le carburant
kar-bew-rah(n)
fuel

la fusée
few-zay
space rocket

le garage
gar-azh
garage

l'horaire
lor-air
timetable

le voyage
vwa-yazh
journey

Combien de roues y a-t-il sur cette page ?

POLICE

l'hélicoptère de police
lay-lee-kop-tair duh po-leess
police helicopter

POLICIA
436

la voiture de police
vwa-tewr duh po-leess
police car

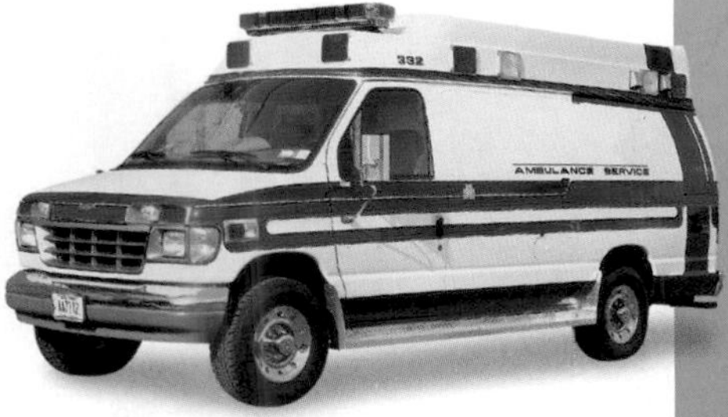

l'ambulance
lahm-bew-lahnss
ambulance

Les animaux de la jungle

Jungle animals

l'oiseau-mouche
lwa-zoh-moosh
hummingbird

la chauve-souris
shohv soo-ree
bat

le chimpanzé
shahm-pahn-zay
chimpanzee

l'aile
wing

le papillon
pa-pee-yo(n)
butterfly

la fourmi
foor-mee
ant

l'araignée
lar-ehn-yay
spider

le gorille
go-ree-ye
gorilla

le papillon de nuit
pa-pee-yo(n) duh nwee
moth

le crocodile
kro-ko-deel
crocodile

Quels animaux peuvent voler sur cette page ?

le perroquet
pair-o-kay
parrot

Le toucan prend la **nourriture** avec son **bec**.
The toucan gets food with its beak.

l'œil
eye
le bec
beak
la griffe
claw

le toucan
too-kah(n)
toucan

Extra words to learn

l'aigle
lay-gluh
eagle

l'arbre
lar-bruh
tree

la forêt tropicale
for-eh tro-pee-kal
rainforest

l'insecte
lan-sekt
insect

le lézard
lay-zar
lizard

le mammifère
ma-mee-fair
mammal

l'oiseau
lwa-zoh
bird

le scarabée
ska-ra-bay
beetle

le serpent
sair-pah(n)
snake

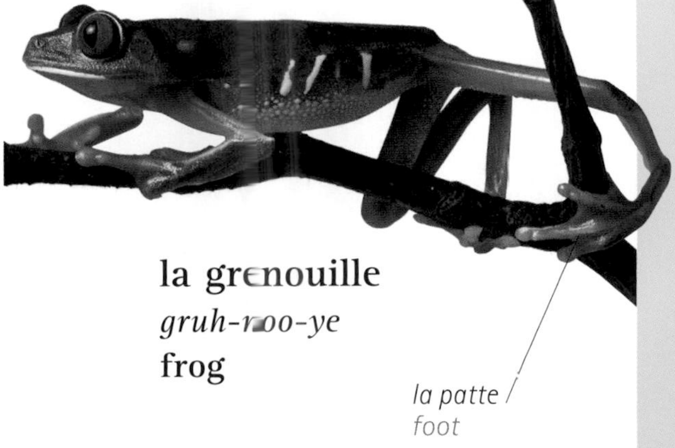

la patte
foot

la grenouille
gruh-noo-ye
frog

les rayures
stripes

le tigre
tee-gruh
tiger

les taches
spots

le léopard
lay-o-par
leopard

Les animaux du monde

World animals

le koala
ko-a-la
koala

le daim
da(m)
deer

la patte
paw

le lion
lee-yo(n)
lion

le panda
pahn-da
panda

La **girafe** a un long **cou!**
The giraffe has a long neck!

la queue
tail

la girafe
zhee-raf
giraffe

l'ours blanc
loorss blah(n)
polar bear

le bec
beak

le pingouin
pah(n)-gwa(h)
penguin

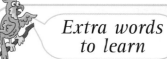

Extra words to learn

l'alligator
lal-ee-gah-tor
alligator

le babouin
ba-bwa(n)
baboon

la chauve-souris
shohv soo-ree
bat

le faucon
foh-ko(n)
hawk

le loup
loo
wolf

le pélican
pay-lee-kah(n)
pelican

le renard
ruh-nar
fox

la tortue de mer
tor-tew duh mair
turtle

Combien d'oiseaux y a-t-il sur cette page ?

L'éléphant prend la **nourriture** avec sa **trompe**.
The elephant gets food with its trunk.

le chameau
sha-moh
camel

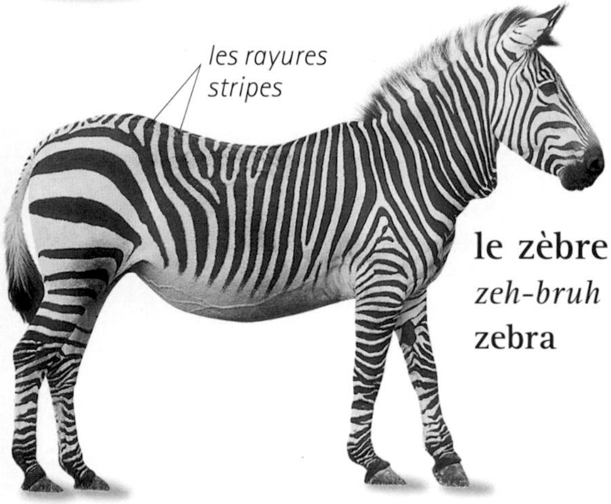

les rayures
stripes

le zèbre
zeh-bruh
zebra

la trompe
trunk

l'éléphant
lay-lay-fah(n)
elephant

la griffe
claw

l'ours
loorss
bear

la queue
tail

le kangourou
kahn-goo-roo
kangaroo

le rhinocéros
ree-no-say-ros
rhinoceros

la palme
flipper

le dauphin
doh-fa(n)
dolphin

À la ferme
On the farm

le tracteur
trak-tuhr
tractor

le chien de berger
shya(n) duh bair-zhay
sheepdog

le champ
shah(m)
field

le blé
blay
wheat

les agneaux
an-yoh
lambs

La **fermière utilise** le **tracteur.**
The farmer uses a tractor.

7110
CASE INTERNATIONAL
MAGNUM

la fermière
fairm-yair
farmer

le mouton
moo-to(n)
sheep

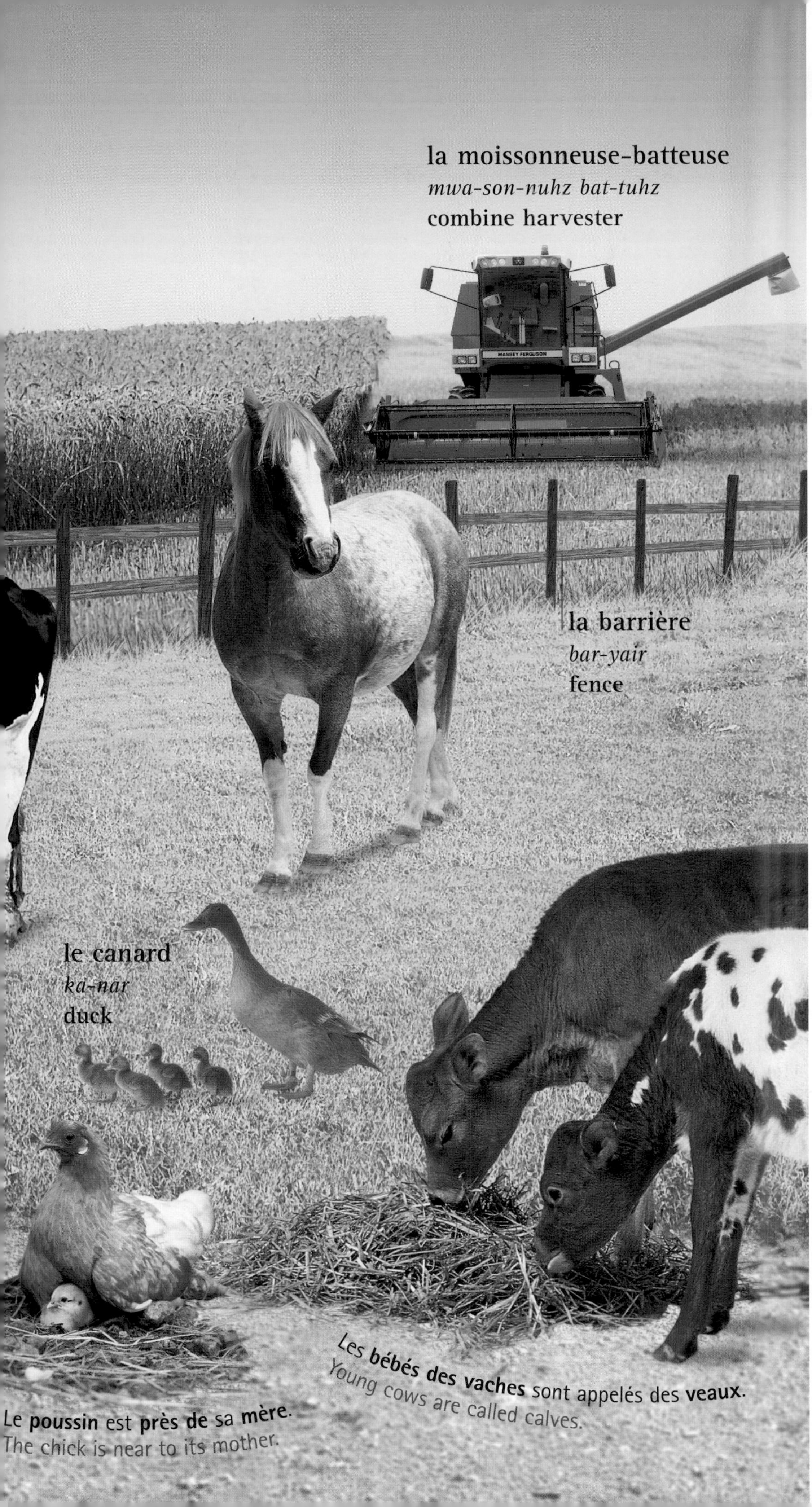

la moissonneuse-batteuse
mwa-son-nuhz bat-tuhz
combine harvester

la barrière
bar-yair
fence

le canard
ka-nar
duck

Les **bébés des vaches** sont appelés des **veaux**.
Young cows are called calves.

Le **poussin** est **près de** sa **mère**.
The chick is near to its mother.

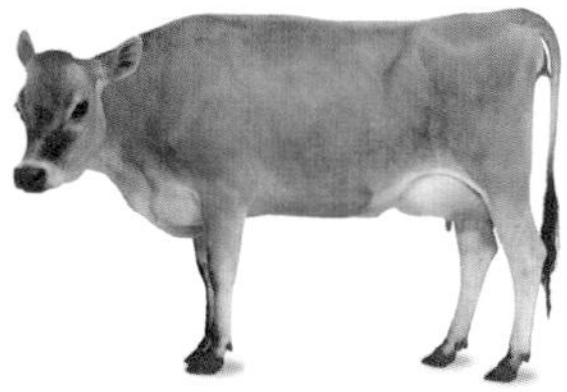

la vache
vash
cow

le foin
fwa(n)
hay

le cheval
shuh-val
horse

le poulet
poo-lay
chicken

les canetons
ka-nuh-to(n)
ducklings

L'océan
Ocean

le bateau de pêche
ba-toh duh pehsh
fishing boat

la mouette
moo-wet
seagull

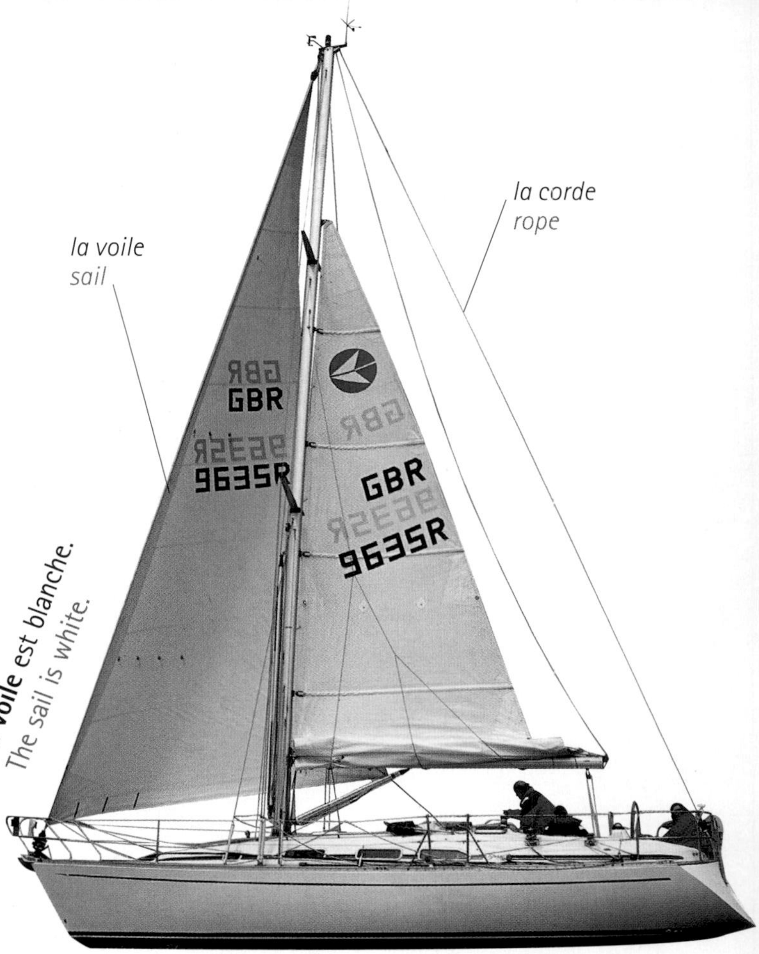
la voile
sail
la corde
rope
La **voile** est blanche.
The sail is white.

le bateau à voiles
ba-toh ah vwal
sailing boat

Extra words to learn

l'ancre
lahn-kruh
anchor

la bouée
boo-way
buoy

le canot
kanoh
rowing boat

la mer
mair
sea

la pêche
pehsh
fishing

le port
por
harbour

la vague
vag
wave

La **baleine nage** dans la **mer**.
The whale swims in the sea.

la baleine
ba-len
whale

la méduse
may-dewz
jellyfish

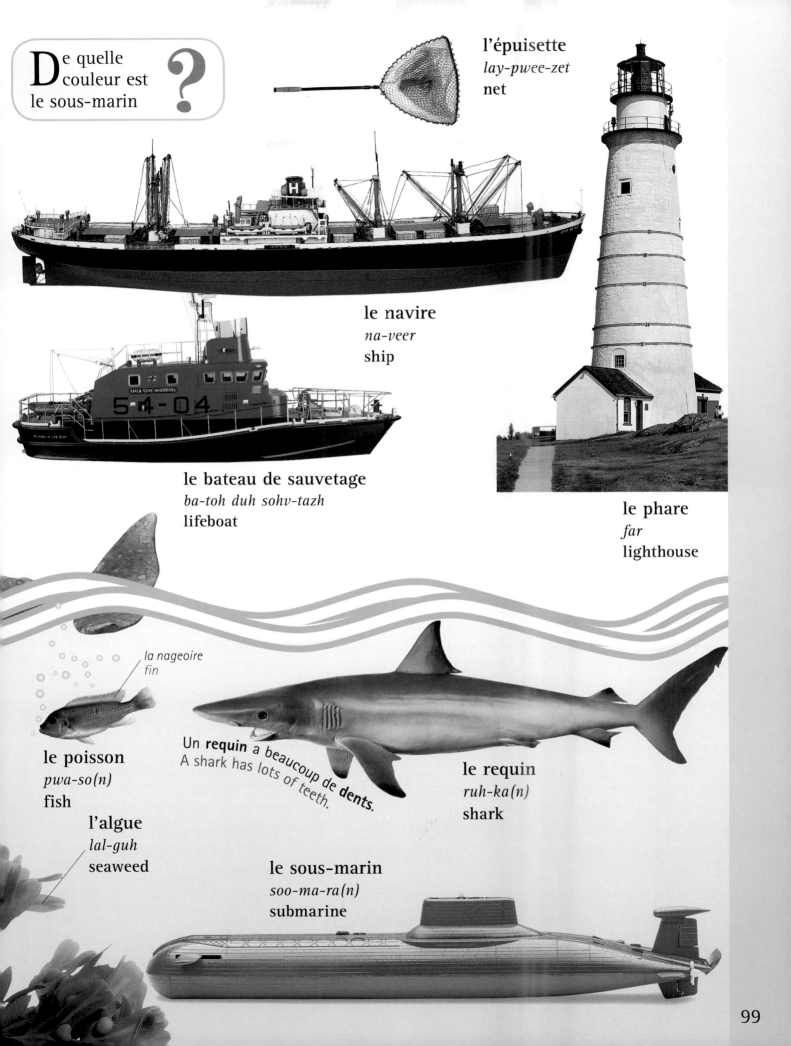

De quelle couleur est le sous-marin ?

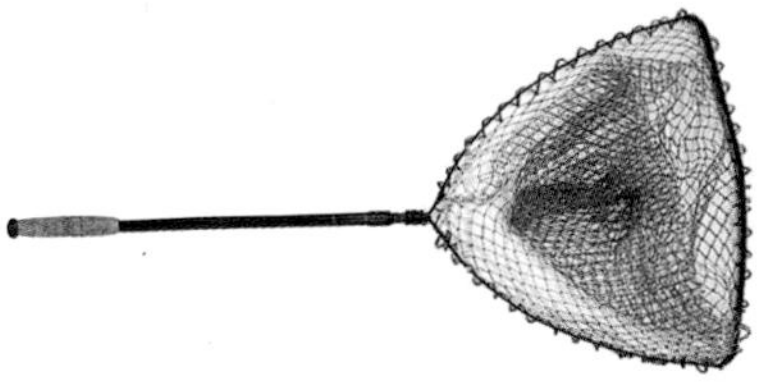

l'épuisette
lay-pwee-zet
net

le navire
na-veer
ship

le bateau de sauvetage
ba-toh duh sohv-tazh
lifeboat

le phare
far
lighthouse

la nageoire
fin

le poisson
pwa-so(n)
fish

Un **requin** a beaucoup de **dents.**
A shark has lots of teeth.

le requin
ruh-ka(n)
shark

l'algue
lal-guh
seaweed

le sous-marin
soo-ma-ra(n)
submarine

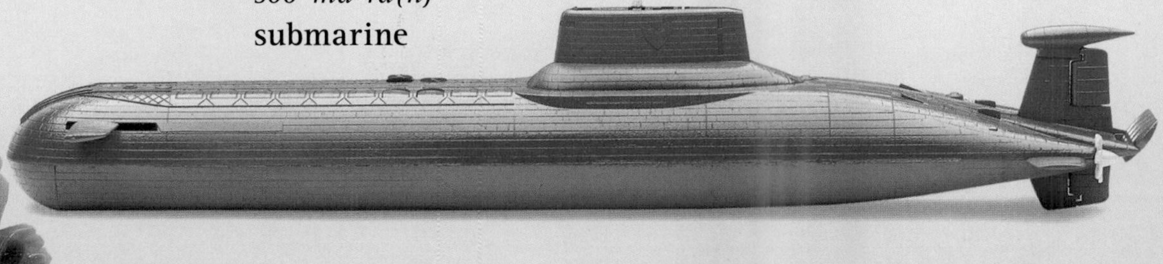

La nature

Nature

la libellule
lee-bel-lewl
dragonfly

Le **nénuphar pousse** dans l'**eau**.
The water lily grows in the water.

le nénuphar
nay-new-far
water lily

le canard
ka-nar
duck

la plante
plahnt
plant

Beaucoup d'**animaux vivent** près des **étangs**.
Many animals live near ponds.

le cygne
seen-ye
swan

le crapaud
kra-poo
toad

le bec
beak

le nid
nee
nest

Les **têtards nagent** dans les **étangs.**
Tadpoles swim in ponds.

les têtards
the-tar
tadpoles

Combien de nénuphars y a-t-il dans l'étang ?

l'antenne
antenna

la guêpe
gehp
wasp

l'aile
wing

la mouche
moosh
fly

l'étang
lay-tah(n)
pond

le hibou
ee-boo
owl

la grenouille
gruh-noo-ye
frog

Extra words to learn

l'eau
loh
water

l'habitat
la-bee-ta
habitat

le héron
air-o(n)
heron

l'insecte
lan-sekt
insect

le lapin
lap-a(n)
rabbit

la mauvaise herbe
moh-vayz airb
weed

l'oiseau
lwa-zoh
bird

le papillon
pa-pee-yo(n)
butterfly

À la plage
At the beach

le seau
soh
bucket

la pelle
pel
spade

le crabe
krab
crab

le coquillage
ko-kee-yazh
shell

les galets
ga-lay
pebbles

J'adore **nager** dans la **mer**!
I love swimming in the sea!
Aimes-tu **aller** à la **plage**?
Do you like going to the beach?
Je **joue** sous mon **parasol**.
I'm playing under my parasol.
le parasol
umbrella
la crème solaire
suncream

le rocher
ro-shay
rock

les mouettes
moo-wet
seagulls

Nous adorons **jouer** avec le **sable**.
We love playing in the sand.

le maillot de bain
swimsuit

l'etoile de mer
lay-twal duh mair
starfish

la glace
glass
ice cream

l'algue
lal-guh
seaweed

Elle **construit** un **château de sable**.
She's building a sandcastle.

les lunettes de natation
lew-net duh na-ta-syo(n)
goggles

le chapeau
sha-poh
sunhat

la chaise longue
shayz long-uh
deck chair

le sable
sah-bluh
sand

le château de sable
sha-toh duh sah-bluh
sandcastle

L'école

School

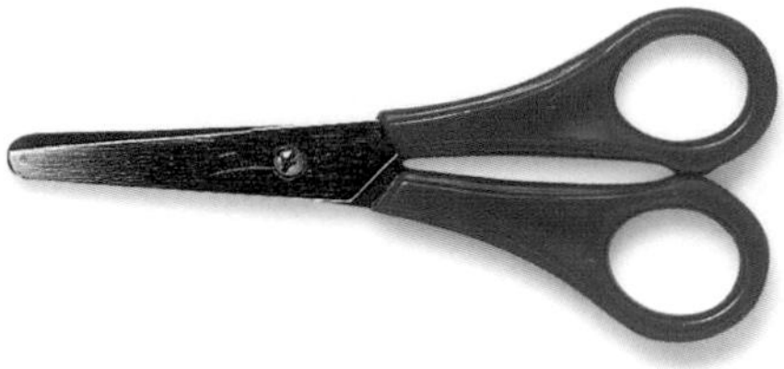

les ciseaux
see-zoh
scissors

les crayons de couleur
kra-yo(n) duh koo-luhr
coloured pencils

le tableau
tab-loh
blackboard

la règle
reh-gluh
ruler

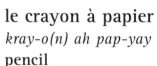

la gomme
gom
rubber

le crayon à papier
kray-o(n) ah pap-yay
pencil

le stylo
stee-loh
pen

le carnet
notebook

le bureau
bew-roh
desk

Les enfants s'assoient à des **bureaux**.
The children sit at desks.

Extra words to learn

l'alphabet
lal-fa-bay
alphabet

la chaise
shehz
chair

le dessin
de-sa(n)
drawing

l'écriture
lay-kree-tewr
writing

la lecture
lek-tewr
reading

le maître/la maîtresse
meh-truh/meh-tress
teacher

la salle de classe
sal duh klahss
classroom

les sciences
see-yahnss
science

Vois-tu la **pomme** dans le **panier repas**?
Can you see the apple in the lunch box?

le panier repas
pan-yay ruh-pah
lunch box

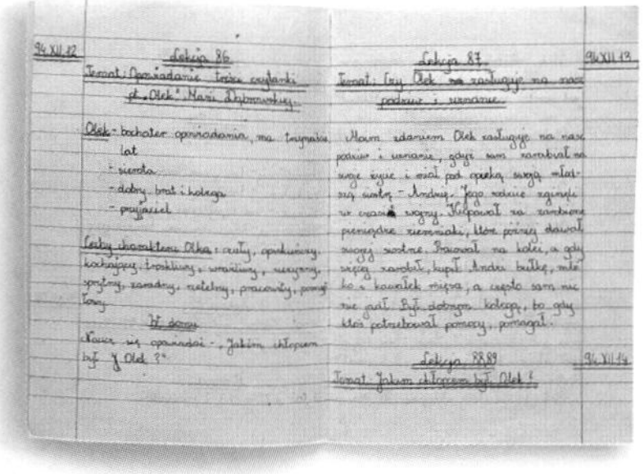

le cahier
ka-yay
exercise book

le cartable
school bag

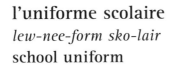

l'uniforme scolaire
lew-nee-form sko-lair
school uniform

les livres
leev-ruh
books

Combien de livres y a-t-il sur cette page ?

les feutres
fuh-truh
felt-tips

Trouve ton **pays** sur le **globe**.
Find your country on the globe.

le globe
glob
globe

l'ordinateur
lor-dee-na-tuhr
computer

Les sports

Sports

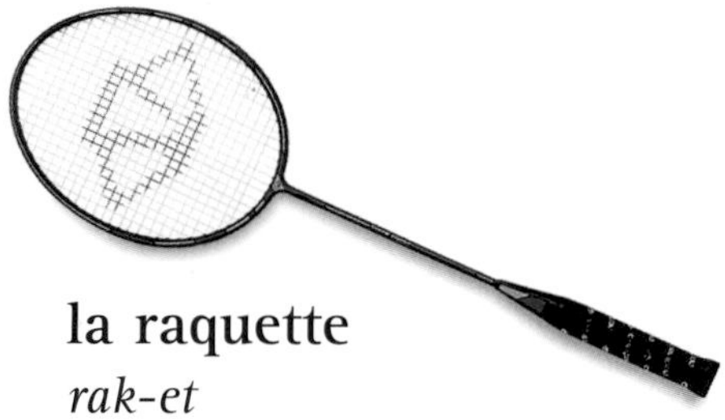

la raquette
rak-et
racket

Je porte un **casque**.
I'm wearing a helmet.

le casque
helmet
la roue
wheel

faire du vélo
fair dew vay-lo
cycling

le ski
skee
skiing

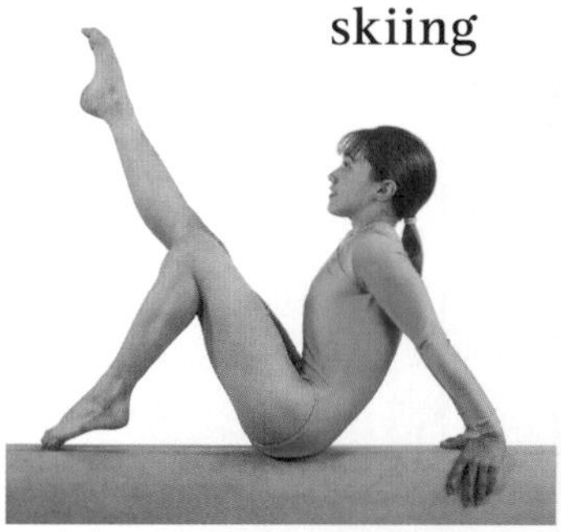

la gymnastique
zheem-nas-teek
gymnastics

le patinage sur glace
pa-tee-nazh
soor glass
ice skating

Nous **jouons** au **basket-ball.**
We're playing basketball.

le short
shorts
les baskets
trainers

le basket
basket
basketball

le tee-shirt
T-shirt

le golf
golf
golf

Delphine **veut marquer** un **but**.
Delphine wants to score a goal.

le foot
foot
football

Extra words to learn

l'athlétisme
lat-lay-tee-smah
athletics

le base-ball
bayz-bohl
baseball

l'exercice
lek-sair-seess
exercise

le hockey
ok-ay
hockey

le hockey sur glace
ok-ay soor glass
ice hockey

le judo
zhew-do
judo

le karaté
ka-ra-tay
karate

la natation
na-ta-syo(n)
swimming

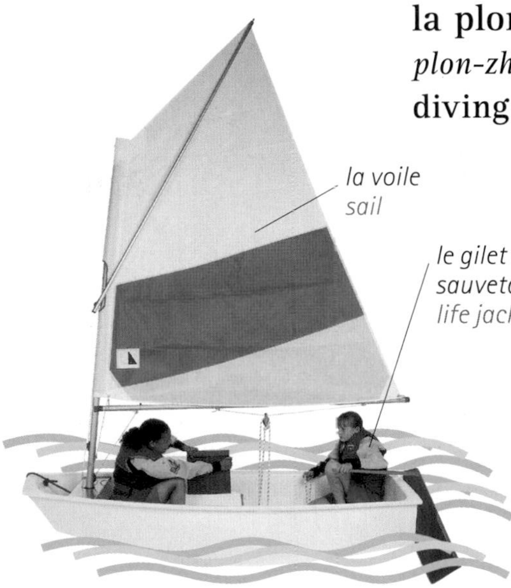
la voile
sail
le gilet de sauvetage
life jacket

faire de la voile
fair duh la vwal
sailing

la plongée
plon-zhay
diving

Aimes-tu faire du sport ?

Je **tire** sur les **rames**.
I'm pulling on the oars.

la rame
oar

faire de l'aviron
fair duh lav-ee-ro(n)
rowing

la balle
ball
le gant
glove

la batte
bat
bat

le rugby
rewg-bee
rugby

la course à pied
koorss ah pyay
running

le cheval
horse

l'équitation
lay-keet-a-syo(n)
horse riding

la raquette
racket

le tennis
ten-neess
tennis

Les animaux familiers

Pets

la nourriture
food

le chiot
shyoh
puppy

Mon **chien** s'appelle Toby.
My dog's called Toby.

le hamster
am-stair
hamster

Une **tortue bouge** très **lentement**.
A tortoise moves very slowly.

la tortue
tor-tew
tortoise

le lapin
lap-(a)n
rabbit

le cochon d'Inde
ko-sho(n) dand
guinea pig

le collier
collar

le chat
sha
cat

le poisson rouge
pwa-so(n) roozh
goldfish

De quelles couleurs sont les poils du cochon d'Inde ?

les poils
fur

le chaton
sha-to(n)
kitten

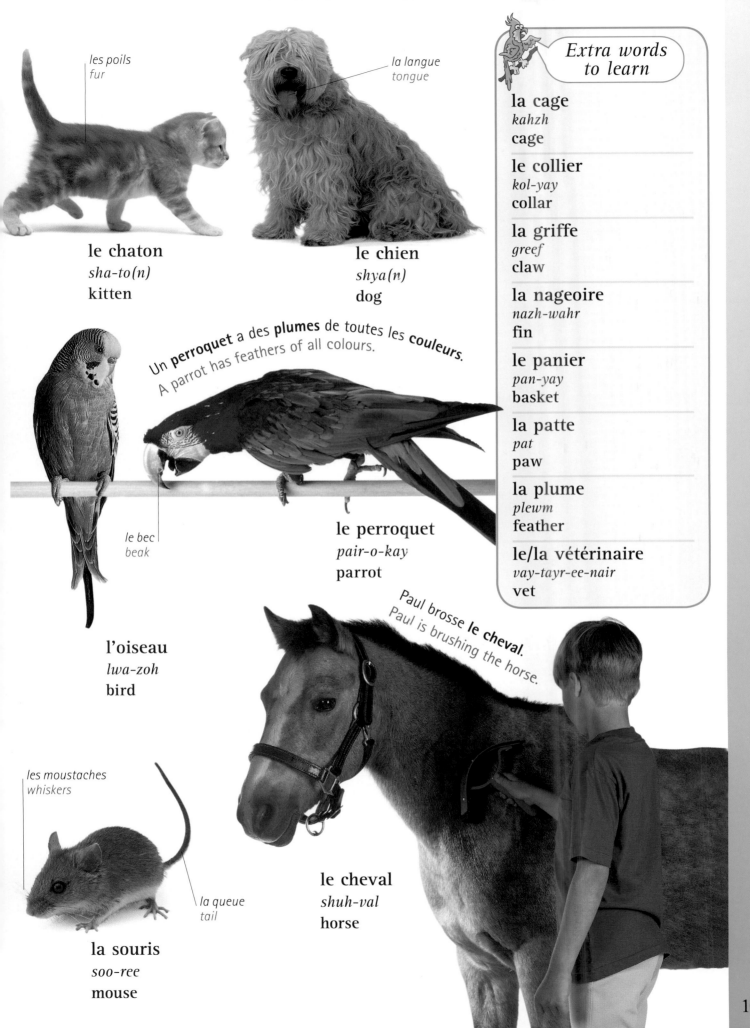

la langue
tongue

le chien
shya(n)
dog

Un **perroquet** a des **plumes** de toutes les **couleurs.**
A parrot has feathers of all colours.

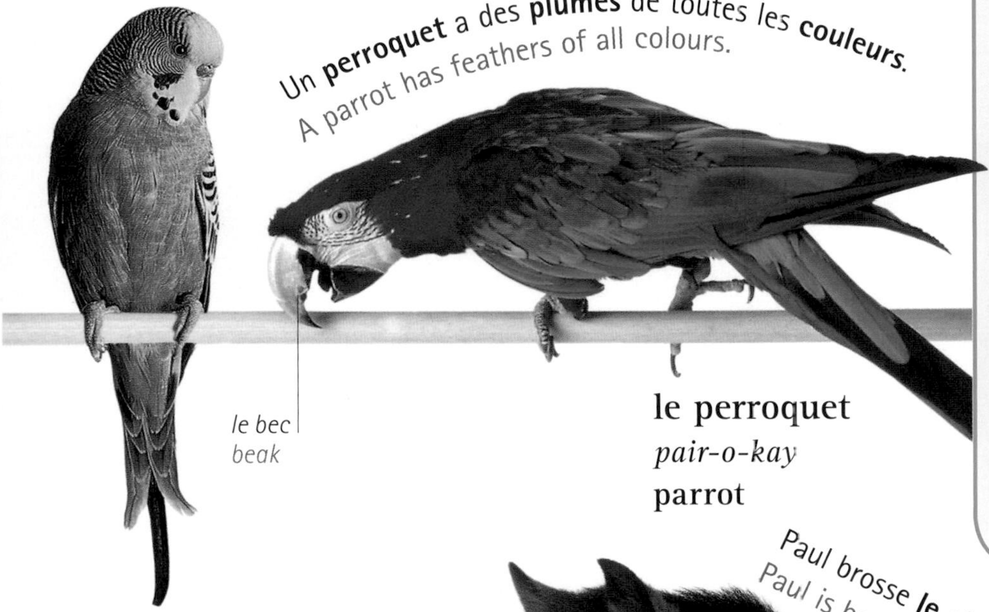
le bec
beak

le perroquet
pair-o-kay
parrot

l'oiseau
lwa-zoh
bird

Extra words to learn

la cage
kahzh
cage

le collier
kol-yay
collar

la griffe
greef
claw

la nageoire
nazh-wahr
fin

le panier
pan-yay
basket

la patte
pat
paw

la plume
plewm
feather

le/la vétérinaire
vay-tayr-ee-nair
vet

Paul brosse **le cheval.**
Paul is brushing the horse.

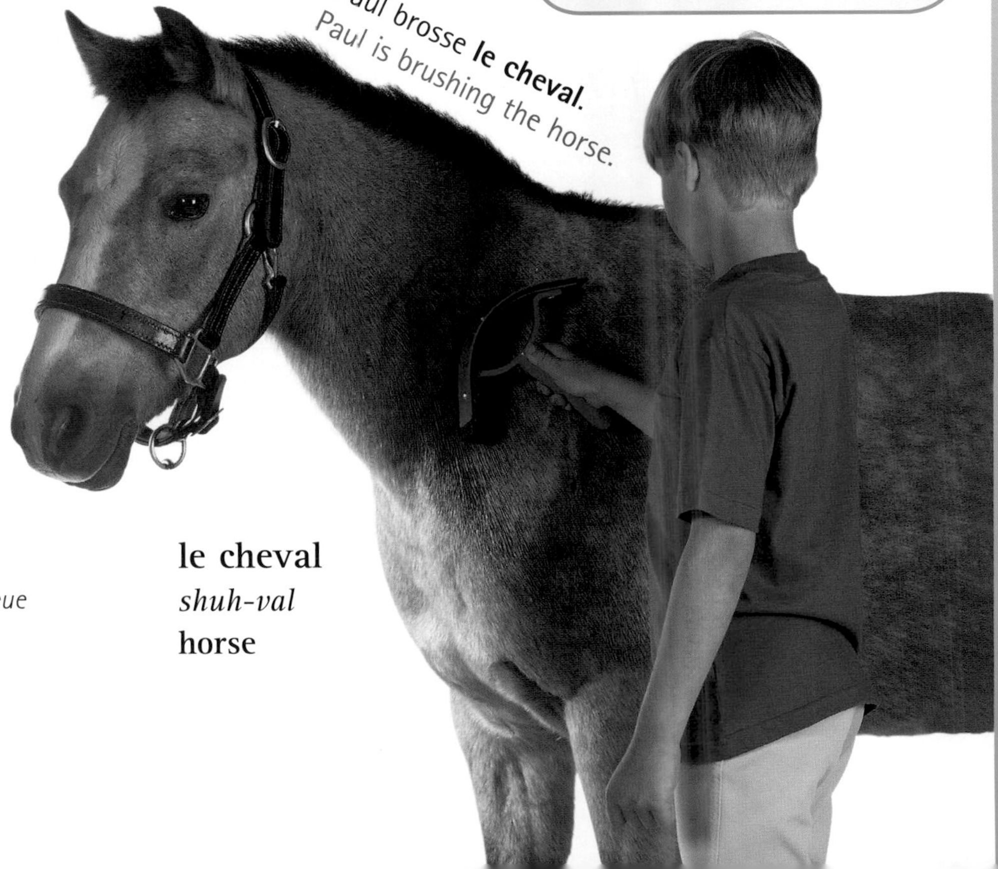

le cheval
shuh-val
horse

les moustaches
whiskers
la queue
tail

la souris
soo-ree
mouse

Les couleurs et les formes

Colours and shapes

rouge
roozh
red

orange
or-ahnzh
orange

jaune
zhohn
yellow

vert
vair
green

bleu
bluh
blue

violet
vyo-lay
purple

rose
rohz
pink

marron
mar-o(n)
brown

noir
nwahr
black

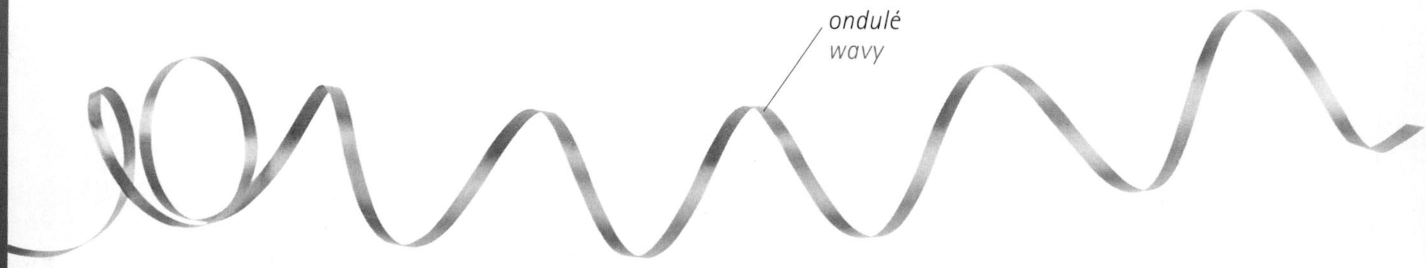
ondulé
wavy

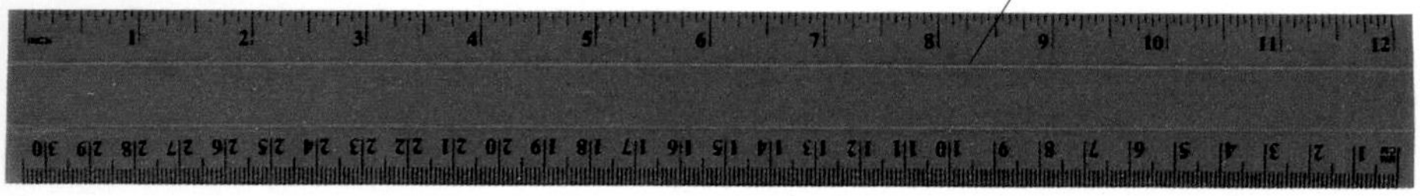
droit
straight

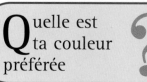

Quelle est ta couleur préférée?

le carré
kar-ray
square

le cercle
sair-kluh
circle

l'arc-en-ciel
rainbow

le triangle
tree-yahn-gluh
triangle

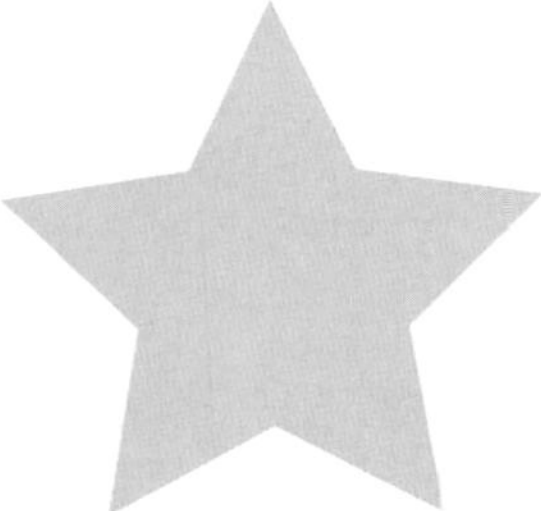

l'étoile
lay-twal
star

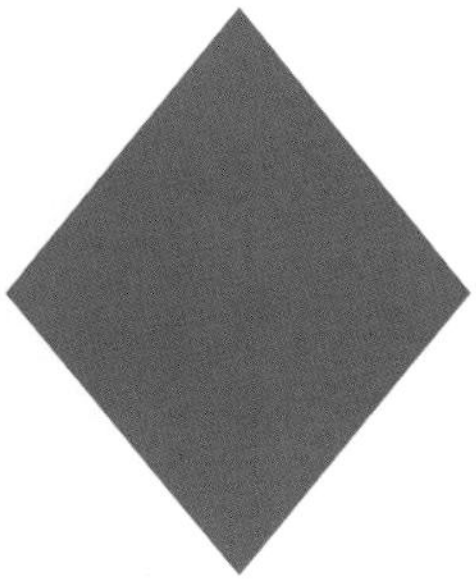

le losange
lo-zahnzh
diamond

le rectangle
rek-tahn-gluh
rectangle

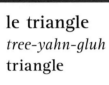

un hexagone
ecks-a-gon
hexagon

le pentagone
pahn-ta-gon
pentagon

Extra words to learn

blanc
blah(n)
white

le cœur
kuhr
heart

coloré
ko-lo-ray
colourful

courbé
koor-bay
curved

le demi-cercle
duh-mee sair-kluh
semicircle

droit
drwa
straight

l'ovale
lo-val
oval

rond
ro(n)
round

le cube
kewb
cube

le ballon
bal-o(n)
ball

Les contraires

Opposites

Ouvre grand !
Open wide!

ouvert
oo-vair
open

fermé
fair-may
closed

rugueux
rew-ghuh
rough

lisse
leess
smooth

mouillé
moo-yay
wet

sec
sec
dry

sale
sal
dirty

propre
prop-ruh
clean

Extra words to learn

léger
lay-zhay
light (weight)

lent
lah(n)
slow

lourd
loor
heavy

nouveau
noo-voh
new

plein
pla(n)
full

rapide
rap-eed
fast

vide
veed
empty

vieux
vyuh
old

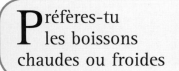

Préfères-tu les boissons chaudes ou froides ?

froid
frwa
cold

chaud
shoh
hot

Une **citrouille** devient **grosse** en **automne**.
A pumpkin gets big in the autumn.

gros
groh
fat

Ce **légume** est très **fin**.
This vegetable is very thin.

fin
fa(n)
thin

doux
doo
soft

dur
dewr
hard

Le tournesol a une **grande** tige.
The sunflower has a long stem.

grand
grah(n)
tall

Cette fleur a une **tige courte**.
This flower has a short stem.

court
koor
short

petit
puh-tee
small

grand
grah(n)
big

Le temps qu'il fait

Weather

le bonhomme de neige
bon-om duh nehzh
snowman

la neige
nehzh
snow

le bonnet
bon-nay
woolly hat

Il y a beaucoup de **vent.**
It's very windy.

le parapluie
pa-ra-plwee
umbrella

l'automne
loh-ton
autumn

l'hiver
lee-vair
winter

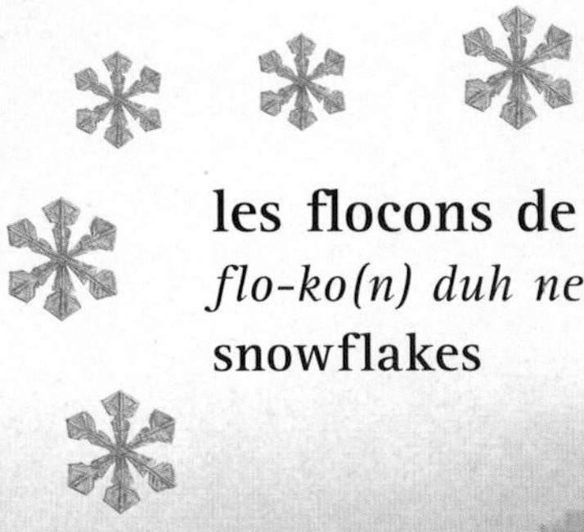

les flocons de neige
flo-ko(n) duh nehzh
snowflakes

J'ai fait un **bonhomme de neige.**
I'm building a snowman.
Je porte un **bonnet,** une **écharpe** et des **gants.**
I'm wearing a hat, scarf, and gloves.

le printemps
pran-tah(m)
spring

J'ai un **parapluie** jaune.
I've got a yellow umbrella.

l'été
lay-tay
summer

le soleil
so-laye
sun

Il fait ***chaud*** *au* ***soleil.***
It's hot in the sun.

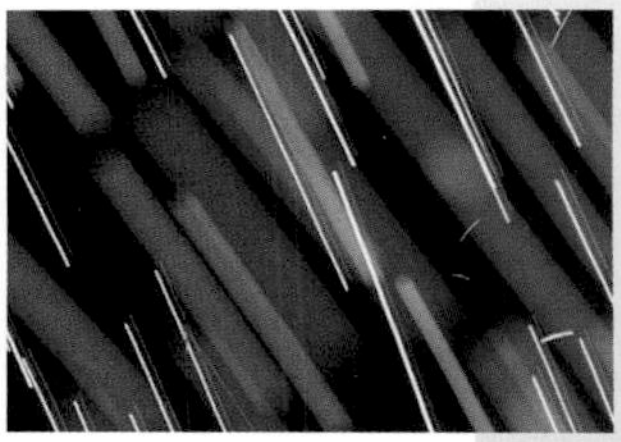

la pluie
plwee
rain

le nuage
new-azh
cloud

l'arc-en-ciel
lark-ah(n)-syel
rainbow

les lunettes de soleil
lew-net duh so-laye
sunglasses

la casquette
kas-ket
cap

Les nombres

Numbers

0	zéro *zay-roh* zero	
1	un *a(n)* one	
2	deux *duh* two	
3	trois *trwa* three	
4	quatre *kat-ruh* four	
5	cinq *sank* five	
6	six *seess* six	
7	sept *set* seven	
8	huit *weet* eight	
9	neuf *nuhf* nine	
10	dix *deess* ten	
11	onze *onz* eleven	
12	douze *dooz* twelve	
13	treize *trez* thirteen	
14	quatorze *kat-orz* fourteen	
15	quinze *kanz* fifteen	
16	seize *sez* sixteen	
17	dix-sept *dees-set* seventeen	
18	dix-huit *deez-weet* eighteen	
19	dix-neuf *dees-nuhf* nineteen	
20	vingt *va(n)* twenty	
21	vingt et un *vant ay a(n)* twenty-one	
30	trente *trahnt* thirty	
40	quarante *kar-ahnt* forty	
50	cinquante *sank-ahnt* fifty	
60	soixante *swa-sahnt* sixty	
70	soixante-dix *swa-sahnt-dees* seventy	
80	quatre-vingts *kat-ruh-va(n)* eighty	
90	quatre-vingt-dix *kat-ruh-va(n)-deess* ninety	
100	cent *sah(n)* hundred	

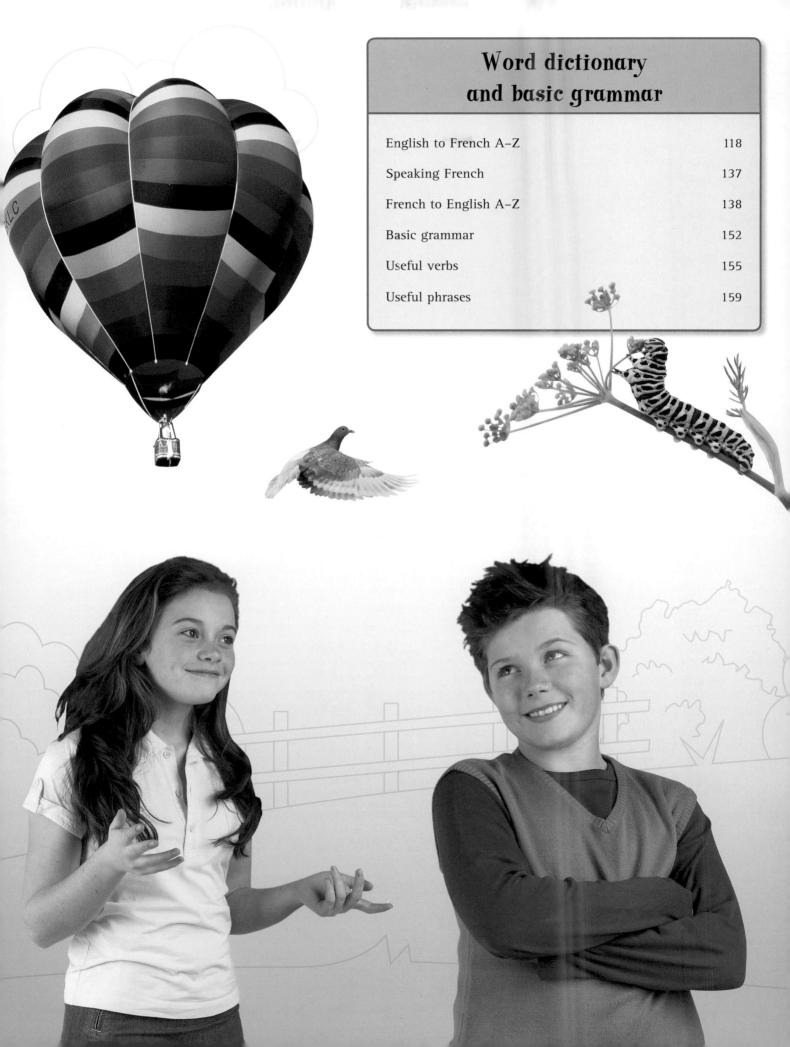

Word dictionary and basic grammar

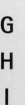

A B C D E F G H I J K L M N O P Q R S T U V W X Y Z

English A–Z

In this section, the English words are given in alphabetical order, followed by the French translation. There is information after each English word to show you what type of word it is. In French, nouns (naming words) are either masculine or feminine. If the French word has *un* or *le* before it, it is masculine (m), if it has *une* or *la*, it is feminine (f).

(n) = noun (a naming word). Nouns are either masculine or feminine. Feminine nouns usually have an "e" at the end.

(adj) = adjective (a describing word). These words can change depending on whether the noun they are describing is masculine (m) or feminine (f).

(adv) = adverb (a word that gives more information about a verb, an adjective, or another adverb).

(conj) = conjunction (a joining word, eg, *and*).

(prep) = preposition (eg, *about*).

(pron) = pronoun (eg, *he*, *she*, *it*).

(article) = (eg, *a*, *an*, *the*).

A

a (article)
un/une
a(n)/ewn

about (adv)
environ
ahn-veer-o(n)

about (prep)
sur
soor

above (prep)
au-dessus de
oh duhs-ew duh

accident (n)
un accident
ak-see-dah(n)

acrobat (n)
un/une acrobate
ak-ro-bat

across (prep)
de l'autre côté de
duh loh-truh koh-tay duh

action (n)
une action
ak-syo(n)

activity (n)
une activité
ak-tee-vee-tay

actor (n)
un acteur (m)
ak-tuhr

actress (n)
une actrice (f)
ak-treess

address (n)
une adresse
a-dress

adult (n)
un/une adulte
ad-ewlt

adventure (n)
une aventure
av-ahn-tewr

aeroplane (n)
un avion
av-yo(n)

after (prep)
après
ap-reh

afternoon (n)
un après-midi
ap-reh mee-dee

again (adv)
encore
ahn-kor

against (prep)
contre
kon-truh

age (n)
l'âge (m)
lahzh

ahead (prep)
devant
duh-vah(n)

air (n)
l'air (m)
lair

airport (n)
un aéroport
a-ay-ro-por

alarm clock (n)
un réveil
ray-vaye

alien (n)
un/une extraterrestre
ek-stra-tair-es-truh

alive (adj)
vivant (m)
vivante (f)
vee-vah(n)/vee-vahnt

all (adj)
tout (m) toute (f)
too/toot

alligator (n)
un alligator
al-ee-gah-tor

almost (adv)
presque
presk

alone (adj)
seul (m) seule (f)
suhl

alphabet (n)
l'alphabet (m)
lal-fa-bay

already (adv)
déjà
day-zha

also (adv)
aussi
oh-see

although (conj)
bien que
bya(n) kuh

always (adv)
toujours
too-zhoor

amazing (adj)
incroyable
an-krwa-ya-bluh

ambulance (n)
une ambulance
ahm-bew-lahnss

among (prep)
entre
ahn-truh

amount (n)
une quantité
kahn-tee-tay

an (article)
un/une
a(n)/ewn

anchor (n)
une ancre
ahn-kruh

and (conj)
et
eh

angry (adj)
en colère
ah(n) ko-lehr

animal (n)
un animal
an-ee-mal

ankle (n)
une cheville
shuh-vee-ye

another (adj)
autre
oh-truh

answer (n)
une réponse
ray-ponss

ant (n)
une fourmi
foor-mee

antenna (n)
une antenne
ahn-ten

anybody (pron)
n'importe qui
nam-port kee

anything (pron)
n'importe quoi
nam-port kwa

apart (adv)
séparément
say-pa-ray-mah(n)

apartment (n)
un appartement
ap-par-tuh-mah(n)

ape (n)
un singe (m)
sanzh

appearance (n)
une apparence
ap-par-ahnss

apple (n)
une pomme
pom

apple juice (n)
le jus de pomme
zhew duh pom

apricot (n)
un abricot
ab-ree-koh

apron (n)
un tablier
tab-lee-yay

arch (n)
une arche
arsh

architect (n)
un/une architecte
ar-shee-tekt

area (n)
une région
ray-zhyo(n)

arm (n)
un bras
bra

armchair (n)
un fauteuil
foh-tuh-ye

army (n)
une armée
ar-may

around (prep)
autour de
oh-toor duh

arrival (n)
l'arrivée (f)
lar-ree-vay

arrow (n)
une flèche
flehsh

art (n)
l'art (m)
lar

art (n) (school)
le dessin
de-sa(n)

artist (n)
un/une artiste
ar-teest

assistant (n)
un assistant
a-seess-tah(n)
une assistante
a-seess-tahnt

astronaut (n)
un/une astronaute
astro-noht

astronomer (n)
un/une astronome
astro-nom

athletics (n)
l'athlétisme (m)
lat-lay-tee-smah

atlas (n)
un atlas
at-lahs

attic (n)
un grenier
gruhn-yay

audience (n)
les spectateurs (m)
spek-ta-tuhr

aunt (n)
une tante
tahnt

author (n)
un auteur
oh-tuhr

autumn (n)
l'automne (m)
loh-ton

avocado (n)
un avocat
av-o-ka

away (adj)
absent (m)
ap-sah(n)
absente (f)
ap-sahnt

B

baboon (n)
un babouin
ba-bwa(n)

baby (n)
un bébé
bay-bay

back (body) (n)
un dos
do

back (adv)
à l'arrière
ah lar-yehr

backpack (n)
un sac à dos
sak ah do

backwards (adv)
en arrière
ah(n) ar-yehr

bacon (n)
le bacon
bay-kon

bad (adj)
mauvais (m)
moh-vay
mauvaise (f)
moh-vayz

badge (n)
un insigne
an-seen-ye

badminton (n)
le badminton
bad-meen-ton

bag (n)
un sac
sak

bakery (n)
une boulangerie
boo-lahn-zhree

balcony (n)
un balcon
bal-ko(n)

bald (adj)
chauve
shohv

ball (n)
un ballon
bal-o(n)
une balle
bal

ballet dancer (n)
un danseur classique
dahn-suhr kla-seek
une danseuse classique
dahn-suhz kla-seek

balloon (n)
un ballon
bal-o(n)

banana (n)
une banane
ba-nan

band (n)
une bande
bahnd

bank (money) (n)
une banque
bahnk

bank (river) (n)
une rive
reev

barbecue (n)
un barbecue
bar-buhk-yew

barn (n)
une grange
grahnzh

baseball (n)
le base-ball
bayz-bohl

basket (n)
un panier
pan-yay

basketball (n)
le basket-ball
basket-bohl

bat (animal) (n)
une chauve-souris
shohv soo-ree

bat (sports) (n)
une batte
bat

bath (n)
une baignoire
bayn-wahr

bathroom (n)
une salle de bain
sal duh ba(n)

battery (n)
une pile
peel

battle (n)
une bataille
bat-ah-ye

beach (n)
une plage
plazh

bead (n)
une perle
pairl

beak (n)
un bec
behk

beans (n)
les haricots
ar-ee-koh

bear (n)
un ours
oorss

beard (n)
une barbe
barb

beautiful (adj)
beau (m)
belle (f)
boh/bell

beauty (n)
la beauté
boh-tay

because (conj)
parce que
par-suh-kuh

bed (n)
un lit
lee

bedroom (n)
une chambre
shahm-bruh

bee (n)
une abeille
a-baye

beetle (n)
un scarabée
ska-ra-bay

before (prep)
avant
av-ah(n)

beginner (n)
un débutant
day-bew-tah(n)
une débutante
day-bew-tahnt

behind (prep)
derrière
dair-yehr

bell (n)
une cloche
klosh

below (prep)
au-dessous de
oh-duh-soo duh

belt (n)
une ceinture
san-tewr

bench (n)
un banc
bah (n)

beneath (prep)
sous/au-dessous
soo/oh-duh-soo

beside (prep)
à côté de
ah koh-tay duh

best (adj)
mieux
myuh

better (adj)
meilleur (m)
meilleure (f)
may-yuhr

between (prep)
entre
ahn-truh

big (large) (adj)
gros (m)
grosse (f)
groh/grohss

big (tall) (adj)
grand (m)
grah(n)
grande (f)
grahnd

bike (n)
un vélo
vay-lo

bill (n)
une addition
ad-dee-syo(n)

billion
milliard
meel-yar

bin (n)
une poubelle
poo-bell

binoculars (n)
les jumelles
zhew-mel

bird (n)
un oiseau
wa-zoh

birthday (n)
un anniversaire
an-ee-vair-sair

birthday cake (n)
un gâteau d'anniversaire
gah-toh dan-ee-vair-sair

birthday card (n)
une carte d'anniversaire
kart dan-ee-vair-sair

biscuit (n)
un biscuit
bee-skwee

bitter (adj)
amer (m)
amère (f)
am-air

black (adj)
noir (m)
noire (f)
nwahr

blackboard (n)
un tableau
tab-loh

blanket (n)
une couverture
koo-vair-tewr

blonde (adj)
blond (m)
bloh(n)
blonde (f)
blohnd

blood (n)
le sang
sah(n)

blouse (n)
un chemisier
shuh-meez-yay

blue (adj)
bleu (m)
bleue (f)
bluh

board (notice) (n)
un panneau
pan-noh

board game (n)
un jeu de société
zhuh duh so-see-ay-tay

boat (n)
un bateau
ba-toh

body (n)
un corps
kor

bone (n)
un os
oss

book (n)
un livre
leev-ruh

bookshop (n)
une librairie
leeb-rair-ee

boot (n)
une botte
bot

boring (adj)
ennuyeux (m)
ahn-wee-yuh
ennuyeuse (f)
ahn-wee-yuhz

bottle (n)
une bouteille
boo-taye

A B C D E F G H I J K L M N O P Q R S T U V W X Y Z

bottom (n)
le fond
foh(n)

bowl (cereal) (n)
un bol
bol

box (n)
une boîte
bwat

boy (n)
un garçon
gar-so(n)

boyfriend (n)
un petit ami
puh-tee-ta-mee

bracelet (n)
un bracelet
bra-slay

brain (n)
un cerveau
sair-voh

branch (n)
une branche
brahnsh

brave (adj)
courageux (m)
koor-a-zhuh
courageuse (f)
koor-a-zhuhz

bread (n)
le pain
pa(n)

break (n)
une pause
pohz

breakfast (n)
le petit-déjeuner
puh-tee day-zhuh-nay

breath (n)
un souffle
soo-fluh

breeze (n)
une brise
breez

bridge (n)
un pont
po(n)

bright (adj)
brillant (m)
bree-yah(n)
brillante (f)
bree-yahnt

broken (adj)
cassé (m)
cassée (f)
kah-say

broom (n)
un balai
ba-lay

brother (n)
un frère
frair

brown (adj)
marron
mar-o(n)

bruise (n)
un bleu
bluh

bubble (n)
une bulle
bewl

bucket (n)
un seau
soh

bug (illness) (n)
un microbe
meek-rohb

bug (insect) (n)
un insecte
an-sekt

buggy (pushchair) (n)
une poussette
poo-set

builder (n)
un ouvrier
oov-ree-yay
une ouvrière
oov-ree-yair

building (n)
un bâtiment
bah-tee-mah(n)

bulb (light) (n)
une ampoule
ahm-pool

bulb (plant) (n)
un bulbe
bewlb

bunk beds (n)
les lits superposés (m)
lee soo-pair-poh-zay

buoy (n)
une bouée
boo-way

bus (n)
un autobus
ohto-bews

bus stop (n)
un arrêt de bus
ar-reh duh bews

bush (n)
un buisson
bwee-so(n)

business (n)
les affaires
a-fair

busy (adj)
occupé (m)
occupée (f)
ok-ew-pay

but (conj)
mais
may

butcher's shop (n)
une boucherie
boosh-ree

butter (n)
le beurre
buhr

butterfly (n)
un papillon
pa-pee-yo(n)

button (n)
un bouton
boo-to(n)

C

cabbage (n)
un chou
shoo

café (n)
un café
ka-fay

cage (n)
une cage
kahzh

cake (n)
un gâteau
gah-toh

calculator (n)
une calculatrice
kal-kew-la-treess

calendar (n)
un calendrier
kal-ahn-dree-yay

calf (n)
un veau
voh

calm (adj)
calme
kalm

camel (n)
un chameau
sha-moh

camera (n)
un appareil photo
ap-pa-ray fo-toh

campsite (n)
un camping
kahm-peeng

can (n)
un bidon
bee-do(n)

candle (n)
une bougie
boo-zhee

canoe (n)
un canoë
kan-o-ay

cap (n)
une casquette
kas-ket

capital (n)
une capitale
ka-pee-tal

car (n)
une voiture
vwah-tewr

caravan (n)
une caravane
ka-ra-van

card (n)
une carte
kart

cardboard (n)
le carton
kar-to(n)

cards (n)
les carte
kart

careful (adj)
prudent (m)
prew-dah(n)
prudente (f)
prew-dahnt

carnival (n)
un carnaval
kar-na-val

carpet (n)
une moquette
moh-ket

carrot (n)
une carotte
ka-rot

cart (n)
une charrette
sha-ret

cartoon (drawing) (n)
une bande dessinée
bahnd dess-ee-nay

cartoon (film) (n)
un dessin animé
de-san an-ee-may

cartwheel (movement) (n)
une roue
roo

cash (n)
en espèces
ah(n) es-pehss

cassette (n)
une cassette
ka-set

castle (n)
un château
sha-toh

cat (n)
un chat
sha

caterpillar (n)
une chenille
shuh-nee-ye

cathedral (n)
une cathédrale
ka-tay-dral

cattle (n)
le bétail
bay-tye

cauliflower (n)
un chou-fleur
shoo-fluhr

cave (n)
une grotte
grot

CD (n)
un CD
say-day

CD player (n)
un lecteur de CD
lek-tuhr duh say-day

ceiling (n)
le plafond
pla-fo(n)

celebration (n)
une célébration
say-lay-bra-syo(n)

cellar (n)
une cave
kav

centre (n)
le centre
sahn-truh

cereal (n)
une céréale
sair-ay-al

certain (adj)
certain (m)
sair-ta(n)
certaine (f)
sair-tehn

chain (n)
une chaîne
shehn

chair (n)
une chaise
shehz

challenge (n)
un défi
day-fee

chance (n)
une chance
shahns

change (n)
un changement
shahnzh-mah(n)

cheap (adj)
bon marché
bo(n) mar-shay

checkout (n)
une caisse
kehss

cheek (body) (n)
la joue
zhoo

cheese (n)
un fromage
fro-mazh

cheetah (n)
un guépard
gay-par

chef (n)
un/une chef
shef

chemist (shop) (n)
une pharmacie
far-ma-see

cherry (n)
une cerise
sair-eez

chess (n)
les échecs
ay-shek

chest (n)
une poitrine
pwa-treen

chest of drawers (n)
une commode
kom-mod

chewing gum (n)
un chewing-gum
shweeng gom

chick (n)
un poussin
poo-sa(n)

chicken (n)
un poulet
poo-lay

child (n)
un/une enfant
ahn-fah(n)

children (n)
les enfants
ahn-fah(n)

chimney (n)
une cheminée
shuh-mee-nay

chimpanzee (n)
un chimpanzé
shahm-pahn-zay

chin (n)
un menton
mahn-to(n)

chips (n)
les frites
freet

chocolate (n)
le chocolat
sho-ko-la

choice (n)
un choix
shwa

Christmas (n)
Noël
no-el

church (n)
une église
ayg-leess

cinema (n)
un cinéma
see-nay-ma

circle (n)
un cercle
sair-kluh

circus (n)
un cirque
seerk

city (n)
une ville
veel

class (school) (n)
une classe
klass

classroom (n)
une salle de classe
sal duh klahss

claw (n)
une griffe
greef

clean (adj)
propre
prop-ruh

clear (adj)
clair (m)
claire (f)
klair

clever (adj)
intelligent (m)
an-tel-lee-zhah(n)
intelligente (f)
an-tel-lee-zhahnt

cliff (n)
une falaise
fa-lehz

cloak (n)
une cape
kap

clock (n)
une horloge
or-lozh

close (near) (adj)
proche
prosh

closed (adj)
fermé (m) fermée (f)
fair-may

cloth (n)
un tissu
tee-soo

clothes (n)
les vêtements
veht-mah(n)

cloud (n)
un nuage
new-azh

cloudy (adj)
nuageux (m)
new-azh-uh
nuageuse (f)
new-azh-uhz

clown (n)
un clown
kloon

club (n)
un club
kluhb

clumsy (adj)
maladroit (m)
mal-a-drwa
maladroite (f)
mal-a-drwat

coach (n)
un autocar
ohto-kar

coast (n)
une côte
koht

coat (n)
un manteau
mahn-toh

coat hanger (n)
un cintre
san-truh

coffee (n)
le café
ka-fay

coin (n)
une pièce
pyehs

cold (adj)
froid (m)
frwa
froide (f)
frwad

cold (n)
un rhume
rewm

collar (n)
un collier
kol-yay

colour (n)
une couleur
koo-luhr

coloured pencil (n)
un crayon de couleur
kra-yo(n) duh koo-luhr

colourful (adj)
coloré (m)
colorée (f)
ko-lo-ray

comb (n)
un peigne
pain-ye

combine harvester (n)
une moissonneuse-batteuse
mwa-son-nuhz bat-tuhz

comfortable (adj)
confortable
kon-for-ta-bluh

comic (n)
un comique
ko-meek

compass (n)
une boussole
boo-sol

competition (n)
une compétition
kom-pay-tee-syo(n)

computer (n)
un ordinateur
or-dee-na-tuhr

computer game (n)
un jeu électronique
zhuh ay-lek-tro-neek

concert (n)
un concert
kon-sair

continent (n)
un continent
kon-tee-nah(n)

controls (n)
les commandes
ko-mahnd

conversation (n)
une conversation
kon-vair-sa-syo(n)

cooker (n)
une cuisinière
kwee-zeen-yair

cool (adj)
frais (m)
fray
fraîche (f)
frehsh

corner (n)
un coin
kwa(n)

correct (adj)
juste
zhewst

corridor (n)
un couloir
kool-wahr

costume (n)
un costume
kos-tewm

cotton (n)
le coton
ko-to(n)

cough (n)
une toux
too

country (n)
un pays
pay-ee

countryside (n)
la campagne
kahm-pan-ye

cousin (n)
un cousin
koo-za(n)
une cousine
koo-zeen

cow (n)
une vache
vash

cowboy (n)
un cow-boy
koh-boye

crab (n)
un crabe
krab

crane (n)
une grue
grew

crayon (n)
un crayon de couleur
kray-o(n) duh koo-luhr

cream (n)
la crème
krehm

creature (n)
une bête
beht

crew (n)
l'équipage (m)
ay-kee-pazh

crisps (n)
les chips (f)
sheeps

crocodile (n)
un crocodile
kro-ko-deel

crop (n)
une récolte
ray-kolt

crossing (n)
un carrefour
kar-foor

crowd (n)
la foule
fool

crowded (adj)
bondé (m)
bondée (f)
bon-day

crown (n)
une couronne
koo-ron

cruel (adj)
cruel (m) cruelle (f)
krew-ell

cube (n)
un cube
kewb

cucumber (n)
un concombre
kon-kom-bruh

cup (n)
une tasse
tahss

cupboard (n)
un placard
pla-kar

cupboard (tall) (n)
une armoire
arm-wahr

curious (adj)
curieux (m)
kew-ree-uh
curieuse (f)
kew-ree-uhz

curly (adj)
frisé (m) frisée (f)
free-zay

curtain (n)
un rideau
ree-doh

curved (adj)
courbé(e)
koor-bay

cushion (n)
un coussin
koo-sa(n)

customer (n)
un client
klee-ah(n)
une cliente
klee-ahnt

D

dad (n)
papa
pa-pa

dairy (adj)
laitier (m) laitière (f)
layt-yay/layt-yair

daisy (n)
une pâquerette
pak-uh-ret

dancer (n)
un danseur
dahn-suhr
une danseuse
dahn-suhz

dandelion (n)
un pissenlit
pee-sahn-lee

danger (n)
le danger
dahn-zhay

dangerous (adj)
dangereux (m)
dahn-zhay-ruh
dangereuse (f)
dahn-zhay-ruhz

dark (adj)
sombre
som-bruh

dark (hair) (adj)
foncé (m) foncée (f)
fon-say

date (n)
une date
dat

daughter (n)
une fille
fee-ye

day (n)
un jour
zhoor

dawn (n)
l'aube (f)
lohb

dead (adj)
mort (m) morte (f)
mor/mort

deaf (adj)
sourd (m) sourde (f)
soor/soord

dear (special, expensive) (adj)
cher (m) chère (f)
shair

deck (boat) (n)
un pont
po(n)

deck chair (n)
une chaise longue
shayz long-uh

decoration (n)
une décoration
day-ko-ra-syo(n)

deep (adj)
profond (m)
pro-fo(n)
profonde (f)
pro-fond

deer (n)
un daim
da(m)

delicious (adj)
délicieux (m)
day-lee-syuh
délicieuse (f)
day-lee-syuhz

dentist (n)
un/une dentiste
dahn-teest

desert (n)
un désert
day-zair

desk (n)
un bureau
bew-roh

dessert (n)
un dessert
duh-sair

detective (n)
un détective
day-tek-teev

diagram (n)
un diagramme
dya-gram

diamond (shape) (n)
un losange
lo-zahnzh

diary (n)
un journal
zhoor-nal

dice (n)
les dés
day

dictionary (n)
un dictionnaire
deek-syo-nair

different (adj)
différent (m)
dee-fay-rah(n)
différente (f)
dee-fay-rahnt

difficult (adj)
difficile
dee-fee-seel

digital (adj)
digital (m)
digitale (f)
dee-zhee-tal

dining room (n)
une salle à manger
sal ah mahn-zhay

dinner (n)
un dîner
dee-nay

dinosaur (n)
un dinosaure
dee-noh-zor

direction (n)
une direction
dee-rek-syo(n)

directly (adv)
directement
dee-rek-tuh-mah(n)

dirty (adj)
sale
sal

disabled (adj)
handicapé (m)
handicapée (f)
ahn-dee-ka-pay

disaster (n)
une catastrophe
ka-ta-strof

disco (n)
une discothèque
dee-sko-tek

disease (n)
une maladie
ma-la-dee

disguise (n)
un déguisement
day-gheez-mah(n)

dishwasher (n)
un lave-vaisselle
lav vay-sel

distance (n)
une distance
dee-stahnss

diving (n)
la plongée
plon-zhay

divorced (adj)
divorcé (m)
divorcée (f)
dee-vor-say

doctor (n)
un médecin
may-duh-sa(n)

dog (n)
un chien
shya(n)

doll (n)
une poupée
poo-pay

dolphin (n)
un dauphin
doh-fa(n)

dome (n)
un dôme
dohm

door (n)
une porte
port

downstairs (adv)
au rez-de-chaussée
oh ray-du-shoh-say

dragon (n)
un dragon
dra-go(n)

dragonfly (n)
une libellule
lee-bel-lewl

drawer (n)
un tiroir
teer-wahr

drawing (act of) (n)
le dessin
de-sa(n)

drawing pin (n)
une punaise
pew-nehz

dream (n)
un rêve
rehv

dress (n)
une robe
rob

drink (n)
une boisson
bwa-so(n)

drinking straw (n)
une paille
pah-ye

drop (n)
une goutte
goot

drum (n)
un tambour
tahm-boor

drum kit (n)
une batterie
bat-tree

dry (adj)
sec (m)
sèche (f)
sek/sehsh

duck (n)
un canard
ka-nar

duckling (n)
un caneton
ka-nuh-to(n)

during (prep)
pendant
pahn-dah(n)

dusk (n)
le crépuscule (m)
kray-pew-skewl

dust (n)
la poussière
poo-syair

duvet (n)
une couette
koo-et

DVD (n)
un DVD
day-vay-day

DVD player (n)
un lecteur
de DVD
lek-tuhr duh day-vay-day

E

each (adj)
chaque
shak

eagle (n)
un aigle
ay-gluh

ear (n)
une oreille
o-raye

earache (n)
une otite
o-teet

early (adv)
tôt
toh

earring (n)
une boucle d'oreille
book-luh do-raye

Earth (planet) (n)
la Terre
tair

earthquake (n)
un tremblement de terre
trahm-bluh-mah(n) duh tair

earthworm (n)
un ver de terre
vair duh tair

east (n)
l'est (m)
lest

easy (adj)
facile
fa-seel

echo (n)
un écho
ay-ko

edge (n)
le bord
bor

education (n)
l'éducation (f)
lay-dew-ka-syo(n)

effect (n)
un effet
ay-fay

egg (n)
un œuf
uhf

elbow (n)
un coude
kood

electrical (adj)
électrique
ay-lek-treek

electricity (n)
l'électricité (f)
lay-lek-tree-see-tay

elephant (n)
un éléphant
ay-lay-fah(n)

email (n)
un e-mail
ee-mail

email address (n)
une adresse électronique
a-dress ay-lek-tro-neek

emergency (n)
une urgence
ewr-zhahnss

empty (adj)
vide
veed

encyclopedia (n)
une encyclopédie
ahn-see-klo-pay-dee

end (final part) (n)
la fin
fa(n)

enemy (n)
un ennemi
une ennemie
en-mee

energy (n)
l'énergie (f)
lay-nair-zhee

English (n)
l'anglais (m)
lahn-glay

enormous (adj)
énorme
ay-norm

enough (adj)
assez
a-say

enthusiastic (adj)
enthousiaste
ahn-too-zee-ast

entrance (n)
l'entrée (f)
lahn-tray

envelope (n)
une enveloppe
ahn-vlop

environment (n)
l'environnement (m)
lahn-vee-ron-mah(n)

equal (adj)
égal (m)
égale (f)
ay-gal

equator (n)
l'équateur (m)
lay-kwa-tuhr

equipment (n)
le matériel
ma-tay-ree-el

even (adv)
même
mehm

evening (n)
un soir
swahr

event (n)
un événement
ay-vayn-mah(n)

every (adj)
tous
too

everybody (pron)
tout le monde
too luh mond

everyday (adv)
tous les jours
too lay zhoor

everything (pron)
tout
too

everywhere (adv)
partout
par-too

evil (adj)
mauvais (m)
moh-vay
mauvaise (f)
moh-vayz

exactly (adv)
exactement
eg-zak-tuh-mah(n)

exam (n)
un examen
eg-za-ma(n)

example (n)
un exemple
eg-zahm-pluh

excellent (adj)
excellent (m)
ek-say-lah(n)
excellente (f)
ek-say-lahnt

exchange (n)
un échange
ay-shahnzh

excited (adj)
excité (m)
excitée (f)
ek-see-tay

exercise (n)
un exercice
ek-sair-seess

exercise book (n)
un cahier
ka-yay

excuse (n)
une excuse
ek-skewz

exhibition (n)
une exposition
ek-spoh-zee-syo(n)

exit (n)
la sortie
sor-tee

expedition (n)
une expédition
ek-spay-dee-syo(n)

expensive (adj)
cher (m)
chère (f)
shair

experiment (n)
une expérience
ek-spay-ree-ahnss

expert (n)
un expert
ek-spair
une experte
ek-spairt

explorer (n)
un explorateur
ek-splor-a-tuhr
une exploratrice
ek-splor-a-treess

explosion (n)
une explosion
ek-sploh-zyo(n)

extinct (adj)
éteint (m)
ay-ta(n)
éteinte (f)
ay-tant

extra (adj)
supplémentaire
soo-play-mahn-tair

extremely (adv)
extrêmement
ek-streh-muh-mah(n)

eye (n)
un œil
uh-ye

eyebrow (n)
un sourcil
soor-seel

eyelash (n)
un cil
seel

F

fabulous (adj)
fabuleux (m)
fa-bew-luh
fabuleuse (f)
fa-bew-luhz

face (n)
le visage
vee-zazh

fact (n)
un fait
fay

factory (n)
une usine
ew-zeen

faint (pale) (adj)
faible
fay-bluh

fair (n)
une foire
fwahr

false (adj)
faux (m) fausse (f)
foh/fohss

family (n)
une famille
fa-mee-ye

famous (adj)
célèbre
say-lay-bruh

fancy dress (n)
un déguisement
day-gheez-mah(n)

fantastic (adj)
fantastique
fan-tas-teek

far (adv)
loin
lwa(n)

farm (n)
une ferme
fairm

farmer (n)
un fermier
fairm-yay
une fermière
fairm-yair

fashion (n)
la mode
mod

fashionable (adj)
à la mode
ah la mod

fast (adv)
rapide
rap-eed

fat (adj)
gros (m) grosse (f)
groh/grohss

father (n)
un père
pair

favourite (adj)
préféré (m)
préférée (f)
pray-fair-ay

feast (n)
un banquet
bahn-kay

A B C D E F G H I J K L M N O P Q R S T U V W X Y Z

feather (n)
une plume
plewm

felt-tip pen (n)
un feutre
fuh-truh

female (human) (n)
une femme
fam

fence (n)
une barrière
bar-yair

ferry (n)
un ferry
fay-ree

festival (n)
une fête
feht

field (n)
un champ
shah(m)

fierce (adj)
féroce
fair-os

film (n)
un film
feelm

film star (n)
une vedette de cinéma
vuh-det duh see-nay-ma

fin (n)
une nageoire
nazh-wahr

fine (adv)
bien
bya(n)

finger (n)
un doigt
dwa

fingernail (n)
un ongle
ong-luh

fingerprint (n)
une empreinte
ahm-prant

fire (n)
le feu
fuh

fire engine (n)
un camion de pompier
kam-yo(n) duh pomp-yay

firefighter (n)
un pompier
pomp-yay
une femme pompier
fam pomp-yay

firework (n)
un feu d'artifice
fuh dar-tee-feess

first (adv)
d'abord
da-bor

first (adj)
premier (m)
pruhm-yay
première (f)
pruhm-yair

first aid (n)
les premiers secours
pruhm-yay suh-koor

fish (n)
un poisson
pwa-so(n)

fishing (n)
la pêche
pehsh

fishing boat (n)
un bateau de pêche
ba-toh duh pehsh

fit (adj)
en forme
ah(n) form

fizzy (adj)
gazeux (m)
gaz-uh
gazeuse (f)
gaz-uhz

flag (n)
un drapeau
dra-poh

flame (n)
une flamme
flahm

flannel (n)
une serviette de toilette
sair-vee-et duh twa-let

flat (building) (n)
un appartement
ap-par-tuh-mah(n)

flat (adj)
plat (m) plate (f)
pla/plat

fleece (n)
une polaire
po-lair

flight (n)
un vol
vol

flipper (n)
une palme
palm

flock (of sheep) (n)
un troupeau
troo-poh

flood (n)
une inondation
in-on-da-syo(n)

floor (n)
le sol
sol

flour (n)
la farine
far-een

flower (n)
une fleur
fluhr

flu (n)
la grippe
la greep

flute (n)
une flûte
flewt

fly (n)
une mouche
moosh

fog (n)
le brouillard
broo-yar

food (n)
la nourriture
noo-ree-tewr

foot (human) (n)
le pied
pyay

foot (animal) (n)
une patte
pat

football (ball) (n)
un ballon de football
ba-lo(n) duh foot-bohl

football (game) (n)
le football
foot-bohl

foreign (adj)
étranger (m)
ay-trahn-zhay
étrangère (f)
ay-trahn-zhair

forest (n)
une forêt
fo-reh

fork (n)
une fourchette
foor-shet

forward (adv)
en avant
ah(n) av-ah(n)

fountain (n)
une fontaine
fon-tehn

fox (n)
un renard
ruh-nar

frame (n)
un cadre
kah-druh

freckle (n)
une tache de rousseur
tash duh roo-suhr

free (adj)
libre
lee-bruh

free time (n)
le temps libre
tah(n) lee-bruh

freedom (n)
la liberté
lee-bair-tay

freezer (n)
un congélateur
kon-zhay-la-tuhr

French (n)
le français
frahn-say

fresh (adj)
frais (m)
fraîche (f)
fray/frehsh

fridge (n)
un réfrigérateur
ray-free-zhair-a-tuhr

friend (n)
un ami, une amie
a-mee

friendly (adj)
amical (m)
amicale (f)
a-mee-kal

frightened (adj)
effrayé (m)
effrayée (f)
eh-fray-yay

frog (n)
une grenouille
gruh-noo-ye

from (prep)
de
duh

front door (n)
une porte d'entrée
port dahn-tray

frosty (weather) (adj)
glacial (m)
glaciale (f)
glass-yal

frozen (adj)
gelé (m) gelée (f)
zhuh-lay

fruit (n)
un fruit
frwee

fruit salad (n)
une salade de fruits
sal-ad duh frwee

frying pan (n)
une poêle
pwal

fuel (n)
le carburant
kar-bew-rah(n)

full (adj)
plein (m)
pleine (f)
pla(n)/plen

fun (n)
un amusement
am-ewz-mah(n)

fun (adj)
rigolo
ree-go-loh

funny (adj)
drôle
drohl

fur (n)
les poils
pwal

furniture (n)
les meubles
muh-bluh

future (n)
l'avenir (m)
lav-neer

G

galaxy (n)
une galaxie
gal-ak-see

gale (n)
un grand vent
grah(n) vah(n)

game (n)
un jeu
zhuh

gang (n)
une bande
bahnd

garage (n)
un garage
gar-azh

garden (n)
un jardin
zhar-da(n)

gardener (n)
un jardinier
zhar-deen-yay
une jardinière
zhar-deen-yair

gardening (n)
le jardinage
zhar-dee-nazh

gas (n)
le gaz
gahz

gate (n)
une barrière
bar-yair

gentle (adj)
doux (m)
douce (f)
doo/dooss

gently (adv)
doucement
dooss-mah(n)

geography (n)
la géographie
zhay-o-gra-fee

germ (n)
un microbe
meek-rohb

giant (n)
un géant
zhay-ah(n)

gift (n)
un cadeau
ka-doh

giraffe (n)
une girafe
zhee-raf

girl (n)
une fille
fee-ye

girlfriend (n)
une petite amie
puh-teet a-mee

glacier (n)
un glacier
glass-yay

glass (drink) (n)
un verre
vair

glasses (n)
les lunettes
lew-net

globe (n)
un globe
glob

glove (n)
un gant
gah(n)

glue (n)
la colle
kol

goal (n)
un but
bewt

goat (n)
une chèvre
shay-vruh

God (n)
Dieu
dyuh

goggles (n)
les lunettes de natation
lew-net duh na-ta-syo(n)

gold (n)
l'or (m)
lor

goldfish (n)
un poisson rouge
pwa-so(n) roozh

golf (n)
le golf
golf

good (adj)
bon (m) bonne (f)
bo(n)/bon

gorilla (n)
un gorille
go-ree-ye

government (n)
le gouvernement
goo-vairn-mah(n)

grandchildren (n)
les petits-enfants (m)
puh-teez ahn-fah(n)

granddaughter (n)
une petite-fille
puh-teet fee-ye

grandfather (n)
un grand-père
grah(n)-pair

grandmother (n)
une grand-mère
grah(n)-mair

grandparents (n)
les grands-parents
grah(n)-par-ah(n)

grandson (n)
un petit-fils
puh-tee feess

grape (n)
le raisin
ray-za(n)

grass (n)
l'herbe (f)
lairb

grasshopper (n)
une sauterelle
soht-rel

gravity (n)
la pesanteur
puh-xahn-tuhr

great (adj)
formidable
for-mee-da-bluh

green (adj)
vert (m) verte (f)
vair/vairt

greenhouse (n)
une serre
sair

grey (adj)
gris (m)
gree
grise (f)
greez

ground (n)
la terre
tair

group (n)
un groupe
groop

guard (n)
un garde
gard

guest (n)
un invité
une invitée
an-vee-tay

guide (n)
un guide
gheed

guidebook (n)
un guide
gheed

guinea pig (n)
un cochon d'Inde
ko-sho(n) dand

guitar (n)
une guitare
ghee-tar

gymnastics (n)
la gymnastique
zheem-nas-teek

H

habit (n)
l'habitude (f)
lab-ee-tewd

habitat (n)
un habitat
a-bee-ta

hair (n)
les cheveux
shuh-vuh

hairbrush (n)
une brosse à cheveux
bros ah shuh-vuh

hairdresser (n)
un coiffeur
kwa-fuhr
une coiffeuse
kwa-fuhz

hairy (adj)
poilu (m)
poilue (f)
pwa-lew

half (n)
une moitié
mwat-yay

hall (n)
un couloir
kool-wahr

hamster (n)
un hamster
am-stair

hand (n)
une main
ma(n)

handbag (n)
un sac à main
sak ah ma(n)

handkerchief (n)
un mouchoir
moosh-wahr

handsome (adj)
beau (m)
boh
belle (f)
bell

hang-glider (n)
un deltaplane
delta-plan

happy (adj)
content (m)
kon-tah(n)
contente (f)
kon-tahnt

harbour (n)
un port
por

hard (adj)
dur (m)
dure (f)
dewr

hard drive (n)
un disque dur
deesk dewr

hare (n)
un lièvre
lyeh-vruh

harm (n)
le mal
mal

harvest (n)
une moisson
mwa-so(n)

hat (n)
un chapeau
sha-poh

hawk (n)
un faucon
foh-ko(n)

hay (n)
le foin
fwa(n)

he (pron)
il
eel

head (n)
la tête
teht

headache (n)
un mal de tête
mal duh teht

headphones (n)
les casques (m)
kask

healthy (adj)
en bonne santé
ah(n) bon sahn-tay

heart (n)
le cœur
kuhr

heat (n)
la chaleur
sha-luhr

heavy (adj)
lourd (m) lourde (f)
loor/loord

heel (n)
un talon
tal-o(n)

helicopter (n)
un hélicoptère
ay-lee-kop-tair

helmet (n)
un casque
kask

help (n)
une aide
ehd

her/his (adj)
son (m)
sa (f)
so(n)/sa

her/him (pron)
la (her) le (him)
l' (before a vowel)
la/luh/l

here (adv)
ici
ee-see

hero (n)
un héros
air-o

heron (n)
un héron
air-o(n)

hers/his (pron)
le sien (m)
luh sya(n)
la sienne (f)
la syen

hi
salut
sa-lew

A B C D E F G H I J K L M N O P Q R S T U V W X Y Z

A B C D E F G H I J K L M N O P Q R S T U V W X Y Z

hide-and-seek (n)
cache-cache
kash-kash

high (adj)
haut (m)
haute (f)
oh/oht

hill (n)
une colline
kol-leen

hip (n)
une hanche
ahnsh

hippopotamus (n)
un hippopotame
eep-o-po-tam

historical (adj)
historique
ee-stor-eek

history (n)
l'histoire (f)
leest-wahr

hive (n)
une ruche
rewsh

hobby (n)
un loisir
lwa-zeer

hockey (n)
le hockey
ok-ay

hole (n)
un trou
troo

holiday (n)
les vacances
vak-ahnss

home (n)
la maison
may-zo(n)

homework (n)
les devoirs
duhv-wahr

honey (n)
le miel
myel

hood (n)
une capuche
kap-ewsh

hoof (n)
un
sabot
sa-boh

horn (n)
une corne
korn

horrible (adj)
horrible
o-ree-bluh

horse (n)
un cheval
shuh-val

horse riding (n)
l'équitation (f)
lay-keet-a-syo(n)

hospital (n)
un hôpital
o-pee-tal

hot (adj)
chaud (m)
shoh
chaude (f)
shohd

hot-air balloon (n)
une montgolfière
mohn-golf-yair

hot chocolate (n)
un chocolat chaud
sho-ko-la shoh

hot dog (n)
un hot-dog
ot-dog

hotel (n)
un hôtel
o-tel

hour (n)
l'heure (f)
luhr

house (n)
une maison
may-zo(n)

how (adv)
comment
ko-mah(n)

huge (adj)
énorme
ay-norm

human (n)
un être humain
eh-truh ew-ma(n)

hummingbird (n)
un oiseau-mouche
wa-zoh-moosh

hungry (adj)
affamé (m)
affamée (f)
af-fa-may

hurricane (n)
un ouragan
oo-ra-gah(n)

husband (n)
un mari
ma-ree

hut (n)
une cabane
ka-ban

I

I (pron)
je/j'
zhuh/zh

ice (n)
la glace
glass

ice cream (n)
une glace
glass

ice cube (n)
un glaçon
glass-o(n)

ice hockey (n)
le hockey
sur glace
ok-ay soor glass

ice lolly (n)
un esquimau
es-kee-moh

ice skating (n)
le patinage sur
glace
pa-tee-nazh soor glass

idea (n)
une idée
ee-day

ill (adj)
malade
ma-lad

illness (n)
une maladie
ma-la-dee

illustration (n)
une illustration
eel-lew-stra-syo(n)

immediately (adv)
tout de suite
too-duh-sweet

important (adj)
important (m)
am-por-tah(n)
importante (f)
am-por-tahnt

impossible (adj)
impossible
am-po-see-bluh

information (n)
une information
an-for-ma-syo(n)

ingredient (n)
un ingrédient
an-gray-diah(n)

injury (n)
une blessure
bless-ewr

ink (n)
l'encre (f)
lahn-kruh

insect (n)
un insecte
an-sekt

inside (prep)
à l'intérieur de
ah lan-tayr-yuhr duh

instruction (n)
une instruction
an-strewk-syo(n)

instrument (n)
un instrument
an-strew-mah(n)

interesting (adj)
intéressant (m)
an-tair-ay-sah(n)
intéressante (f)
an-tair-ay-sahnt

international (adj)
international (m)
internationale (f)
an-tair-na-syo-nal

Internet (n)
l'Internet (m)
lin-tair-net

into (prep)
dans
dah(n)

introduction (n)
une présentation
pray-zahn-ta-syo(n)

invention (n)
une invention
an-vahn-syo(n)

invisible (adj)
invisible
an-vee-zee-bluh

invitation (n)
une invitation
an-vee-ta-syo(n)

iron (clothes) (n)
un fer à repasser
fair ah ruh-pah-say

island (n)
une île
eel

IT (information technology) (n)
l'informatique (f)
lan-for-ma-teek

its (adj)
son (m) sa (f)
so(n)/sa

it's (it is)
c'est
say

J

jacket (n)
un blouson
bloo-zo(n)

jam (n)
la confiture
kon-fee-tewr

jaw (n)
une mâchoire
mash-wahr

jeans (n)
un jean
jeen

jellyfish (n)
une méduse
may-dewz

jet (n)
un avion à réaction
av-yo(n) ah ray-ak-syo(n)

jewel (n)
un bijou
bee-zhoo

jewellery (n)
les bijoux
bee-zhoo

jigsaw (n)
un puzzle
puh-zluh

job (n)
un emploi
am-plwa

joke (n)
une blague
blag

journey (n)
un voyage
vwa-yazh

judo (n)
le judo
zhew-doh

jug (n)
une cruche
krewsh

juice (n)
le jus
zhew

jumper (n)
un pull-over
pewl-o-vair

jungle (n)
la jungle
zhahn-gluh

junk (n)
le bric-à-brac
breek-ah-brak

just (adv)
juste
zhewst

K

kangaroo (n)
un kangourou
kahn-goo-roo

karate (n)
le karaté
ka-ra-tay

kettle (n)
une bouilloire
booy-wahr

key (n)
une clé/clef
klay

keyboard (n)
un clavier
klav-yay

kilogram (n)
un kilogramme
kee-lo-gram

kilometre (n)
un kilomètre
kee-lo-meh-truh

kind (gentle) (adj)
gentil (m)
zhahn-tee
gentille (f)
zhahn-teeye

kind (type) (n)
une sorte
sort

king (n)
un roi
rwa

kiss (n)
un baiser
bay-zay

kitchen (n)
une cuisine
kwee-zeen

kite (n)
un cerf-volant
sair-vo-lah(n)

kitten (n)
un chaton
sha-to(n)

knee (n)
le genou
zhuh-noo

knife (n)
un couteau
koo-toh

knight (n)
un chevalier
shuh-val-yay

knot (n)
un nœud
nuh

knowledge (n)
la connaissance
kon-nehs-sahns

koala (n)
un koala
ko-a-la

L

ladder (n)
une échelle
ay-shell

ladybird (n)
une coccinelle
kok-see-nel

lake (n)
un lac
lak

lamb (n)
un agneau
an-yoh

lamp (n)
une lampe
lahmp

land (n)
un terrain
tair-ra(n)

language (n)
une langue
lahn-guh

laptop (n)
un ordinateur portable
or-dee-na-tuhr por-ta-bluh

large (adj)
gros (m)
groh
grosse (f)
grohss

laser (n)
un laser
laz-air

last (adj)
dernier (m)
dairn-yay
dernière (f)
dairn-yair

late (adv)
en retard
ah(n) ruh-tar

law (n)
une loi
lwa

lawn (n)
la pelouse/le gazon
puh-looz/gah-zo(n)

lawn mower (n)
une tondeuse à gazon
ton-duhz ah gah-zo(n)

lazy (adj)
paresseux (m)
pa-re-suh
paresseuse (f)
pa-re-suhz

leader (n)
le chef
shef

leaf (n)
une feuille
fuh-ye

leather (adj)
en cuir
ah(n) kweer

left (adj)
gauche
gohsh

left-handed (adj)
gaucher (m)
goh-shay
gauchère (f)
goh-shair

leg (n)
une jambe
zhahmb

legs (animal) (n)
les pattes (f)
pat

lemon (n)
un citron
see-tro(n)

lemonade (n)
une limonade
lee-mon-ad

leopard (n)
un léopard
lay-o-par

lesson (n)
une leçon
le-so(n)

letter (n)
une lettre
let-truh

letter box (n)
une boîte aux lettres
bwat oh let-truh

lettuce (n)
une laitue
lay-tew

level (adj)
plat (m) plate (f)
pla/plat

library (n)
une bibliothèque
bee-blee-yo-tek

lid (n)
un couvercle
koo-vair-kluh

life (n)
la vie
vee

lifeboat (n)
un bateau de sauvetage
ba-toh duh sohv-tazn

lifeguard (n)
un surveillant de baignade
soor-vay-ah(n) duh bayn-yad

life jacket (n)
un gilet de sauvetage
zhee-lay duh sohv-tazh

lift (n)
un ascenseur
a-sahn-suhr

light (not heavy) (adj)
léger (m)
légère (f)
lay-zhay/lay-zhehr

light (pale) (adj)
clair (m)
claire (f)
klair

light (n)
une lumière
lewm-yair

lighthouse (n)
un phare
far

lightning (n)
un éclair
ay-klair

like (prep)
comme
kom

line (n)
une ligne
leen-ye

lion (n)
un lion
lee-yo(n)

lips (n)
les lèvres (f)
leh-vruh

liquid (n)
un liquide
lee-keed

list (n)
une liste
leest

litre (n)
un litre
lee-truh

little (adj)
petit (m)
petite (f)
puh-tee/puh-teet

living room (n)
un salon
sal-o(n)

lizard (n)
un lézard
lay-zar

lock (n)
une serrure
sair-rewr

locomotive (n)
une locomotive
lo-ko-mo-teev

log (wood) (n)
une bûche
bewsh

long (adj)
long (m)
longue (f)
lo(n)/lon-guh

loose (adj)
ample
ahm-pluh

lorry (n)
un camion
kam-yo(n)

lost (adj)
perdu (m)
perdue (f)
pair-dew

(a) lot (adj)
beaucoup
boh-koo

loud (adj)
bruyant (m)
brew-yah(n)
bruyante (f)
brew-yahnt

loudspeaker (n)
un haut-parleur
oh par-luhr

lovely (adj)
adorable
a-do-ra-bluh

low (adj)
bas (m)
basse (f)
bah/bahss

lucky (adj)
chanceux (m)
shahn-suh
chanceuse (f)
shahn-suhz

luggage (n)
les bagages
bag-azh

lunch (n)
le déjeuner
day-zhuh-nay

lunch box (n)
un panier repas
pan-yay ruh-pah

lungs (n)
les poumons (m)
poo-mo(n)

A B C D E F G H I J K L M N O P Q R S T U V W X Y Z

M

machine (n)
une machine
ma-sheen

mad (adj)
fou (m)
foo
folle (f)
fol

magazine (n)
un magazine
ma-ga-zeen

magician (n)
un magicien
ma-zhee-sya(n)
une magicienne
ma-zhee-syen

magnet (n)
un aimant
eh-mah(n)

magnetic (adj)
magnétique
man-yet-eek

magnifying glass (n)
une loupe
loop

mail (n)
la poste
post

main (adj)
principal (m)
principale (f)
prahn-see-pal

make-up (n)
le maquillage
ma-kee-yazh

male (human) (n)
un homme
om

mammal (n)
un mammifère
ma-mee-fair

man (n)
un homme
om

map (n)
une carte
kart

marbles (toy) (n)
les billes
bee-ye

mark (n)
une note
noht

market (n)
le marché
mar-shay

marriage (n)
le mariage
mar-yazh

married (adj)
marié (m) mariée (f)
mar-yay

mask (n)
un masque
mask

mat (n)
un petit tapis
puh-tee ta-pee

match (football) (n)
un match
match

matchbox (n)
une boîte d'allumettes
bwat dal-lew-met

maths (n)
les mathématiques
ma-tay-ma-teek

mattress (n)
un matelas
mat-la

maybe (adv)
peut-être
puht-eh-truh

me (pron)
me/m' (vowel)
muh/m

meal (n)
un repas
ruh-pah

meaning (n)
le sens
sahnss

measles (n)
la rougeole
la roozh-ol

measurement (n)
une mesure
muh-zewr

meat (n)
la viande
vyahnd

medal (n)
une médaille
may-da-ye

medicine (n)
un médicament
may-dee-ka-mah(n)

medium (adj)
moyen (m)
mwa-ya(n)
moyenne (f)
mwa-yen

melon (n)
un melon
muh-lo(n)

memory (n)
la mémoire
may-mwahr

menu (n)
la carte
kart

mess (n)
le désordre
day-zor-druh

message (n)
un message
mess-azh

metre (n)
un mètre
meh-truh

microchip (n)
une puce (f)
poos

microscope (n)
un microscope
mee-kro-skop

microwave (n)
un micro-ondes
mee-kro-ond

middle (n)
le milieu
meel-yuh

midnight (n)
minuit
mee-nwee

milk (n)
le lait
lay

milk shake (n)
un milk-shake
meelk-shayk

million
million
meel-yo(n)

millipede (n)
un mille-pattes (m)
meel-pat

mineral (n)
un minéral
mee-nay-ral

minute (n)
une minute
mee-newt

mirror (n)
un miroir
meer-wahr

miserable (adj)
malheureux (m)
mal-uhr-uh
malheureuse (f)
mal-uhr-uhz

mistake (n)
une erreur
er-ruhr

misty (adj)
brumeux (m)
brew-muh
brumeuse (f)
brew-muhz

mitten (n)
une mitaine
mee-tehn

mixture (n)
un mélange
may-lahnzh

mobile phone (n)
un téléphone
portable/
un portable
tay-lay-fon por-ta-bluh

modelling clay (n)
la pâte
à modeler
paht ah mod-lay

moment (n)
un instant (m)
an-stah(n)

money (n)
l'argent (m)
lar-zhah(n)

monkey (n)
un singe
sanzh

monster (n)
un monstre
mon-struh

month (n)
un mois
mwa

moon (n)
la lune
lewn

more than
plus que
plews kuh

morning (n)
le matin
ma-ta(n)

mosque (n)
une mosquée
mos-kay

mosquito (n)
un moustique
moos-teek

moth (n)
un papillon
de nuit
pa-pee-yo(n)
duh nwee

mother (n)
une mère
mair

motor (n)
un moteur
mo-tuhr

motorbike (n)
une moto
moh-toh

motorway (n)
une autoroute
oh-toh-root

mountain (n)
une montagne
mon-tan-ye

mountain bike (n)
un V. T. T.
vay-tay-tay

mouse (animal) (n)
une souris
soo-ree

mouse (computer) (n)
une souris
soo-ree

mouse mat (n)
un tapis de souris
ta-pee duh soo-ree

moustache (n)
une moustache
moo-stash

mouth (n)
une bouche
boosh

mud (n)
la boue
boo

muddy (adj)
boueux (m)
boo-uh
boueuse (f)
boo-uhz

mug (n)
une tasse
tahss

mum (n)
maman
mah-mah(n)

muscle (n)
un muscle
mew-skluh

museum (n)
un musée
mew-zay

mushroom (n)
un champignon
shahm-peen-yo(n)

music (n)
la musique
mew-zeek

musician (n)
un musicien
mew-zee-sya(n)
une musicienne
mew-zee-syen

my (adj)
mon (m)
ma (f)
mo(n)/ma

N

nail (n)
un ongle
ong-luh

name (n)
un nom
no(m)

narrow (adj)
étroit (m) étroite (f)
ay-trwa/ay-trwat

nasty (unkind) (adj)
méchant (m)
may-shah(n)
méchante (f)
may-shahnt

nature (n)
la nature
nat-ewr

naughty (adj)
vilain (m)
vee-la(n)
vilaine (f)
veelehn

near (prep)
près de
preh duh

nearly (adv)
presque
presk

neck (n)
un cou
koo

necklace (n)
un collier
kol-yay

needle (n)
une aiguille
ehg-wee-ye

neighbour (n)
un voisin
vwa-za(n)
une voisine
vwa-zeen

nephew (n)
un neveu
nuh-vuh

nerves (n)
les nerfs (m)
nair

nest (n)
un nid
nee

net (n)
une épuisette
ay-pwee-zet

never (adv)
jamais
zha-may

new (adj)
nouveau (m)
noo-voh
nouvelle (f)
noo-vel

news (n)
les nouvelles
noo-vel

newspaper (n)
un journal
zhoor-nal

next (adj)
prochain (m)
prosh-a(n)
prochaine (f)
prosh-ehn

nice (adj)
sympathique
sam-pa-teek

nickname (n)
un surnom
soor-no(m)

niece (n)
une nièce
nyehs

night (n)
la nuit
nwee

no (adv)
non
no(n)

nobody (pron)
personne
pair-son

noisy (adj)
bruyant (m)
brew-yah(n)
bruyante (f)
brew-yahnt

noodles (n)
les nouilles
noo-ye

north (n)
le nord
nor

nose (n)
un nez
nay

nostril (n)
une narine
nar-een

note (n)
un billet
bee-yay

notebook (n)
un carnet
kar-nay

nothing (n/pron)
rien
rya(n)

now (adv)
maintenant
mehn-tuh-nah(n)

nowhere (adv)
nulle part
newl par

number (n)
un nombre
nom-bruh

nurse (n)
une infirmière
an-feerm-yair

nursery (n)
une crèche
krehsh

O

oar (n)
une rame
ram

oasis (n)
une oasis
o-az-eess

object (n)
un objet
ob-zhay

ocean (n)
un océan
o-say-ah(n)

octopus (n)
une pieuvre
pyuh-vruh

odd (strange) (adj)
bizarre
bee-zar

office (n)
un bureau
bew-roh

office worker (n)
employé (m) de bureau
employée (f) de bureau
ahm-plwa-yay duh bew-roh

often (adv)
souvent
soo-vah(n)

oil (n)
l'huile (f)
lweel

old (adj)
vieux (m)
vieille (f)
vyuh/vyay

old-fashioned (adj)
démodé (m)
démodée (f)
day-mo-day

old person (n)
une personne âgée
pair-son ah-zhay

Olympic Games (n)
les Jeux olympiques
zhuz o-leem-peek

omelette (n)
une omelette
om-let

on foot (adv)
à pied
ah pyay

on top of (prep)
sur
soor

once (adv)
une fois
ewn fwa

onion (n)
un oignon
ohn-yo(n)

only (adv)
seulement
suhl-mah(n)

open (adj)
ouvert (m)
oo-vair
ouverte (f)
oo-vairt

opening hours (n)
le heures d'ouverture
uhr doo-vair-tewr

operation (n)
une opération
o-pair-a-syo(n)

opposite (n)
le contraire
kon-trair

opposite (prep)
en face de
ah(n) fass duh

or (conj)
ou
oo

orange (colour) (adj)
orange
or-ahnzh

orange (fruit) (n)
une orange
or-ahnzh

orange juice (n)
un jus d'orange
zhew dor-ahnzh

orchestra (n)
un orchestre
or-ke-struh

organic (adj)
biologique
byo-lo-zheek

ornament (n)
un bibelot
beeb-loh

ostrich (n)
une autruche
oh-trewsh

other (adj)
autre
oh-truh

ouch!
aïe!
eye-ye

our (adj)
notre (m/f)
no-truh

out of (prep)
hors de
or duh

outside (adv)
dehors
duh-or

oval (n)
un ovale
o-val

oven (n)
un four
foor

oven glove (n)
un gant de cuisine
gah(n) duh kwee-zeen

over there (adv)
là-bas
la-bah

owl (n)
un hibou
ee-boo

own (adj)
propre
pro-pruh

oxygen (n)
l'oxygène (m)
lok-see-zhen

ozone layer (n)
la couche d'ozone
koosh doh-zohne

P

padlock (n)
un cadenas
kad-na

page (n)
une page
pazh

paint (n)
la peinture
pan-tewr

paint brush (n)
un pinceau
pan-soh

A B C D E F G H I J K L M N O P Q R S T U V W X Y Z

paint tin (n)
un pot
de peinture
poh duh pan-tewr

pair (n)
une paire
pair

pale (adj)
pâle
pahl

palm tree (n)
un palmier
palm-yay

pancake (n)
une crêpe
krehp

panda (n)
un panda
pahn-da

paper (n)
le papier
pap-yay

paper clip (n)
un trombone
trom-bon

paper towel (n)
un essuie-tout
es-swee too

parachute (n)
un parachute
pa-ra-shewt

parade (n)
un défilé
day-fee-lay

parcel (n)
un colis
ko-lee

parent (n)
un parent
par-ah(n)

park (n)
un parc
park

parrot (n)
un perroquet
pair-o-kay

part (n)
une pièce
pee-ess

partner (n)
un/une camarade
ka-ma-rad

party (n)
une fête
feht

passenger (n)
un passager
pah-sa-zhay
une passagère
pah-sa-zhair

passport (n)
un passeport
pah-spor

past (history) (n)
le passé
pah-say

past (prep)
après
ap-reh

pasta (n)
les pâtes
paht

path (n)
un chemin
shuh-ma(n)

patient (adj)
patient (m)
pa-sya(n)
patiente (f)
pa-syant

pattern (n)
un motif
mo-teef

pavement (n)
le trottoir
trot-wahr

paw (n)
une patte
pat

pay (n)
un salaire
sa-lair

PC (personal computer) (n)
un PC
pay-say

PE (physical education) (n)
l'éducation
physique (f)
lay-dew-ka-syo(n) fee-zeek

pea (n)
un petit pois
puh-tee pwa

peace (n)
la paix
pay

peaceful (adj)
tranquille
trahn-keel

peanut (n)
une cacahuète
ka-ka-weht

pear (n)
une poire
pwahr

pearl (n)
une perle
pairl

pebble (n)
un galet
ga-lay

pedal (n)
une pédale
pay-dal

pelican (n)
un pélican
pay-lee-kah(n)

pen (n)
un stylo
stee-loh

pencil (n)
un crayon
à papier
kray-o(n) ah pap-yay

pencil case (n)
une trousse
trooss

penguin (n)
un pingouin
pa(n)-gwa(n)

people (n)
les gens (pl)
zhah(n)

pepper (n)
le poivre
pwa-vruh

perfect (adj)
parfait (m)
par-fay
parfaite (f)
par-feht

perhaps (adv)
peut-être
puh-teh-truh

person (n)
une personne
pair-son

pet (n)
un animal familier
an-ee-mal fa-meel-yay

petrol (n)
l'essence (f)
le-sahns

phone (n)
un téléphone
tay-lay-fon

photo (n)
une photo
fo-toh

piano (n)
un piano
piano

picnic (n)
un pique-nique
peek-neek

picture (n)
une image
ee-mazh

piece (n)
un morceau
mor-soh

pig (n)
un cochon
ko-sho(n)

pillow (n)
un oreiller
o-ray-yay

pilot (n)
un pilote
pee-lot

pineapple (n)
un ananas
an-an-ass

pinecone (n)
une pomme de pin
pom duh pa(n)

pine tree (n)
un pin
pa(n)

pink (adj)
rose
rohz

pirate (n)
un pirate
pee-rat

pizza (n)
une pizza
peed-za

place (n)
un endroit
ahn-drwa

plan (n)
un plan
plah(n)

plane (n)
un avion
av-yo(n)

planet (n)
une planète
plan-eht

plant (n)
une plante
plahnt

plastic (adj)
en plastique
ah(n) plas-teek

plastic bag (n)
un sac en plastique
sak ah(n) plas-teek

plate (n)
une assiette
a-syet

platform (n)
un quai
kay

play (n)
une pièce de théâtre
pyehs duh tay-a-truh

player (n)
un joueur
zhoo-uhr
une joueuse
zhoo-uhz

playground (n)
une cour de
récréation
koor duh ray-kray-a-syo(n)

playtime (n)
la récréation
ray-kray-a-syo(n)

please (adv)
s'il te plaît/
s'il vous plaît
seel tuh pleh/seel voo pleh

plug (for bath) (n)
un bouchon
boo-sho(n)

plug (electric) (n)
une prise
électrique
preez ay-lek-treek

plum (n)
une prune
prewn

pocket (n)
une poche
posh

pocket money (n)
l'argent de poche (m)
lar-zhah(n) duh posh

point (n)
un point
pwa(n)

pointed (adj)
pointu (m)
pointue (f)
pwan-tew

polar bear (n)
un ours blanc
oorss blah(n)

pole (post) (n)
un poteau
po-toh

police (n)
la police
po-leess

police car (n)
une voiture
de police
vwa-tewr duh po-leess

police helicopter (n)
un hélicoptère
de police
ay-lee-kop-tair duh po-leess

police officer (n)
un policier
po-lee-syay
une femme policier
fam po-lee-syay

polite (adj)
poli (m) polie (f)
po-lee

pollution (n)
la pollution
pol-lew-syo(n)

pond (n)
un étang
ay-tah(n)

pony (n)
un poney
po-nay

poor (adj)
pauvre
poh-vruh

popular (adj)
populaire
po-pew-lair

population (n)
la population
po-pew-la-syo(n)

port (n)
un port
por

portrait (n)
un portrait
por-tray

position (n)
une position
poh-zee-syo(n)

possible (adj)
possible
po-see-bluh

postbox (n)
une boîte aux lettres
bwat oh let-truh

postcard (n)
une carte postale
kart pos-tal

postcode (n)
un code postal
kohd pos-tal

poster (n)
une affiche
af-feesh

postman (n)
un facteur
fak-tuhr
une factrice
fak-treess

post office (n)
un bureau de poste
bew-roh duh post

potato (n)
une pomme de terre
pom duh tair

pottery (n)
une poterie (f)
pot-ree

powder (n)
la poudre
poo-druh

powerful (adj)
puissant (m)
pwee-sah(n)
puissante (f)
pwee-sahnt

practice (n)
la répétition
ray-pay-tee-syo(n)

prawn (n)
une crevette
kruh-vet

preparations (n)
les préparatifs (m)
pray-para-teef

present (n)
un cadeau
ka-doh

president (n)
un président
pray-zee-dah(n)

pretty (adj)
joli (m) jolie (f)
zho-lee

prey (n)
la proie
prwa

price (n)
un prix
pree

prince (n)
un prince
pranss

princess (n)
une princesse
pran-sess

print-out (n)
une impression
am-preh-syo(n)

private (adj)
privé (m) privée (f)
pree-vay

prize (n)
un prix
pree

probably (adv)
probablement
pro-bab-luh-mah(n)

problem (n)
un problème
prob-lehm

programme (TV) (n)
une émission
ay-mee-syo(n)

project (n)
un projet
pro-zhay

proud (adj)
fier (m)
fyer
fière (f)
fy-air

public (adj)
public (m)
publique (f)
pewb-leek

pudding (n)
un dessert
duh-sair

pumpkin (n)
une citrouille
see-troo-ye

pupil (n)
un/une élève
ay-lehv

puppet (n)
une marionnette
mar-yon-net

puppet show (n)
un spectacle de marionnettes
spek-tak-luh duh mar-yon-net

puppy (n)
un chiot
shyoh

purple (adj)
violet (m)
violette (f)
vyo-lay/vyo-let

purse (n)
un porte-monnaie
port-mo-nay

puzzle (n)
un puzzle
puh-zluh

pyjamas (n)
un pyjama
pee-zha-ma

pyramid (n)
une pyramide
pee-ra-meed

Q

quantity (n)
une quantité
kahn-tee-tay

quarrel (n)
une dispute
dee-spewt

quarter (n)
un quart
kar

queen (n)
une reine
rehn

question (n)
une question
kest-yo(n)

queue (n)
une queue
kuh

quickly (adv)
vite
veet

quiet (adj)
silencieux (m)
see-lahn-syuh
silencieuse (f)
see-lahn-syuhz

quietly (adv)
tranquillement
trahn-keel-mah(n)

quiz (n)
un quiz
kweez

R

rabbit (n)
un lapin
lap-a(n)

race (n)
une course
koorss

racing car (n)
une voiture de course
vwa-tewr duh koorss

racket (n)
une raquette
rak-et

radio (n)
une radio
rad-yo

railway station (n)
une gare
gar

rain (n)
la pluie
plwee

rainbow (n)
un arc-en-ciel
ark-ah(n)-syel

raincoat (n)
un imperméable
am-pair-may-a-bluh

rainforest (n)
la forêt tropicale
for-eh tro-pee-kal

rake (n)
un râteau
rah-toh

ranch (n)
un ranch
rahnch

rare (adj)
rare
rahr

raspberry (n)
une framboise
frahm-bwaz

rat (n)
un rat
ra

raw (adj)
cru (m) crue (f)
krew

reading (n)
la lecture
lek-tewr

ready (adj)
prêt (m)
preh
prête (f)
preht

real (adj)
réel (m)
réelle (f)
ray-el

really (adv)
vraiment
vray-mah(n)

receipt (n)
un ticket de caisse
tee-kay duh kess

recipe (n)
une recette
ruh-set

rectangle (n)
un rectangle
rek-tahn-gluh

red (adj)
rouge
roozh

referee (n)
un arbitre
ar-bee-truh

religion (n)
la religion
ruh-lee-zhyo(n)

remote control (n)
une télécommande
tay-lay-kom-mahnd

report (for school) (n)
un exposé
ek-spoh-zay

rescue (n)
les secours
suh-koor

restaurant (n)
un restaurant
res-tor-ah(n)

reward (n)
une récompense
ray-kom-pahns

A B C D E F G H I J K L M N O P Q R S T U V W X Y Z

rhinoceros (n)
un rhinocéros
ree-no-say-ros

ribbon (n)
un ruban
rew-bah(n)

rice (n)
le riz
ree

rich (adj)
riche
reesh

riding (n)
l'équitation (f)
lay-kee-ta-syo(n)

right (not left) (adj)
droit (m)
droite (f)
drwa/drwat

right (correct) (adj)
exact (m)
exacte (f)
eg-zakt

ring (n)
une bague
bag

ripe (adj)
mûr (m) mûre (f)
mewr

river (n)
une rivière
reev-yehr

road (n)
une route
root

robot (n)
un robot
ro-boh

rock (n)
un rocher
ro-shay

rocket (n)
une fusée
few-zay

roll (n)
un petit pain
puh-tee pa(n)

rollerblades (n)
les rollerblades (m)
rollerblades

rollerskates (n)
les patins à roulettes (m)
pa-ta-(n) ah roo-let

roof (n)
un toit
twa

room (n)
une pièce
pyehs

root (n)
une racine
ra-seen

rope (n)
une corde
cord

rose (n)
une rose
rohz

rough (adj)
rugueux (m)
rew-ghuh
rugueuse (f)
rew-ghuhz

round (adj)
rond (m)
ro(n)
ronde (f)
rond

roundabout (n)
un tourniquet
toor-nee-kay

route (n)
un trajet
tra-zhay

row (line) (n)
une rangée
rahn-zhay

rowing boat (n)
un canot
kanoh

rubber (eraser) (n)
une gomme
gom

rubber band (n)
un élastique
ay-la-steek

rubbish (n)
les ordures
or-dewr

rucksack (n)
un sac à dos
sak ah doh

rug (n)
un tapis
ta-pee

rugby (n)
le rugby
rewg-bee

ruler (measure) (n)
une règle
reh-gluh

running (n)
la course à pied
koorss ah pyay

runway (n)
une piste
peest

S

sack (n)
un sac
sak

sad (adj)
triste
treest

saddle (n)
une selle
sel

safari park (n)
une réserve
ray-zairv

safe (adj)
en sécurité
ah(n) say-kew-ree-tay

sail (n)
une voile
vwal

sailing boat (n)
un bateau à voiles
ba-toh ah vwal

sailor (n)
un marin
mar-a(n)

salad (n)
une salade
sal-ad

salt (n)
le sel
sel

same (adj)
même
mehm

sand (n)
le sable
sah-bluh

sandals (n)
les sandales (f)
sahn-dal

sandcastle (n)
un château de sable
sha-toh duh sah-bluh

sandwich (n)
un sandwich
sahnd-weetsh

satellite dish (n)
une antenne parabolique
ahn-ten pa-ra-bo-leek

satellite TV (n)
la télévision par satellite
tay-lay-vee-zyo(n) par sa-teh-leet

saucepan (n)
une casserole
kass-rol

sausage (n)
une saucisse
soh-seess

scar (n)
une cicatrice
see-ka-treess

scarf (n)
une écharpe
ay-sharp

school (n)
l'école (f)
lay-kol

school bag (n)
un cartable
kar-ta-bluh

school uniform (n)
un uniforme scolaire
ew-nee-form sko-lair

science (n)
les sciences
see-yahnss

scientist (n)
un/une scientifique
see-yahn-tee-feek

scissors (n)
les ciseaux
see-zoh

score (n)
un score
skor

screen (n)
un écran
ay-krah(n)

sea (n)
la mer
mair

seafood (n)
les fruits de mer
frwee duh mair

seagull (n)
une mouette
moo-wet

seal (n)
un phoque
fok

sea lion (n)
un lion de mer
lee-yo(n) duh mair

seaside (n)
le bord de la mer
bor duh la mair

season (n)
une saison
seh-zo(n)

seat (n)
un siège
syezh

seat belt (n)
une ceinture de sécurité
san-tewr duh say-kew-ree-tay

seaweed (n)
une algue
al-guh

second (2nd) (adj)
deuxième
duhz-yehm

second (time) (n)
une seconde
suh-go(n)

secret (n)
un secret
suh-kray

seed (n)
une graine
grehn

semicircle (n)
un demi-cercle
duh-mee sair-kluh

shadow (n)
une ombre
om-bruh

shallow (adj)
peu profond (m)
puh pro-fo(n)
peu profonde (f)
puh pro-fond

shampoo (n)
un shampooing
shahm-pwa(n)

shape (n)
une forme
form

shark (n)
un requin
ruh-ka(n)

sharp (adj)
aigu (m) aiguë (f)
ehg-ew

she (pron)
elle
el

sheep (n)
un mouton
moo-to(n)

sheepdog (n)
un chien de berger
shya(n) duh bair-zhay

sheet (for bed) (n)
un drap
dra

shelf (n)
une étagère
ay-ta-zhehr

shell (n)
un coquillage
ko-kee-yazh

shiny (adj)
brillant (m)
bree-yah(n)
brillante (f)
bree-yahnt

ship (n)
un navire
na-veer

shirt (n)
une chemise
shuh-meez

shoe (n)
une chaussure
shoh-soor

shop (n)
un magasin
ma-ga-za(n)

shop assistant (n)
un vendeur
vahn-duhr
une vendeuse
vahn-duhz

shopper (n)
un acheteur
ash-tuhr
une acheteuse
ash-tuhz

shopping (n)
les courses
koorss

shopping bag (n)
un sac
sak

shopping list (n)
une liste de courses
leest duh koorss

short (adj)
court (m) courte (f)
koor/koort

shorts (n)
un short
short

shoulder (n)
une épaule
ay-pohl

show (n)
un spectacle
spek-ta-kluh

shower (n)
une douche
doosh

shy (adj)
timide
tee-meed

sick (adj)
malade
ma-lad

sign (n)
un panneau
pan-noh

silence
le silence (m)
luh see-lahns

silly (adj)
bête
beht

silver (n)
l'argent
lar-zhah(n)

simple (adj)
simple
sam-pluh

since (prep)
depuis
duh-pwee

singing (n)
le chant
shah(n)

sink (n)
un évier
ayv-yay

sister (n)
une sœur
suhr

size (n)
la taille
tah-ye

skate (n)
un roller
ro-lair

skateboard (n)
un skate-board
skate-board

skeleton (n)
un squelette
skuh-let

skiing (n)
le ski
skee

skin (n)
la peau
poh

skipping rope (n)
une corde à sauter
kord ah soh-tay

skirt (n)
une jupe
zhewp

skull (n)
un crâne
kran

sky (n)
le ciel
syel

skyscraper (n)
un gratte-ciel
grat-syel

sledge (n)
une luge
lewzh

sleeping bag (n)
un sac de couchage
sak duh koosh-azh

sleeve (n)
une manche
mahnsh

sleigh (n)
un traîneau
treh-noh

slipper (n)
une pantoufle
pahn-too-fluh

slippery (adj)
glissant (m)
glee-sah(n)
glissante (f)
glee-sahnt

slow (adj)
lent (m)
lente (f)
lah(n)/lahnt

slowly (adv)
lentement
lahn-tuh-mah(n)

slug (n)
une limace
lee-mass

small (adj)
petit (m)
petite (f)
puh-tee/puh-teet

smart (adj)
élégant (m)
ay-lay-gah(n)
élégante (f)
ay-lay-gahnt

smell (n)
une odeur
o-duhr

smile (n)
un sourire
soo-reer

smoke (n)
la fumée
few-may

smooth (adj)
lisse
leess

snail (n)
un escargot
es-kar-goh

snake (n)
un serpent
sair-pah(n)

snow (n)
la neige
nehzh

snowball (n)
une boule de neige
bool duh nehzh

snowboard (n)
un snow-board
snow-board

snowflake (n)
un flocon de neige
flo-ko(n) duh nehzh

snowman (n)
un bonhomme de neige
bon-om duh nehzh

soap (n)
le savon
sa-vo(n)

sock (n)
une chaussette
shoh-set

sofa (n)
un canapé
ka-na-pay

soft (adj)
doux (m) douce (f)
doo/dooss

soil (n)
la terre
tair

soldier (n)
un soldat (m)
sol-da
une femme soldat (f)
fam sol-da

solid (n)
un solide
sol-eed

some (adj)
quelques
kel-kuh

someone (pron)
quelqu'un
kel-ka(n)

something (pron)
quelque chose
kel-kuh shohz

sometimes (adv)
quelquefois
kel-kuh fwa

somewhere (adv)
quelque part
kel-kuh par

son (n)
un fils
feess

song (n)
une chanson
shahn-so(n)

soon (adv)
bientôt
byan-toh

sound (noise) (n)
un son
so(n)

soup (n)
la soupe
la soop

sour (adj)
acide
ass-eed

south (n)
le sud
sood

souvenir (n)
un souvenir
soov-neer

space (n)
l'espace (m)
less-pass

space rocket (n)
une fusée
few-zay

spade (n)
une pelle
pel

spaghetti (n)
les spaghettis
spa-get-ee

Spanish (n)
l'espagnol (m)
le-span-yol

special (adj)
particulier (m)
par-tee-kewl-yay
particulière (f)
par-tee-kewl-yair

speech (n)
un discours
dee-skoor

speed (n)
la vitesse
vee-tess

spider (n)
une araignée
ar-ehn-yay

sponge (n)
une éponge
ay-ponzh

spoon (n)
une cuillère
kwee-yehr

sport (n)
un sport
spor

spots (n)
les taches
tash

spring (season) (n)
le printemps
pran-tah(m)

spy (n)
un espion
es-pyo(n)
une espionne
es-pyon

square (n)
un carré
kar-ray

squirrel (n)
un écureuil
ay-kew-ruh-ye

A B C D E F G H I J K L M N O P Q R S T U V W X Y Z

stadium (n)
un stade
stad

stage (theatre) (n)
la scène
sehn

stairs (n)
un escalier
es-kal-yay

stamp (n)
un timbre
tam-bruh

star (n)
une étoile
ay-twal

starfish (n)
une étoile de mer
ay-twal duh mair

station (n)
une gare
gar

steak (n)
le steak
stek

steam (n)
la buée
bway

steep (adj)
raide
rehd

stem (n)
une tige
teezh

step (n)
un pas
pa

stepfather (n)
un beau-père
boh-pair

stepmother (n)
une belle-mère
bel-mair

stick (n)
un bâton
bah-to(n)

sticker (n)
un autocollant
oh-to-ko-lah(n)

sticky (adj)
collant (m)
ko-lah(n)
collante (f)
ko-lahnt

still (adj)
immobile
im-mob-eel

stocking (n)
un bas
bah

stomach (n)
l'estomac (m)
es-to-ma

stone (n)
une pierre
pyair

storey (n)
un étage
ay-tazh

stormy (adj)
orageux (m)
or-azh-uh
orageuse (f)
or-azh-uhz

story (n)
une histoire
eest-wahr

straight (adj)
droit (m) droite (f)
drwa/drwat

straight (hair) (adj)
raide
rehd

strange (adj)
étrange
ay-trahnzh

straw (n)
la paille
pah-ye

strawberry (n)
une fraise
frehz

stream (n)
un ruisseau
rwee-soh

street (n)
une rue
rew

street light (n)
un réverbère
ray-vair-bair

strict (adj)
sévère
say-vehr

string (n)
une ficelle
fee-sel

stripes (n)
les rayures
ray-ewr

strong (adj)
fort (m)
forte (f)
for/fort

student (n)
un/une élève
ay-lehv

studio (n)
un studio
stew-dyoh

stupid (adj)
stupide
stoo-peed

subject (n)
un sujet
soo-zhay

submarine (n)
un sous-marin
soo-ma-ra(n)

subway (underground) (n)
un métro
may-troh

suddenly (adv)
tout à coup
toot ah koo

sugar (n)
le sucre
soo-kruh

suit (n)
un costume
kos-tewm

suitcase (n)
une valise
val-eez

summer (n)
l'été (m)
lay-tay

sun (n)
le soleil
so-laye

suncream (n)
la crème solaire
krehm so-lair

sunflower (n)
un tournesol
toor-nuh-sol

sunglasses (n)
les lunettes de soleil
lew-net duh so-laye

sunhat (n)
un chapeau
sha-poh

sunny (adj)
ensoleillé (m)
ensoleillée (f)
ahn-so-lay-yay

sunrise (n)
le lever de soleil
luh-vay duh so-laye

sunset (n)
le coucher de soleil
koo-shay duh so-laye

supermarket (n)
un supermarché
soo-pair-mar-shay

sure (adj)
sûr (m) sûre (f)
soor

surface (n)
une surface
soor-fass

surfboard (n)
une planche de surf
plahnsh duh surf

surfing (n)
le surf
surf

surgery (place) (n)
un cabinet médical
ka-bee-nay may-dee-kal

surname (n)
le nom de famille
no(m) duh fa-mee-ye

surprise (n)
une surprise
soor-preez

surprising (adj)
étonnant (m)
ay-ton-nah(n)
étonnante (f)
ay-ton-nahnt

swan (n)
un cygne
seen-ye

sweater (n)
un pull
pewl

sweatshirt (n)
un sweat-shirt
swet-shurt

sweet (n)
un bonbon
bo(n)-bo(n)

swimming (n)
la natation
na-ta-syo(n)

swimming pool (n)
une piscine
pee-seen

swimsuit (n)
un maillot de bain
ma-yoh duh ba(n)

swing (n)
une balançoire
ba-lahn-swahr

T

table (n)
une table
tab-luh

table tennis (n)
le tennis de table
ten-neess duh tab-luh

tadpole (n)
un têtard
teh-tar

tail (n)
une queue
kuh

tall (adj)
grand (m)
grah(n)
grande (f)
grahnd

tap (n)
un robinet
ro-bee-nay

tape measure (n)
un mètre
meh-truh

taxi (n)
un taxi
tak-see

tea (n)
le thé
tay

teacher (n)
un maître (m)
meh-truh
une maîtresse (f)
meh-tress

team (n)
une équipe
ay-keep

tea towel (n)
un torchon
tor-sho(n)

teddy bear (n)
un ours en peluche
oorss ah(n) puh-lewsh

teenager (n)
un adolescent (m)
une adolescente (f)
ado-less-ah(n)/ado-less-ahnt

telescope (n)
un télescope
tay-leh-skop

television (n)
une télévision
tay-lay-vee-zyo(n)

temperature (n)
la température
tahm-pair-a-tewr

tennis (n)
le tennis
ten-neess

tent (n)
une tente
tahnt

term (n)
un mot
moh

terrible (adj)
terrible
tair-ee-bluh

test (n)
un contrôle
kon-trohl

text message (n)
un texto
teks-toh

that one (pron)
celui-là
suhl-wee-la

the (article)
le (m) la (f)
l'(vowel)
luh/la/l

theatre (n)
le théâtre
tay-a-truh

their (adj)
leur (m/f)
luhr

then (conj)
alors
al-or

there (adv)
là
la

thermometer (n)
un thermomètre
tair-mo-meh-truh

they (pron)
ils (m) elles (f)
eel/el

thick (adj)
épais (m)
épaisse (f)
ay-pay/ay-pehss

thin (adj)
fin (m) fine (f)
fa(n)/feen

thin (slim) (adj)
mince
manss

thing (n)
une chose
shohz

third (adj)
troisième
trwaz-yehm

thirsty (adj)
assoiffé (m)
assoiffée (f)
a-swa-fay

this one (pron)
celui-ci
suhl-wee-see

thought (n)
une pensée
pahn-say

thousand
mille
meel

throat (n)
la gorge
gorzh

throne (n)
un trône
trohn

through (prep)
à travers
ah tra-vair

thumb (n)
un pouce
pooss

thunderstorm (n)
un orage
or-azh

ticket (n)
un billet
bee-yay

tide (n)
la marée
ma-ray

tie (n)
une cravate
kra-vat

tiger (n)
un tigre
tee-gruh

tight (adj)
serré (m) serrée (f)
sair-ray

tights (n)
les collants
ko-lah(n)

till (cash register) (n)
une caisse
kess

time (n)
l'heure (f)
luhr

timetable (n)
un horaire
or-air

tiny (adj)
minuscule
mee-new-skewl

tired (adj)
fatigué (m) atiguée(f)
fa-tee-gay

tissues (n)
les mouchoirs en
papier
moosh-wahrs ah(n) pap-yay

toad (n)
un crapaud
kra-poh

toaster (n)
un grille-pain
gree-ye-pa(n)

today (adv)
aujourd'hui
oh-zhoor-dwee

toe (n)
un orteil
or-teye

together (adv)
ensemble
ahn-sahm-bluh

toilet (n)
les toilettes
twa-let

toilet paper (n)
le papier toilette
pap-yay twa-let

tomato (n)
une tomate
tom-at

tomorrow (adv)
demain
duh-ma(n)

tongue (n)
une langue
lahn-guh

tonight (adv)
cette nuit
set nwee

too (adv)
aussi
oh-see

tool (n)
un outil
oo-tee

tooth (n)
une dent
dah(n)

toothbrush (n)
une brosse à dents
bros ah dah(n)

toothpaste (n)
le dentifrice
dahn-tee-freess

top (n)
le haut
oh

torch (n)
une lampe de poche
lahmp duh posh

tornado (n)
une tornade
tor-nad

tortoise (n)
une tortue
tor-tew

toucan (n)
un toucan
too-kah(n)

tough (adj)
dur (m)
dure (f)
dewr

tourist (n)
un/une touriste
too-reest

towards (prep)
vers
vair

towel (n)
une serviette
sair-vee-et

town (n)
une ville
veel

toy (n)
un jouet
zhoo-way

toy box (n)
un coffre à
jouets
kof-fruh ah zhoo-way

toy bricks (n)
les cubes
kewb

tracksuit (n)
un survêtement
soor-veht-mah(n)

tractor (n)
un tracteur
trak-tuhr

traffic (n)
la circulation
seer-kew-lah-syo(n)

traffic lights (n)
les feux de
signalisation
fuh duh seen-ya-lee-za-
syo(n)

train (n)
un train
tra(n)

trainers (n)
les baskets
bas-ket

train set (toy) (n)
un train
tra(n)

trampoline (n)
un trampoline
trahm-po-leen

transport (n)
le transport
trahn-spor

tray (n)
un plateau
pla-toh

tree (n)
un arbre
ar-bruh

triangle (n)
un triangle
tree-yahn-gluh

trip (n)
un voyage
vwa-yazh

trolley (supermarket) (n)
un caddie
ka-dee

tropical (adj)
tropical (m)
tropicale (f)
tro-pee-kal

trouble (n)
un ennui
ahn-wwee

trousers (n)
un pantalon
pahn-ta-lo(n)

trowel (n)
un déplantoir
day-plahnt-wahr

truck (n)
un camion
kam-yo(n)

true (adj)
vrai (m)
vraie (f)
vray

trunk (animal) (n)
une trompe
tromp

trunk (tree) (n)
un tronc
tro(n)

trunks (n)
un maillot de bain
ma-yoh duh ba(n)

truth (n)
la vérité
vay-ree-tay

T-shirt (n)
un tee-shirt
tee-shirt

tube (n)
un tube
tewb

tummy (n)
un ventre
vahn-truh

tune (n)
un air
air

tunnel (n)
un tunnel
tew-nel

turkey (n)
un dindon
dan-do(n)

turn (bend) (n)
un tournant
toor-nah(n)

turtle (n)
une tortue
de mer
tor-tew duh mair

twice (adv)
deux fois
duh fwa

twin (n)
un jumeau
zhew-moh
une jumelle
zhew-mel

tyre (n)
un pneu
p-nuh

U

ugly (adj)
laid (m) laide (f)
lay/lehd

umbrella (rain) (n)
un parapluie
pa-ra-plwee

umbrella (sun) (n)
un parasol
pa-ra-sol

uncle (n)
un oncle
onk-luh

uncomfortable (adj)
inconfortable
an-kon-for-ta-bluh

under (prep)
sous
soo

underneath (prep)
au-dessous de
oh duh-soo duh

underwear (n)
les sous-vêtements
soo-veht-mah(n)

unfair (adj)
injuste
an-zhewst

uniform (n)
un uniforme
ew-nee-form

universe (n)
l'univers (m)
lew-nee-vair

university (n)
l'université (f)
lew-nee-vair-see-tay

until (prep)
jusqu'à
zhew-ska

unusual (adj)
inhabituel (m)
inhabituelle (f)
een-ab-ee-tew-el

upside down (adv)
à l'envers
ah lahn-vair

upstairs (adv)
en haut
ah(n) oh

useful (adj)
utile
ew-teel

usually (adv)
d'habitude
da-bee-tewd

V

vacuum cleaner (n)
un aspirateur
ass-peer-a-tuhr

valley (n)
une vallée
va-lay

van (n)
une camionnette
kam-yon-net

vegetable (n)
un légume
lay-gewm

vegetarian (n)
un végétarien
vay-zhay-ta-rya(n)
une végétarienne
vay-zhay-ta-ryen

verb (n)
un verbe
vairb

very (adv)
très
treh

vet (n)
un/une vétérinaire
vay-tair-ee-nair

video game (n)
un jeu vidéo
zhuh vee-day-oh

video player (n)
un magnétoscope
man-yay-to-skop

village (n)
un village
vee-lazh

violin (n)
un violon
vyo-lo(n)

virtual reality (n)
la réalité
virtuelle
ray-a-lee-tay
veer-tew-ell

vocabulary (n)
le vocabulaire
vo-ka-bew-lair

voice (n)
la voix
vwa

vulture (n)
un vautour
voh-toor

W

waist (n)
la taille
tah-ye

waiter (n)
un garçon de café
gar-so(n) duh ka-fay

waitress (n)
une serveuse
sair-vuhz

walk (n)
une promenade
pro-muh-nad

wall (n)
un mur
mewr

wallet (n)
un portefeuille
por-tuh-fuh-ye

war (n)
une guerre
gair

wardrobe (n)
une armoire
arm-wahr

warm (adj)
chaud (m)
chaude (f)
shoh/shohd

warning (n)
un avertissement
av-air-tee-smah(n)

washbasin (n)
un lavabo
la-va-boh

washing machine (n)
une machine
à laver
ma-sheen ah la-vay

washing-up (n)
la vaisselle
vay-sel

wasp (n)
une guêpe
gehp

watch (n)
une montre
mon-truh

water (n)
l'eau (f)
loh

watering can (n)
un arrosoir
ar-rohz-wahr

water lily (n)
un nénuphar
nay-new-far

watermelon (n)
une pastèque
pas-tehk

waterproof (adj)
imperméable
am-pair-may-a-bluh

wave (n)
une vague
vag

wavy (hair) (adj)
bouclé (m)
bouclée (f)
boo-klay

way in (n)
l'entrée (f)
lahn-tray

way out (n)
la sortie
sor-tee

we (pron)
nous
noo

weak (adj)
faible
fay-bluh

weather (n)
le temps
tah(n)

website (n)
un site web
seet web

weed (n)
une mauvaise
herbe
moh-vayz airb

week (n)
une semaine
suh-mehn

weekend (n)
un week-end
week-end

weight (n)
le poids
pwa

welcome (adj)
bienvenu (m)
bienvenue (f)
byan-vuh-new

well (adj)
bien
bya(n)

west (n)
l'ouest (m)
lwest

wet (adj)
mouillé (m)
mouillée (f)
moo-yay

whale (n)
une baleine
ba-len

wheat (n)
le blé
blay

wheel (n)
une roue
roo

wheelbarrow (n)
une brouette
broo-et

wheelchair (n)
un fauteuil
roulant
foh-tuh-ye roo-lah(n)

when (adv)
quand
kah(n)

where (adv)
où
oo

while (conj)
pendant que
pahn-dah(n) kuh

whisker (n)
une moustache
moo-stash

whistle (n)
un sifflement
see-fluh-mah(n)

white (adj)
blanc (m)
blanche (f)
blah(n)/blahnsh

who (pron)
qui
kee

why (adv)
pourquoi
poor-kwa

wide (adj)
large
larzh

wife (n)
une épouse
ay-pooz

wig (n)
une perruque
pair-ewk

wind (n)
le vent
vah(n)

window (n)
une fenêtre
fuh-neh-truh

windy (adj)
il y a du vent
eel ya dew vah(n)

wing (n)
une aile
ehl

winner (n)
un gagnant
gan-yah(n)
une gagnante
gan-yahnt

winter (n)
l'hiver (m)
lee-vair

wise (adj)
sage
sazh

wish (n)
un souhait
sway

with (prep)
avec
av-ek

without (prep)
sans
sah(n)

wolf (n)
un loup
loo

woman (n)
une femme
fam

wood (n)
le bois
bwa

wooden (adj)
en bois
ah(n) bwa

wool (n)
la laine
lehn

woolly hat (n)
un bonnet
bon-nay

word (n)
un mot
moh

work (n)
le travail
tra-vye

world (n)
un monde
mond

worm (n)
un ver
vair

worst (adj)
pire
peer

wound (n)
une blessure
bless-ewr

wrist (n)
le poignet
pwan-ye

writing (act of) (n)
l'écriture (f)
lay-kree-tewr

X

x-ray (n)
une radiographie
rad-yo-gra-fee

Y

yes (adv)
oui
wee

Z

zebra (n)
un zèbre
zeh-bruh

zebra crossing (n)
un passage clouté
pa-sazh kloo-tay

zero (n)
zéro
zay-roh

zip (n)
une fermeture éclair
fair-muh-tewr ay-klair

zone (n)
une zone
zohn

zoo (n)
un zoo
zoh

Speaking French

In this dictionary, we have spelled out each French word in a way that will help you pronounce it. Use this guide to help you understand how the word should sound when you say it. Some French words look the same as English, but sound very different!

Letter	Pronunciation	Our spelling	Example
a, à, â	between the *a* n klh*a*t and f*a*r	*a* or *ah*	**adresse** *a-dreys*
ch	like *sh* in *sh*ip	*sh*	**changer** *shahn-zhay*
ç	like *s* in *s*it	*s*	**garçon** *gar-so(n)*
é	like *ay* in d*ay*	*ay*	**café** *ka-fay*
è, ê	ike *e* in m*e*t	*eh*	**crème** *krehm*
e	ike *er* in oth*er*	*uh*	**de** *duh*
gn	like the *ni* in o*ni*on	*nye*	**ligne** *leen-ye*
i, y	like *ee* in f*ee*t	*ee*	**fille** *fee-ye*
j, and sometimes g	like *s* in mea*s*ure	*zh*	**bonjour** *bon-zhoor*
qu	like *k* in *k*ing	*k*	**queue** *kuh*
o, ô	ike *o* in m*o*re	*o* or *oh*	**porte** *port*
r	say *ruh* at the back of your throat, as if you're gargling	*r*	**fleur** *fluhr*
u	like *ew* in f*ew*	*ew*	**tu** *tew*
an, en, ien, in, ain, ein, on, un, am, em, im, aim, eim, om, um	the *n* is not pronounced, but the vowel in front of it should have a nasal sound, as if the word ended in *ng*. For example, as if you said *song*, but stopped before saying the final *ng*	*a(n), ah(n), o(n)*	**bien** *bya(n)*

A B C D E F G H I J K L M N O P Q R S T U V W X Y Z

French A–Z

In this section, the French words are given in alphabetical order. They are followed by the English translation and a few letters to show what type of word it is – a noun (n) or adjective (adj), for example. Look at page 152 to see a list of the different types of words.

Nouns in French are either masculine or feminine. We have used the abbreviations (m) and (f) to tell you which they are. Sometimes a word in French might mean more than one thing in English, so there might be two translations underneath.

Most of the nouns (naming words) here are singular (only one of the object). To make a noun plural (for more than one thing) you usually just add an "s" – the same as in English. In French though, the other words in the sentence change too – *le* and *la* become *les*. The adjectives also change, usually getting an extra "s" at the end.

A

à côté de (prep)
beside

à l'arrière (adv)
back (opposite of front)

à l'envers (adv)
upside down

à l'intérieur de (prep)
inside

à la mode (adv)
fashionable

à pied (adv)
on foot

à travers (prep)
through

abeille (n) (f)
bee

abricot (n) (m)
apricot

absent/absente (adj)
away

accident (n) (m)
accident

acheteur/acheteuse (n) (m/f)
shopper

acide (adj)
sour

activité (n) (f)
activity

acrobate (n) (m/f)
acrobat

acteur (n) (m)
actor

action (n) (f)
action

actrice (n) (f)
actress

addition (n) (f)
bill

adolescent/adolescente (n) (m/f)
teenager

adorable (adj)
lovely

adresse (n) (f)
address

adresse électronique (n) (f)
email address

adulte (n) (m/f)
adult

aéroport (n) (m)
airport

affaires (n) (f)
business

affamé/affamée (adj)
hungry

affiche (n) (f)
poster

âge (n) (m)
age

agneau (n) (m)
lamb

aide (n) (f)
help

aïe!
ouch!

aigle (n) (m)
eagle

aigu/aiguë (adj)
sharp

aiguille (n) (f)
needle

aile (n) (f)
wing

aimant (n) (m)
magnet

air (n) (m)
air

air (n) (m)
tune

algue (n) (f)
seaweed

alligator (n) (m)
alligator

alors (conj)
then

alphabet (n) (m)
alphabet

ambulance (n) (f)
ambulance

amer/amère (adj)
bitter

ami/amie (n) (m/f)
friend

amical/amicale (adj)
friendly

ample (adj)
loose

ampoule (n) (f)
bulb (light)

amusement (n) (m)
fun

ananas (n) (m)
pineapple

ancre (n) (f)
anchor

anglais (n) (m)
English

animal (n) (m)
animal

animal familier (n) (m)
pet

année/an (n) (f/m)
year

anniversaire (n) (m)
birthday

antenne (n) (f)
antenna

antenne parabolique (n) (f)
satellite dish

appareil photo (n) (m)
camera

apparence (n) (f)
appearance

appartement (n) (m)
flat (apartment)

après (prep)
after, past

après-midi (n) (m)
afternoon

araignée (n) (f)
spider

arbitre (n) (m)
referee

arbre (n) (m)
tree

arc-en-ciel (n) (m)
rainbow

arche (n) (f)
arch

architecte (n) (m/f)
architect

argent (n) (m)
money, silver

argent de poche (n) (m)
pocket money

armée (n) (f)
army

armoire (n) (f)
cupboard (tall)

armoire (n) (f)
wardrobe

arrêt de bus (n) (m)
bus stop

arrivée (n) (f)
arrival

arrosoir (n) (m)
watering can

art (n) (m)
art

artiste (n) (m/f)
artist

ascenseur (n) (m)
lift

aspirateur (n) (m)
vacuum cleaner

assez (adv)
enough

assiette (n) (f)
plate

assistant/assistante (n) (m/f)
assistant

assoiffé/assoiffée (adj)
thirsty

astronaute (n) (m/f)
astronaut

astronome (n) (m/f)
astronomer

athlétisme (n) (m)
athletics

atlas (n) (m)
atlas

aube (n) (f)
dawn

au-dessous de (prep)
below

au-dessus de (prep)
above

aujourd'hui (adv)
today

aussi (adv)
also, too

auteur (n) (m)
author

autobus (n) (m)
bus

autocar (n) (m)
coach

autocollant (n) (m)
sticker

automne (n) (m)
autumn

autoroute (n) (f)
motorway

autour (prep)
around

autre (adj)
other

autruche (n) (f)
ostrich

au rez-de-chaussée (adv)
downstairs

avant (prep)
before

avec (prep)
with

avenir (n) (m)
future

aventure (n) (f)
adventure

avertissement (n) (m)
warning

avion (n) (m)
aeroplane, plane

avion à réaction (n) (m)
jet

avocat (n) (m)
avocado

B

babouin (n) (m)
baboon

bacon (n) (m)
bacon

badminton (n) (m)
badminton

bagages (n) (m)
luggage

bague (n) (f)
ring

baignoire (n) (f)
bath

baiser (n) (m)
kiss

balai (n) (m)
broom

balançoire (n) (f)
swing

balcon (n) (m)
balcony

baleine (n) (f)
whale

balle (n) (f)
ball

ballon (n) (m)
ball, balloon

ballon de football (n) (m)
football (ball)

banane (n) (f)
banana

banc (n) (m)
bench

bande (n) (f)
band

bande (n) (f)
gang

bande dessinée (n) (f)
cartoon (drawing)

banque (n) (f)
bank (money)

banquet (n) (m)
feast

barbe (n) (f)
beard

barbecue (n) (m)
barbecue

barrière (n) (f)
fence, gate

bas/basse (adj)
low

bas (n) (m)
stocking

base-ball (n) (m)
baseball

basket-ball (n) (m)
basketball

baskets (n) (f)
trainers

bataille (n) (f)
battle

bateau (n) (m)
boat

bateau à voiles (n) (m)
sailing boat

bateau de pêche (n) (m)
fishing boat

bateau de sauvetage (n) (m)
lifeboat

bâtiment (n) (m)
building

bâton (n) (m)
stick

batte (n) (f)
bat (sports)

batterie (n) (f)
drum kit

beau/belle (adj)
beautiful, handsome

beaucoup (adv)
(a) lot

beau-père (n) (m)
stepfather

beauté (n) (f)
beauty

bébé (n) (m)
baby

bec (n) (m)
beak

belle-mère (n) (f)
stepmother

bétail (n) (m)
cattle

bête (n) (f)
creature

bête (adj)
silly

beurre (n) (m)
butter

bibelot (n) (m)
ornament

bibliothèque (n) (f)
library

bidon (n) (m)
can

bien (adj)
fine

bien (adv)
well

bien que (conj)
although

bientôt (adv)
soon

bienvenu/bienvenue (adj)
welcome

bijou (n) (m)
jewel

bijoux (n) (m)
jewellery

billes (n) (f)
marbles (toy)

billet (n) (m)
note, ticket

biologique (adj)
organic

biscuit (n) (m)
biscuit

bizarre (adj)
odd (strange)

blague (n) (f)
joke

blanc/blanche (adj)
white

blé (n) (m)
wheat

blessure (n) (f)
injury,wound

bleu (n) (m)
bruise

bleu/bleue (adj)
blue

blond/blonde (adj)
blonde

blouson (n) (m)
jacket

bois (n) (m)
wood

boisson (n) (f)
drink

boîte (n) (f)
box

boîte aux lettres (n) (f)
letter box, postbox

boîte d'allumettes (n) (f)
matchbox

bol (n) (m)
bowl (cereal)

bon/bonne (adj)
good

bonbon (n) (m)
sweet

bondé/bondée (adj)
crowded

bonhomme de neige (n) (m)
snowman

bon marché (adj)
cheap

bonnet (n) (m)
woolly hat

bord (n) (m)
edge

bord de la mer (n) (m)
seaside

botte (n) (f)
boot

bouche (n) (f)
mouth

boucherie (n) (f)
butcher's shop

bouclé/bouclée (adj)
wavy (hair)

boucle d'oreille (n) (f)
earring

bouchon (n) (m)
plug (for bath)

boue (n) (f)
mud

bouée (n) (f)
buoy

boueux/boueuse (adj)
muddy

bougie (n) (f)
candle

bouilloire (n) (f)
kettle

boulangerie (n) (f)
bakery

boule de neige (n) (f)
snowball

boussole (n) (f)
compass

bouteille (n) (f)
bottle

bouton (n) (m)
button

bracelet (n) (m)
bracelet

branche (n) (f)
branch

bras (n) (m)
arm

bric-à-brac (n) (m)
junk

brillant/brillante (adj)
bright, shiny

brise (n) (f)
breeze

brosse à cheveux (n) (f)
hairbrush

brosse à dents (n) (f)
toothbrush

brouette (n) (f)
wheelbarrow

brouillard (n) (m)
fog

brumeux/brumeuse (adj)
misty

bruyant/bruyante (adj)
loud, noisy

bûche (n) (f)
log (wood)

buée (n) (f)
steam

buisson (n) (m)
bush

bulbe (n) (m)
bulb (plant)

bulle (n) (f)
bubble

bureau (n) (m)
desk, office

bureau de poste (n) (m)
post office

but (n) (m)
goal

C

c'est
it's (it is)

cabane (n) (f)
hut

cabinet médical (n) (m)
surgery (place)

cadeau (n) (m)
gift

cacahuète (n) (f)
peanut

cache-cache (n) (m)
hide-and-seek

caddie (n) (m)
trolley (supermarket)

cadeau (n) (m)
present

cadenas (n) (m)
padlock

cadre (n) (m)
frame

café (n) (m)
café, coffee

cage (n) (f)
cage

cahier (n) (m)
exercise book

caisse (n) (f)
checkout, till

calculatrice (n) (f)
calculator

calendrier (n) (m)
calendar

calme (adj)
calm

camarade (n) (m/f)
partner

camion (n) (m)
lorry, truck

camion de pompier (n) (m)
fire engine

camionnette (n) (f)
van

campagne (n) (f)
countryside

camping (n) (m)
campsite

canapé (n) (m)
sofa

canard (n) (m)
duck

caneton (n) (m)
duckling

canoë (n) (m)
canoe

canot (n) (m)
rowing boat

cape (n) (f)
cloak

capitale (n) (f)
capital

capuche (n) (f)
hood

carburant (n) (m)
fuel

caravane (n) (f)
caravan

carnaval (n) (m)
carnival

carnet (n) (m)
notebook

carotte (n) (f)
carrot

carré (n) (m)
square

carrefour (n) (m)
crossing

cartable (n) (m)
school bag

carte (n) (f)
card, map, menu

carte d'anniversaire (n) (f)
birthday card

carte postale (n) (f)
postcard

cartes (n) (f)
cards

carton (n) (m)
cardboard

casque (n) (m)
helmet

casque (n) (m)
headphones

casquette (n) (f)
cap

cassé/cassée (adj)
broken

casserole (n) (f)
saucepan

cassette (n) (f)
cassette

catastrophe (n) (f)
disaster

cathédrale (n) (f)
cathedral

cave (n) (f)
cellar

CD (n) (m)
CD

ceinture (n) (f)
belt

ceinture de sécurité (n) (f)
seat belt

célébration (n) (f)
celebration

célèbre (adj)
famous

celui-ci (pron)
this one

celui-là (pron)
that one

centre (n) (m)
centre

cercle (n) (m)
circle

céréale (n) (f)
cereal

cerf-volant (n) (m)
kite

cerise (n) (f)
cherry

certain/certaine (adj)
certain

cerveau (n) (m)
brain

cette nuit
tonight

chaîne (n) (f)
chain

chaise (n) (f)
chair

chaise longue (n) (f)
deck chair

chaleur (n) (f)
heat

chambre (n) (f)
bedroom

chameau (n) (m)
camel

champ (n) (m)
field

champignon (n) (m)
mushroom

chance (n) (f)
chance

chanceux/chanceuse (adj)
lucky

changement (n) (m)
change

chance (n) (f)
chance

chanson (n) (f)
song

chant (n) (m)
singing

chapeau (n) (m)
hat, sunhat

chaque (adj)
each

charrette (n) (f)
cart

chat (n) (m)
cat

château (n) (m)
castle

château de sable (n) (m)
sandcastle

chaton (n) (m)
kitten

chaud/chaude (adj)
hot, warm

chaussette (n) (f)
sock

chaussure (n) (f)
shoe

chauve (adj)
bald

chauve-souris (n) (f)
bat (animal)

chef (n) (m/f)
chef

chef (n) (m)
leader

chemin (n) (m)
path

cheminée (n) (f)
chimney

chemise (n) (f)
shirt

chemisier (n) (m)
blouse

chenille (n) (f)
caterpillar

cher/chère (adj)
dear (special, expensive)

cheval (n) (m)
horse

chevalier (n) (m)
knight

cheveux (n) (m)
hair

cheville (n) (f)
ankle

chèvre (n) (f)
goat

chewing-gum (n) (m)
chewing gum

chien (n) (m)
dog

chien de berger (n) (m)
sheepdog

chimpanzé (n) (m)
chimpanzee

chiot (n) (m)
puppy

chirurgie (n) (f)
surgery (operation)

chocolat (n) (m)
chocolate

chocolat chaud (n) (m)
hot chocolate

choix (n) (m)
choice

chose (n) (f)
thing

chou (n) (m)
cabbage

chou-fleur (n) (m)
cauliflower

cicatrice (n) (f)
scar

ciel (n) (m)
sky

cil (n) (m)
eyelash

cinéma (n) (m)
cinema

cintre (n) (m)
coat hanger

circulation (n) (f)
traffic

cirque (n) (m)
circus

ciseaux (n) (m)
scissors

citron (n) (m)
lemon

citrouille (n) (f)
pumpkin

clair/claire (adj)
clear, light

classe (n) (f)
class (school)

clavier (n) (m)
keyboard

clé (n) (f)
key

client/cliente (n) (m/f)
customer

cloche (n) (f)
bell

clown (n) (m)
clown

club (n) (m)
club

coccinelle (n) (f)
ladybird

cochon (n) (m)
pig

cochon d'Inde (n) (m)
guinea pig

code postal (n) (m)
postcode

cœur (n) (m)
heart

coffre à jouets (n) (m)
toy box

coiffeur/coiffeuse (n) (m/f)
hairdresser

coin (n) (m)
corner

colis (n) (m)
parcel

collant/collante (adj)
sticky

collants (n) (m)
tights

colle (n) (f)
glue

collier (n) (m)
collar, necklace

colline (n) (f)
hill

coloré/colorée (adj)
colourful

comique (n) (m)
comic

commandes (n) (f)
controls

comme (prep)
like

comment (adv)
how

commode (n) (f)
chest of drawers

compétition (n) (f)
competition

concert (n) (m)
concert

concombre (n) (m)
cucumber

confiture (n) (f)
jam

confortable (adj)
comfortable

congélateur (n) (m)
freezer

connaissance (n) (f)
knowledge

content/contente (adj)
happy

continent (n) (m)
continent

contraire (n) (m)
opposite

contre (prep)
against

contrôle (n) (m)
test

conversation (n) (f)
conversation

coquillage (n) (m)
shell

corde (n) (f)
rope

corde à sauter (n) (f)
skipping rope

corne (n) (f)
horn

corps (n) (m)
body

costume (n) (m)
costume, suit

côte (n) (f)
coast

coton (n) (m)
cotton

cou (n) (m)
neck

couche d'ozone (n) (f)
ozone layer

coucher de soleil (n) (m)
sunset

coude (n) (m)
elbow

couette (n) (f)
duvet

couleur (n) (f)
colour

couloir (n) (m)
hall, corridor

cour de récréation (n) (f)
playground

courageux/courageuse (adj)
brave

courbe (adj)
curved

couronne (n) (f)
crown

course (n) (f)
race

course à pied (n) (f)
running

courses (n) (f)
shopping

court/courte (adj)
short

cousin/cousine (n) (m/f)
cousin

coussin (n) (m)
cushion

couteau (n) (m)
knife

couvercle (n) (m)
lid

couverture (n) (f)
blanket

cow-boy (n) (m)
cowboy

crabe (n) (m)
crab

crâne (n) (m)
skull

crapaud (n) (m)
toad

cravate (n) (f)
tie

crayon à papier (n) (m)
pencil

crayon de couleur (n) (m)
coloured pencil, crayon

crèche (n) (f)
nursery

crème (n) (f)
cream

crème solaire (n) (f)
suncream

crêpe (n) (f)
pancake

crépuscule (n) (m)
dusk

crevette (n) (f)
prawn

crocodile (n) (m)
crocodile

cruche (n) (f)
jug

cru/crue (adj)
raw

cruel/cruelle (adj)
cruel

cube (n) (m)
cube

cubes (n) (m)
toy bricks

cuillère (n) (f)
spoon

cuisine (n) (f)
kitchen

cuisinière (n) (f)
cooker

curieux/curieuse (adj)
curious

cygne (n) (m)
swan

D

d'abord (adv)
first

d'habitude (adv)
usually

daim (n) (m)
deer

danger (n) (m)
danger

dangereux/dangereuse (adj)
dangerous

dans (prep)
into

danseur/danseuse (n) (m/f)
dancer

danseur/ danseuse classique (n) (m/f)
ballet dancer

date (n) (f)
date

dauphin (n) (m)
dolphin

de (prep)
from

de l'autre côté de (prep)
across

dé/dés (n) (m)
dice

débutant/débutante (n) (m/f)
beginner

décoration (n) (f)
decoration

défi (n) (m)
challenge

défilé (n) (m)
parade

déguisement (n) (m)
fancy dress, disguise

dehors (adv)
outside

déjà (adv)
already

déjeuner (n) (m)
lunch

délicieux/délicieuse (adj)
delicious

deltaplane (n) (m)
hang-glider

demain (adv)
tomorrow

demi-cercle (n) (m)
semicircle

démodé/démodée (adj)
old-fashioned

dent (n) (f)
tooth

dentifrice (n) (m)
toothpaste

dentiste (n) (m/f)
dentist

déplantoir (n) (m)
trowel

depuis (prep)
since

dernier/dernière (adj)
last

derrière (prep)
behind

désert (n) (m)
desert

désordre (n) (m)
mess

dessert (n) (m)
dessert, pudding

dessin (n) (m)
art, drawing

dessin animé (n) (m)
cartoon (film)

détective (n) (m)
detective

deux fois
twice

deuxième (adj)
second (2nd)

devant (prep)
ahead, in front of

devoirs (n) (m)
homework

diagramme (n) (m)
diagram

A B C D E F G H I J K L M N O P Q R S T U V W X Y Z

dictionnaire (n) (m)
dictionary

Dieu (n) (m)
God

différent/différente (adj)
different

difficile (adj)
difficult

digital/digitale (adj)
digital

dindon (n) (m)
turkey

dîner (n) (m)
dinner

dinosaure (n) (m)
dinosaur

directement (adv)
directly

direction (n) (f)
direction

discothèque (n) (f)
disco

discours (n) (m)
speech

dispute (n) (f)
quarrel

disque dur (n) (m)
hard drive

distance (n) (f)
distance

divorcé/divorcée (adj)
divorced

doigt (n) (m)
finger

dôme (n) (m)
dome

dos (n) (m)
back (body)

doucement (adv)
gently

douche (n) (f)
shower

doux/douce (adj)
gentle, soft

dragon (n) (m)
dragon

drap (n) (m)
sheet

drapeau (n) (m)
flag

droit/droite (adj)
straight, right (not left)

drôle (adj)
funny

dur/dure (adj)
hard, tough

DVD (n) (m)
DVD

E

eau (n) (f)
water

échange (n) (m)
exchange

écharpe (n) (f)
scarf

échecs (n) (m)
chess

échelle (n) (f)
ladder

écho (n) (m)
echo

éclair (n) (m)
lightning

école (n) (f)
school

écran (n) (m)
screen

écriture (n) (f)
writing (act of)

écureuil (n) (m)
squirrel

éducation (n) (f)
education

éducation physique (n) (f)
PE (physical education)

effet (n) (m)
effect

effrayé/effrayée (adj)
frightened

égal/égale (adj)
equal

église (n) (f)
church

élastique (n) (m)
rubber band

électricité (n) (f)
electricity

électrique (adj)
electrical

élégant/élégante (adj)
smart

éléphant (n) (m)
elephant

élève (n) (m/f)
pupil, student

elle (pron)
she

elles (pron)
they

e-mail (n) (m)
email

émission (n) (f)
programme (TV)

employé/employée de bureau (n) (m/f)
office worker

emploi (n) (m)
job

empreinte (n) (f)
fingerprint

en arrière (adv)
backwards

en avant (adv)
forward

en bois
wooden

en bonne santé
healthy

en colère
angry

encore (adj)
another

encore (adv)
again

encre (n) (f)
ink

en cuir
leather

encyclopédie (n) (f)
encyclopedia

en-dessous de (prep)
underneath

endroit (n) (m)
place

énergie (n) (f)
energy

en espèces
(in) cash

en face de (prep)
opposite

enfant/enfants (n) (m/f)
child/children

en forme
fit

en haut (adv)
upstairs

ennemi/ennemie (n) (m/f)
enemy

ennui (n) (m)
trouble

ennuyeux/ennuyeuse (adj)
boring

énorme (adj)
enormous

en plastique
plastic

en retard
late

en sécurité
safe

ensemble (adv)
together

ensoleillé/ensoleillée (adj)
sunny

enthousiaste (adj)
enthusiastic

entre (prep)
among, between

entrée (n) (f)
entrance, way in

enveloppe (n) (f)
envelope

environ (adv)
about

environnement (n) (m)
environment

épais/épaisse (adj)
thick

épaule (n) (f)
shoulder

éponge (n) (f)
sponge

épouse (n) (f)
wife

épuisette (n) (f)
net

équateur (n) (m)
equator

équipage (n) (m)
crew

équipe (n) (f)
team

équitation (n) (f)
horse riding

erreur (n) (f)
mistake

escalier (n) (m)
stairs

escargot (n) (m)
snail

espace (n) (m)
space

espagnol (n) (m)
Spanish

espion/espionne (n) (m/f)
spy

esquimau (n) (m)
ice lolly

essence (n) (f)
petrol

essuie-tout (n) (m)
paper towel

est (n) (m)
east

estomac (n) (m)
stomach

et (conj)
and

étage (n) (m)
storey

étagère (n) (f)
shelf

étang (n) (m)
pond

été (n) (m)
summer

éteint/éteinte (adj)
extinct

étoile (n) (f)
star

étoile de mer (n) (f)
starfish

étonnant/étonnante (adj)
surprising

étrange (adj)
strange

étranger/étrangère (adj)
foreign

être humain (n) (m)
human

étroit/étroite (adj)
narrow

événement (n) (m)
event

évier (n) (m)
sink

exact/exacte (adj)
right (correct)

exactement (adv)
exactly

examen (n) (m)
exam

excellent/excellente (adj)
excellent

excité/excitée (adj)
excited

excuse (n) (f)
excuse

exemple (n) (m)
example

exercice (n) (m)
exercise

expédition (n) (f)
expedition

expérience (n) (f)
experiment

expert/experte (n) (m/f)
expert

explorateur/exploratrice (n) (m/f)
explorer

explosion (n) (f)
explosion

exposé (n) (m)
report (for school)

exposition (n) (f)
exhibition

extraterrestre (n) (m/f)
alien

extrêmement (adv)
extremely

F

fabuleux/fabuleuse (adj)
fabulous

facile (adj)
easy

facteur/factrice (n) (m/f)
postman

faible (adj)
faint (pale), weak

fait (n) (m)
fact

falaise (n) (f)
cliff

famille (n) (f)
family

fantastique (adj)
fantastic

farine (n) (f)
flour

fatigué/fatiguée (adj)
tired

faucon (n) (m)
hawk

fauteuil (n) (m)
armchair

fauteuil roulant (n) (m)
wheelchair

faux/fausse (adj)
false

femme (n) (f)
female (human), woman

fenêtre (n) (f)
window

fer à repasser (n) (m)
iron (clothes)

ferme (n) (f)
farm

fermé/fermée (adj)
closed

fermeture éclair (n) (f)
zip

fermier/fermière (n) (m/f)
farmer

féroce (adj)
fierce

ferry (n) (m)
ferry

fête (n) (f)
festival, celebration

feu (n) (m)
fire

feu d'artifice (n) (m)
firework

feuille (n) (f)
leaf

feutre (n) (m)
felt-tip pen

feux de signalisation (n) (m)
traffic lights

ficelle (n) (f)
string

fier/fière (adj)
proud

fille (n) (f)
daughter, girl

film (n) (m)
film

fils (n) (m)
son

fin (n) (f)
end (final part)

fin/fine (adj)
thin

flamme (n) (f)
flame

flèche (n) (f)
arrow

fleur (n) (f)
flower

flocon de neige (n) (m)
snowflake

flûte (n) (f)
flute

foin (n) (m)
hay

foire (n) (f)
fair

foncé/foncée (adj)
dark (hair)

fond (n) (m)
bottom

fontaine (n) (f)
fountain

football (n) (m)
football (game)

forêt (n) (f)
forest

forêt tropicale (n) (f)
rainforest

forme (n) (f)
shape

formidable (adj)
great

fort/forte (adj)
strong

fou/folle (adj)
mad

foule (n) (f)
crowd

four (n) (m)
oven

fourchette (n) (f)
fork

fourmi (n) (f)
ant

frais/fraîche (adj)
cool, fresh

fraise (n) (f)
strawberry

framboise (n) (f)
raspberry

français (n) (m)
French

frère (n) (m)
brother

frisé/frisée (adj)
curly

frites (n) (f)
chips

froid/froide (adj)
cold

fromage (n) (m)
cheese

fruit (n) (m)
fruit

fruits de mer (n) (m)
seafood

fumée (n) (f)
smoke

fusée (n) (f)
rocket, space rocket

G

gagnant/gagnante (n) (m/f)
winner

galaxie (n) (f)
galaxy

galet (n) (m)
pebble

gant (n) (m)
glove

gant de cuisine (n) (m)
oven glove

garage (n) (m)
garage

garçon (n) (m)
boy

garçon de café (n) (m)
waiter

garde (n) (m)
guard

gare (n) (f)
railway station

gâteau (n) (m)
cake

gâteau d'anniversaire (n) (m)
birthday cake

gauche (adj)
left

gaucher/gauchère (adj)
left-handed

gaz (n) (m)
gas

gazeux/gazeuse (adj)
fizzy

géant (n) (m)
giant

gelé/gelée (adj)
frozen

genou (n) (m)
knee

gens (n) (m)
people

gentil/gentille (adj)
kind (gentle)

géographie (n) (f)
geography

gilet de sauvetage (n) (m)
life jacket

girafe (n) (f)
giraffe

glace (n) (f)
ice, ice cream

glacial/glaciale (adj)
frosty (weather)

glacier (n) (m)
glacier

glaçon (n) (m)
ice cube

glissant/glissante (adj)
slippery

globe (n) (m)
globe

golf (n) (m)
golf

gomme (n) (f)
rubber (eraser)

gorge (n) (f)
throat

gorille (n) (m)
gorilla

goutte (n) (f)
drop

gouvernement (n) (m)
government

graine (n) (f)
seed

grand/grande (adj)
big, tall

grand-mère (n) (f)
grandmother

grand-père (n) (m)
grandfather

grands-parents (n) (m)
grandparents

grand vent (n) (m)
gale

A B C D E F G H I J K L M N O P Q R S T U V W X Y Z

grange (n) (f)
barn

gratte-ciel (n) (m)
skyscraper

grenier (n) (m)
attic

grenouille (n) (f)
frog

griffe (n) (f)
claw

grille-pain (n) (m)
toaster

grippe (n) (f)
flu

gris/grise (adj)
grey

gros/grosse (adj)
big, fat

grotte (n) (f)
cave

groupe (n) (m)
group

grue (n) (f)
crane

guépard (n) (m)
cheetah

guêpe (n) (f)
wasp

guerre (n) (f)
war

guide (n) (m)
guide

guide (n) (m)
guidebook

guitare (n) (f)
guitar

gymnastique (n) (f)
gymnastics

H

habitat (n) (m)
habitat

habitude (n) (f)
habit

hamster (n) (m)
hamster

hanche (n) (f)
hip

handicapé/handicapée (adj)
disabled

haricots (n) (m)
beans

haut/haute (adj)
high

haut-parleur (n) (m)
loudspeaker

hélicoptère (n) (m)
helicopter (n)

hélicoptère de police (n) (m)
police helicopter

herbe (n) (f)
grass

héron (n) (m)
heron

héros (n) (m)
hero

heure (n) (f)
hour, time

heures d'ouverture (n) (f)
opening hours

hibou (n) (m)
owl

hier (adv)
yesterday

hippopotame (n) (m)
hippopotamus

histoire (n) (f)
history, story

historique (adj)
historical

hiver (n) (m)
winter

hockey (n) (m)
hockey

hockey sur glace (n) (m)
ice hockey

homme (n) (m)
male (human), man

hôpital (n) (m)
hospital

horaire (n) (m)
timetable

horloge (n) (f)
clock

horrible (adj)
horrible

hors de (prep)
out of

hot-dog (n) (m)
hot dog

hôtel (n) (m)
hotel

huile (n) (f)
oil

I

ici (adv)
here

idée (n) (f)
idea

il (pron)
he

il y a du vent
windy

île (n) (f)
island

illustration (n) (f)
illustration

ils/elles (pron)
they

image (n) (f)
picture

immobile (adj)
still

imperméable (n) (m)
raincoat

imperméable (adj)
waterproof

important/importante (adj)
important

impossible (adj)
impossible

impression (n) (f)
print-out

inconfortable (adj)
uncomfortable

incroyable (adj)
amazing

infirmière (n) (f)
nurse

information (n) (f)
information

informatique (n) (f)
IT (information technology)

ingrédient (n) (m)
ingredient

inhabituel/inhabituelle (adj)
unusual

injuste (adj)
unfair

inondation (n) (f)
flood

insecte (n) (m)
insect

insigne (n) (m)
badge

instant (n) (m)
moment

instruction (n) (f)
instruction

instrument (n) (m)
instrument

intelligent/intelligente (adj)
clever

intéressant/intéressante (adj)
interesting

international/internationale (adj)
international

Internet (n) (m)
Internet

invention (n) (f)
invention

invisible (adj)
invisible

invitation (n) (f)
invitation

invité/invitée (n) (m/f)
guest

J

jamais (adv)
never

jambe (n) (f)
leg

jardin (n) (m)
garden

jardinier/jardinière (n) (m/f)
gardener

jaune (adj)
yellow

je/j' (pron)
I

jean (n) (m)
jeans

jeu (n) (m)
game

jeu de société (n) (m)
board game

jeu électronique (n) (m)
computer game

jeu vidéo (n) (m)
video game (n)

jeune (adj)
young

Jeux olympiques (n) (m)
Olympic Games

joli/jolie (adj)
pretty

joue (n) (f)
cheek (body)

jouet (n) (m)
toy

joueur/joueuse (n) (m/f)
player

jour (n) (m)
day

journal (n) (m)
diary, newspaper

judo (n) (m)
judo

jumeau/jumelle (n) (m/f)
twin

jumelles (n) (f)
binoculars

jungle (n) (f)
jungle

jupe (n) (f)
skirt

jus (n) (m)
juice

jus de pomme (n) (m)
apple juice

jus d'orange (n) (m)
orange juice

jusqu'à (prep)
until

juste (adj)
correct

juste (adv)
just

K

kangourou (n) (m)
kangaroo

karaté (n) (m)
karate

kilogramme (n) (m)
kilogram

kilomètre (n) (m)
kilometre

koala (n) (m)
koala

L

la/lui/l' (pron)
her

là (adv)
there

là-bas (adv)
over there

lac (n) (m)
lake

laid/laide (adj)
ugly

laine (n) (f)
wool

lait (n) (m)
milk

laitier/laitière (adj)
dairy

laitue (n) (f)
lettuce

lampe (n) (f)
lamp

lampe de poche (n) (f)
torch

langue (n) (f)
language, tongue

lapin (n) (m)
rabbit

large (adj)
wide

laser (n) (m)
laser

lavabo (n) (m)
washbasin

lave-vaisselle (n) (m)
dishwasher

le/lui/l' (pron)
him

le/la/l'/les (article)
the

le sien/la sienne (pron)
hers/his

leçon (n) (f)
lesson

lecteur de CD (n) (m)
CD player

lecteur de DVD (n) (m)
DVD player

lecture (n) (f)
reading

léger/légère (adj)
light (not heavy)

légume (n) (m)
vegetable

lent/lente (adj)
slow

lentement (adv)
slowly

léopard (n) (m)
leopard

lettre (n) (f)
letter (alphabet, post)

leur (adj)
their

lever du soleil (n) (m)
sunrise

lèvres (n) (f)
lips

lézard (n) (m)
lizard

libellule (n) (f)
dragonfly

liberté (n) (f)
freedom

librairie (n) (f)
bookshop

libre (adj)
free

lièvre (n) (m)
hare

ligne (n) (f)
line

limace (n) (f)
slug

limonade (n) (f)
lemonade

lion (n) (m)
lion

lion de mer (n) (m)
sea lion (n)

liquide (n) (m)
liquid (n)

lisse (adj)
smooth

liste (n) (f)
list

liste de courses (n) (f)
shopping list

lit (n) (m)
bed

litre (n) (m)
litre

lits superposés (n) (m)
bunk beds

livre (n) (m)
book

locomotive (n) (f)
locomotive

loi (n) (f)
law

loin (adv)
far

loisir (n) (m)
hobby

long/longue (adj)
long

losange (n) (m)
diamond (shape)

loup (n) (m)
wolf

loupe (n) (f)
magnifying glass

lourd/lourde (adj)
heavy

luge (n) (f)
sledge

lumière (n) (f)
light

lune (n) (f)
moon

lunettes (n) (f)
glasses

lunettes de natation (n) (f)
goggles

lunettes de soleil (n) (f)
sunglasses

M

machine (n) (f)
machine

machine à laver (n) (f)
washing machine

mâchoire (n) (f)
jaw

magasin (n) (m)
shop

magazine (n) (m)
magazine

magicien/magicienne (n) (m/f)
magician

magnétique (adj)
magnetic

magnétoscope (n) (m)
video player

maillot de bain (n) (m)
swimsuit, trunks

main (n) (f)
hand

maintenant (adv)
now

mais (conj)
but

maison (n) (f)
home, house

maître/maîtresse (n) (m/f)
teacher

mal (n) (m)
harm

maladroit/maladroite (adj)
clumsy

mal de tête (n) (m)
headache

malade (adj)
ill, sick

maladie (n) (f)
illness

malheureux/malheureuse (adj)
miserable

maman (n) (f)
mum

mammifère (n) (m)
mammal

manche (n) (f)
sleeve

manteau (n) (m)
coat

maquillage (n) (m)
make-up

marché (n) (m)
market

marée (n) (f)
tide

mari (n) (m)
husband

mariage (n) (m)
marriage

marié/mariée (adj)
married

marin (n) (m)
sailor

marionnette (n) (f)
puppet

marron (adj)
brown

masque (n) (m)
mask

match (n) (m)
match (football)

matelas (n) (m)
mattress

matériel (n) (m)
equipment

mathématiques (n) (f)
maths

matin (n) (m)
morning

mauvais/mauvaise (adj)
bad, evil

mauvaise herbe (n) (f)
weed

me/moi/m' (pron)
me

méchant/méchante (adj)
nasty (unkind)

médaille (n) (f)
medal

médecin (n) (m)
doctor

médicament (n) (m)
medicine

méduse (n) (f)
jellyfish

meilleur/meilleure (adj)
better

mélange (n) (m)
mixture

melon (n) (m)
melon

même (adv)
even

même (adj)
same

mémoire (n) (f)
memory

menton (n) (m)
chin

mer (n) (f)
sea

mère (n) (f)
mother

message (n) (m)
message

mesure (n) (f)
measurement

mètre (n) (m)
tape measure

mètre (n) (m)
metre

métro (n) (m)
subway (underground)

meubles (n) (m)
furniture

microbe (n) (m)
bug (illness)

micro-ondes (n) (m)
microwave

microscope (n) (m)
microscope

miel (n) (m)
honey

mieux (adj)
best

milieu (n) (m)
middle

milk-shake (n) (m)
milk shake

mille
thousand

milliard
billion

million
million

mince (adj)
thin (slim)

minéral (n) (m)
mineral

minuit (n) (m)
midnight

minuscule (adj)
tiny

minute (n) (f)
minute

miroir (n) (m)
mirror

mitaine (n) (f)
mitten

mode (n) (f)
fashion

mois (n) (m)
month

moisson (n) (f)
harvest

moissonneuse-batteuse (n) (f)
combine harvester

moitié (n) (f)
half

mon/ma (adj)
my

monde (n) (m)
world

monstre (n) (m)
monster

montagne (n) (f)
mountain

montgolfière (n) (f)
hot-air balloon

montre (n) (f)
watch

moquette (n) (f)
carpet

morceau (n) (m)
piece

mort/morte (adj)
dead

mosquée (n) (f)
mosque

mot (n) (m)
term, word

moteur (n) (m)
motor

motif (n) (m)
pattern

moto (n) (f)
motorbike

mouche (n) (f)
fly

mouchoir (n) (m)
handkerchief

mouchoirs en papier (n) (m)
tissues

mouette (n) (f)
seagull

mouillé/mouillée (adj)
wet

moustache (n) (f)
moustache, whisker

moustique (n) (m)
mosquito

mouton (n) (m)
sheep

moyen/moyenne (adj)
medium

mur (n) (m)
wall

mûr/mûre (adj)
ripe

muscle (n) (m)
muscle

musée (n) (m)
museum

musicien/musicienne (n) (m/f)
musician

musique (n) (f)
music

N

n'importe qui (pron)
anybody

n'importe quoi (pron)
anything

nageoire (n) (f)
fin

narine (n) (f)
nostril

natation (n) (f)
swimming

nature (n) (f)
nature

navire (n) (m)
ship

neige (n) (f)
snow

nénuphar (n) (m)
water lily

nerfs (n) (m)
nerves

neveu (n) (m)
nephew

nez (n) (m)
nose

nid (n) (m)
nest

nièce (n) (f)
niece

Noël (n) (m)
Christmas

nœud (n) (m)
knot

noir/noire (adj)
black

nom (n) (m)
name

nom de famille (n) (m)
surname

nombre (n) (m)
number

non (adv)
no

nord (n) (m)
north

note (n) (f)
mark

notre (adj)
our

nouilles (n) (f)
noodles

nourriture (n) (f)
food

nous (pron)
we

nouveau/nouvelle (adj)
new

nouvelles (n) (f)
news

nuage (n) (m)
cloud

nuageux/nuageuse (adj)
cloudy

nuit (n) (f)
night

nulle part (adv)
nowhere

O

oasis (n) (f)
oasis

objet (n) (m)
object

occupé/occupée (adj)
busy

océan (n) (m)
ocean

odeur (n) (f)
smell

œil (n) (m)
eye

œuf (n) (m)
egg

oignon (n) (m)
onion

oiseau (n) (m)
bird

oiseau-mouche (n) (m)
hummingbird

ombre (n) (f)
shadow

oncle (n) (m)
uncle

ongle (n) (m)
nail

opération (n) (f)
operation

or (n) (m)
gold

orage (n) (m)
thunderstorm

orageux/orageuse (adj)
stormy

orange (adj)
orange (colour)

orange (n) (f)
orange (fruit)

orchestre (n) (m)
orchestra

ordinateur (n) (m)
computer

ordinateur portable (n) (m)
laptop

ordures (n) (f)
rubbish

oreille (n) (f)
ear

oreiller (n) (m)
pillow

orteil (n) (m)
toe

os (n) (m)
bone

otite (n) (f)
earache

ou (conj)
or

où (adv)
where

ouest (n) (m)
west

oui (adv)
yes

ouragan (n) (m)
hurricane

ours (n) (m)
bear

ours blanc (n) (m)
polar bear

ours en peluche (n) (m)
teddy bear

outil (n) (m)
tool

ouvert/ouverte (adj)
open

ouvrier/ouvrière (n) (m/f)
builder

ovale (n) (m)
oval

oxygène (n) (m)
oxygen

P

page (n) (f)
page

paille (n) (f)
drinking straw, straw

pain (n) (m)
bread

paire (n) (f)
pair

paix (n) (f)
peace

pâle (adj)
pale

palme (n) (f)
flipper

palmier (n) (m)
palm tree

panda (n) (m)
panda

panier (n) (m)
basket

panier repas (n) (m)
lunch box

panneau (n) (m)
board (notice), sign

pantalon (n) (m)
trousers

pantoufle (n) (f)
slipper

papa (n) (m)
dad

papier (n) (m)
paper

papier toilette (n) (m)
toilet paper

papillon (n) (m)
butterfly

papillon de nuit (n) (m)
moth

pâquerette (n) (f)
daisy

parachute (n) (m)
parachute

parapluie (n) (m)
umbrella (for rain)

parasol (n) (m)
umbrella (for sun)

parc (n) (m)
park

parce que (conj)
because

parent (n) (m)
parent

paresseux/paresseuse (adj)
lazy

parfait/parfaite (adj)
perfect

particulier/particulière (adj)
special

partout (adv)
everywhere

pas (n) (m)
step

passage clouté (n) (m)
zebra crossing

passager/passagère (n) (m/f)
passenger

passé (n) (m)
past (history)

passeport (n) (m)
passport

pastèque (n) (f)
watermelon

pâte à modeler (n) (f)
modelling clay

pâtes (n) (f)
pasta

patient/patiente (adj)
patient

patient/patiente (n) (m/f)
patient

patins à roulettes (n) (m)
rollerskates

patinage sur glace (n) (m)
ice skating

patte (n) (f)
foot (animal), paw

pause (n) (f)
break

pauvre (adj)
poor

pays (n) (m)
country

PC (n) (m)
personal computer

peau (n) (f)
skin

pêche (n) (f)
fishing

pédale (n) (f)
pedal

peigne (n) (m)
comb

peinture (n) (f)
paint

pélican (n) (m)
pelican

pelle (n) (f)
spade

pelouse (n) (f)
lawn

pendant (prep)
during

pendant que (conj)
while

pensée (n) (f)
thought

perdu/perdue (adj)
lost

père (n) (m)
father

perle (n) (f)
bead, pearl

perroquet (n) (m)
parrot

perruque (n) (f)
wig

personne (pron)
nobody

personne (n) (f)
person

personne âgée (n) (f)
old person

pesanteur (n) (f)
gravity

petit/petite (adj)
little, small

petit ami (m)
boyfriend

petite-fille (n) (f)
granddaughter

petit-déjeuner (n) (m)
breakfast

petit-fils (n) (m)
grandson

petit pain (m)
(bread) roll

petit pois (m)
pea

petits-enfants (n) (m)
grandchildren

petit tapis (m)
mat

petite amie (f)
girlfriend

peu profond/peu profonde (adj)
shallow

peut-être (adv)
maybe, perhaps

phare (n) (m)
lighthouse

pharmacie (n) (f)
chemist

phoque (n) (m)
seal

photo (n) (f)
photo

piano (n) (m)
piano

piéce (n) (f)
part

pièce (n) (f)
coin, room

pièce de théâtre (n) (f)
play

pied (n) (m)
foot

pierre (n) (f)
stone

pieuvre (n) (f)
octopus

pile (n) (f)
battery

pilote (n) (m)
pilot

pin (n) (m)
pine tree

pinceau (n) (m)
paint brush

pingouin (n) (m)
penguin

pique-nique (n) (m)
picnic

pirate (n) (m)
pirate

pire (adj)
worst

piscine (n) (f)
swimming pool

pissenlit (n) (m)
dandelion

piste (n) (f)
runway

pizza (n) (f)
pizza

placard (n) (m)
cupboard

plafond (n) (m)
ceiling

plage (n) (f)
beach

plan (n) (m)
plan

planche de surf (n) (f)
surfboard

planète (n) (f)
planet

plante (n) (f)
plant

plat/plate (adj)
flat, level

plateau (n) (m)
tray

plein/pleine (adj)
full

plongée (n) (f)
diving

pluie (n) (f)
rain

plume (n) (f)
feather

plus que
more than

pneu (n) (m)
tyre

poche (n) (f)
pocket

poêle (n) (f)
frying pan

poids (n) (m)
weight

poignet (n) (m)
wrist

poils (n) (m)
fur

poilu/poilue (adj)
hairy

point (n) (m)
point

pointu/pointue (adj)
pointed

poire (n) (f)
pear

poisson (n) (m)
fish

poisson rouge (n) (m)
goldfish

poitrine (n) (f)
chest

poivre (n) (m)
pepper

polaire (n) (f)
fleece

poli/polie (adj)
polite

police (n) (f)
police

policier (n) (m)
femme policier (n) (m)
police officer

pollution (n) (f)
pollution

pomme (n) (f)
apple

pomme de pin (n) (f)
pinecone

pomme de terre (n) (f)
potato

pompier (n) (m)
firefighter

poney (n) (m)
pony

pont (n) (m)
bridge, deck (boat)

populaire (adj)
popular

population (n) (f)
population

port (n) (m)
harbour, port

porte (n) (f)
door

porte d'entrée (n) (f)
front door

portefeuille (n) (m)
wallet

porte-monnaie (n) (m)
purse

portrait (n) (m)
portrait

position (n) (f)
position

possible (adj)
possible

poste (n) (f)
mail

pot de peinture (n) (m)
paint tin

potage (n) (m)
soup

poteau (n) (m)
pole

poterie (n) (f)
pottery

poubelle (n) (f)
bin

pouce (n) (m)
thumb

poudre (n) (f)
powder

poulet (n) (m)
chicken

poumon (n) (m)
lung

poupée (n) (f)
doll

pourquoi (adv)
why

poussette (n) (f)
buggy

poussière (n) (f)
dust

poussin (n) (m)
chick

préféré/préférée (adj)
favourite

premier/première (adj)
first

premiers secours (n) (m)
first aid

préparatifs (n) (m)
preparations

près de (prep)
near

présentation (n) (f)
introduction

président/e (n) (m/f)
president

presque (adv)
almost, nearly

prêt/prête (adj)
ready

prince (n) (m)
prince

princesse (n) (f)
princess

principal/principale (adj)
main

printemps (n) (m)
spring (season)

prise électrique (n) (f)
plug (electric)

privé/privée (adj)
private

prix (n) (m)
price, prize

probablement (adv)
probably

problème (n) (m)
problem

prochain/prochaine (adj)
next

proche (adj)
close (near)

profond/profonde (adj)
deep

proie (n) (f)
prey

projet (n) (m)
project

promenade (n) (f)
walk

propre (adj)
clean, own

prudent/prudente (adj)
careful

prune (n) (f)
plum

public/publique (adj)
public

puce (n) (f)
microchip

puissant/puissante (adj)
powerful

pull (n) (m)
sweater

pull-over (n) (m)
jumper

punaise (n) (f)
drawing pin

puzzle (n) (m)
puzzle, jigsaw

pyjama (n) (m)
pyjamas

pyramide (n) (f)
pyramid

Q

quai (n) (m)
platform

quand (adv)
when

quantité (n) (f)
amount/quantity

quart (n) (m)
quarter

quelque chose (pron)
something

quelquefois (adv)
sometimes

quelque part (adv)
somewhere

quelques (adj)
some

quelqu'un (pron)
someone

question (n) (f)
question

queue (n) (f)
queue, tail

qui (pron)
who

quiz (n) (m)
quiz

R

racine (n) (f)
root

radio (n) (f)
radio

radiographie (n) (f)
x-ray

raide (adj)
steep, straight (hair)

raisin (n) (m)
grape

rame (n) (f)
oar

ranch (n) (m)
ranch

rangée (n) (f)
row (line)

rapide (adj)
fast

raquette (n) (f)
racket

rare (adj)
rare

rat (n) (m)
rat

râteau (n) (m)
rake

rayures (n) (f)
stripes

réalité virtuelle (n) (f)
virtual reality

recette (n) (f)
recipe

récolte (n) (f)
crop

récompense (n) (f)
reward

récréation (n) (f)
playtime

rectangle (n) (m)
rectangle

réel/réelle (adj)
real

réfrigérateur (n) (m)
fridge

région (n) (f)
area

règle (n) (f)
ruler (measuring)

reine (n) (f)
queen

religion (n) (f)
religion

renard (n) (m)
fox

repas (n) (m)
meal

répétition (n) (f)
practice

réponse (n) (f)
answer

requin (n) (m)
shark

réserve (n) (f)
safari park

restaurant (n) (m)
restaurant

rêve (n) (m)
dream

réveil (n) (m)
alarm clock

réverbère (n) (m)
street light

rhinocéros (n) (m)
rhinoceros

rhume (n) (m)
cold

riche (adj)
rich

rien (pron)
nothing

rideau (n) (m)
curtain

rigolo (adj)
fun

rive (n) (f)
bank (river)

rivière (n) (f)
river

riz (n) (m)
rice

robe (n) (f)
dress

robinet (n) (m)
tap

robot (n) (m)
robot

rocher (n) (m)
rock

roi (n) (m)
king

rollerblades (n) (m)
rollerblades

rond/ronde (adj)
round

rose (adj)
pink

rose (n) (f)
rose

roue (n) (f)
wheel

roue (n) (f)
cartwheel (movement)

rouge (adj)
red

rougeole (n) (f)
measles

route (n) (f)
road

ruban (n) (m)
ribbon

ruche (n) (f)
hive

rue (n) (f)
street

rugby (n) (m)
rugby

rugueux/rugueuse (adj)
rough

ruisseau (n) (m)
stream

S

s'il te plaît /s'il vous plaît
please

sable (n) (m)
sand

sabot (n) (m)
hoof

sac (n) (m)
bag, sack, shopping bag

sac à dos (n) (m)
backpack, rucksack

sac à main (n) (m)
handbag

sac de couchage (n) (m)
sleeping bag

sac en plastique (n) (m)
plastic bag

sage (adj)
wise

saison (n) (f)
season

salade (n) (f)
salad

salade de fruits (n) (f)
fruit salad

salaire (n) (m)
pay

sale (adj)
dirty

salle à manger (n) (f)
dining room

salle de bain (n) (f)
bathroom

salle de classe (n) (f)
classroom

salon (n) (m)
living room

salut
hi

sandales (n) (f)
sandals

sandwich (n) (m)
sandwich

sang (n) (m)
blood

sans (prep)
without

saucisse (n) (f)
sausage

sauterelle (n) (f)
grasshopper

savon (n) (m)
soap

scarabée (n) (m)
beetle

scène (n) (f)
stage (theatre)

sciences (n) (f)
science

scientifique (n) (m/f)
scientist

score (n) (m)
score

seau (n) (m)
bucket

sec/sèche (adj)
dry

seconde (n) (f)
second (time)

secours (n) (m)
rescue

secret (n) (m)
secret

sel (n) (m)
salt

selle (n) (f)
saddle

semaine (n) (f)
week

sens (n) (m)
meaning

séparément (adv)
apart

serpent (n) (m)
snake

serre (n) (f)
greenhouse

serré/serrée (adj)
tight

serrure (n) (f)
lock

serveuse (n) (f)
waitress

serviette (n) (f)
towel

serviette de toilette (n) (f)
flannel

seul/seule (adj)
alone

seulement (adv)
only

sévère (adj)
strict

shampooing (n) (m)
shampoo

short (n) (m)
shorts

siège (n) (m)
seat

sifflement (n) (m)
whistle

silence (n) (m)
silence

silencieux/silencieuse (adj)
quiet

singe (n) (m)
monkey, ape

site web (n) (m)
website

skate-board (n) (m)
skateboard

ski (n) (m)
skiing

snowboard (n) (m)
snowboard

sœur (n) (f)
sister

soir (n) (m)
evening

sol (n) (m)
floor

soldat/femme soldat (n) (m/f)
soldier

soleil (n) (m)
sun

solide (n) (m)
solid

sombre (adj)
dark

son/sa (adj)
her/his/its

son (n) (m)
sound (noise)

sorte (n) (f)
kind (type)

sortie (n) (f)
way out, exit

souffle (n) (m)
breath

souhait (n) (m)
wish

soupe (n) (f)
soup

sourcil (n) (m)
eyebrow

sourd/sourde (adj)
deaf

sourire (n) (m)
smile

souris (n) (f)
mouse (animal, computer)

sous (prep)
under, beneath

sous-marin (n) (m)
submarine

sous-vêtements (n) (m)
underwear

souvenir (n) (m)
souvenir

souvent (adv)
often

spaghettis (n) (m)
spaghetti

spectacle (n) (m)
show

spectateurs (n) (m)
audience

sport (n) (m)
sport

squelette (n) (m)
skeleton

stade (n) (m)
stadium

steak (n) (m)
steak

studio (n) (m)
studio

stupide (adj)
stupid

stylo (n) (m)
pen

sucre (n) (m)
sugar

sud (n) (m)
south

sujet (n) (m)
subject

supermarché (n) (m)
supermarket

supplémentaire (adj)
extra

sur (prep)
about, on top of

sûr/sûre (adj)
sure

surf (n) (m)
surfing

surface (n) (f)
surface

surnom (n) (m)
nickname

surprise (n) (f)
surprise

surveillant de aignade (n) (m)
lifeguard

survêtement (n) (m)
tracksuit

sweat-shirt (n) (m)
sweatshirt

A B C D E F G H I J K L M N O P Q R S T U V W X Y Z

sympathique (adj)
nice

T

table (n) (f)
table

tableau (n) (m)
picture

tableau (n) (m)
blackboard

tablier (n) (m)
apron

tache de rousseur (n) (f)
freckle

taches (n) (f)
spots

taille (n) (f)
size, waist

talon (n) (m)
heel

tante (n) (f)
aunt

tapis (n) (m)
rug

tapis de souris (n) (m)
mouse mat

tasse (n) (m)
cup, mug

taxi (n) (m)
taxi

tee-shirt (n) (m)
T-shirt

télécommande (n) (f)
remote control

téléphone (n) (m)
phone (n)

téléphone portable (n) (m)
mobile phone

télescope (n) (m)
telescope

télévision (n) (f)
television

télévision par satellite (n) (f)
satellite TV

température (n) (f)
temperature

temps (n) (m)
weather

temps libre (n) (m)
free time

tennis (n) (m)
tennis

tennis de table (n) (m)
table tennis

tente (n) (f)
tent

terrain (n) (m)
land

Terre (n) (f)
Earth (planet)

terre (n) (f)
ground, soil

terrible (adj)
terrible

têtard (n) (m)
tadpole

tête (n) (f)
head

texto (n) (m)
text message

thé (n) (m)
tea

théâtre (n) (m)
theatre

thermomètre (n) (m)
thermometer

ticket de caisse (n) (m)
receipt

tige (n) (f)
stem

tigre (n) (m)
tiger

timbre (n) (m)
stamp

timide (adj)
shy

tiroir (n) (m)
drawer

tissu (n) (m)
cloth

toilettes (n) (f)
toilet

toit (n) (m)
roof

tomate (n) (f)
tomato

tondeuse à gazon (n) (f)
lawn mower

torchon (n) (m)
tea towel

tornade (n) (f)
tornado

tortue (n) (f)
tortoise

tortue de mer (n) (f)
turtle

tôt (adv)
early

toucan (n) (m)
toucan

toujours (adv)
always

touriste (n) (m/f)
tourist

tournant (n) (m)
turn (bend)

tournesol (n) (m)
sunflower

tourniquet (n) (m)
roundabout

tous (adj)
every

tous les jours (adv)
everyday

tout (pron)
everything

tout/toute (adj)
all

tout à coup (adv)
suddenly

tout de suite (adv)
immediately

tout le monde (pron)
everybody

toux (n) (f)
cough

tracteur (n) (m)
tractor

train (n) (m)
train

traîneau (n) (m)
sleigh

trajet (n) (m)
route

trampoline (n) (m)
trampoline

tranquille (adj)
peaceful

tranquillement (adv)
quietly

transport (n) (m)
transport

travail (n) (m)
work

tremblement de terre (n) (m)
earthquake

très (adv)
very

triangle (n) (m)
triangle

triste (adj)
sad

troisième (adj)
third

trombone (n) (m)
paper clip

trompe (n) (f)
trunk (animal)

tronc (n) (m)
trunk (tree)

trône (n) (m)
throne

tropical/tropicale (adj)
tropical

trottoir (n) (m)
pavement

trou (n) (m)
hole

troupeau (n) (m)
flock (of sheep)

trousse (n) (f)
pencil case

tu/vous (pron)
you

tube (n) (m)
tube

tunnel (n) (m)
tunnel

U

un/une (article)
a, an

une fois (adv)
once

uniforme (n) (m)
uniform

uniforme scolaire (n) (m)
school uniform

univers (n) (m)
universe

université (n) (f)
university

urgence (n) (f)
emergency

usine (n) (f)
factory

utile (adj)
useful

V

vacances (n) (f)
holiday

vache (n) (f)
cow

vague (n) (f)
wave

vaisselle (n) (f)
washing-up

valise (n) (f)
suitcase

vallée (n) (f)
valley

vautour (n) (m)
vulture

veau (n) (m)
calf

vedette de cinéma (n) (f)
film star

végétarien/végétarienne (n) (m/f)
vegetarian

vélo (n) (m)
bike

vendeur/vendeuse (n) (m/f)
shop assistant

vent (n) (m)
wind

ventre (n) (m)
tummy

ver (n) (m)
worm

ver de terre (n) (m)
earthworm

verbe (n) (m)
verb

vérité (n) (f)
truth

verre (n) (m)
glass (drink)

vers (prep)
towards

vert/verte (adj)
green

vêtements (n) (m)
clothes

vétérinaire (n) (m/f)
vet

viande (n) (f)
meat

vide (adj)
empty

vie (n) (f)
life

vieux/vieille (adj)
old

vilain/vilaine (adj)
naughty

village (n) (m)
village

ville (n) (f)
city, town

violet/violette (adj)
purple

violon (n) (m)
violin

visage (n) (m)
face

vite (adv)
quickly

vitesse (n) (f)
speed

vivant/vivante (adj)
alive

vocabulaire (n) (m)
vocabulary

voile (n) (f)
sail

voisin/voisine (n) (m/f)
neighbour

voiture (n) (f)
car

voiture de course (n) (f)
racing car

voiture de police (n) (f)
police car

voix (n) (f)
voice

vol (n) (m)
flight

votre (adj)
your

voyage (n) (m)
journey, trip

vrai/vraie (adj)
true

vraiment (adv)
really

V. T. T. (n) (m)
mountain bike

W

week-end (n) (m)
weekend

Y

yacht (n) (m)
yacht

yaourt (n) (m)
yoghurt

Z

zèbre (n) (m)
zebra

Basic grammar

Le, la, l'

Every noun (naming word) in French is either masculine or feminine. The word for "the" is either **le** (before masculine nouns) or **la** (before feminine nouns). Le or la become **l'** if the noun begins with a vowel (or with a silent "h"):

Le jardin
The garden
La fenêtre
The window
L'école
The school
L'horloge
The clock

Les

The word for "the" before plural nouns is always **les** (whether the noun is masculine or feminine):

Les jardins
The gardens
Les fenêtres
The windows
Les écoles
The schools
Les horloges
The clocks

To make a noun plural, you usually add an "s" to the end of the word. However, words that end in **-eau** usually take an "x" in the plural:

L'oiseau
Bird
Les oiseaux
Birds

In French, **le**, **la**, **l'** and **les** are often used before nouns where there is no word for "the" in English:

Aimes-tu le jus de pomme?
Do you like apple juice? (singular)
Aimes-tu les bananes?
Do you like bananas? (plural)

To reply to the questions above, you can use **le**, **la**, **l'** or **les** to replace the noun:

Oui, je l'aime
Yes, I like it
Non, je ne les aime pas
No, I don't like them

Un, une

The word for "a" or "an" is **un** (before masculine nouns) or **une** (before feminine nouns):

Un jardin
A garden
Une fenêtre
A window

Au, aux

When **à** is followed by **le** or **les**, it changes:

à + le becomes **au**
à + les becomes **aux**

Je vais au cinéma
I'm going to the cinema
J'ai mal aux dents
I've got toothache

Du, des

When de is followed by **le** or **les**, it changes:

De + le becomes **du**
De + les becomes **des**

Avez-vous du pain?
Do you have any bread?
Avez-vous des tomates?
Do you have any tomatoes?

But when you make the sentence negative, you change **des** to **de**:

Je n'ai pas de frères
I haven't got any brothers
Il n'a pas d'ailes
It hasn't got any wings

Adjectives

In French, adjectives (describing words) change their endings depending on whether the noun they are describing is masculine, feminine, or plural. You add an "e" to most adjectives that describe a feminine noun (unless the adjective already ends in "e") and you add an "s" to adjectives that describe a plural noun:

Il est grand
He's tall
Elle est grande
She's tall
Les garçons sont grands
The boys are tall
Les filles sont grandes
The girls are tall

Some adjectives have different spellings for the masculine and feminine forms, eg, **vieux/vieille** (old). The masculine and feminine endings of adjectives are given in the Word dictionary.

In French, adjectives usually come after the noun they are describing:

Les garçons grands
The tall boys
Les filles grandes
The tall girls

Colours change their endings in the same way as other adjectives:

Une porte verte
A green door
Les stylos bleus
The blue pens

Pronouns

Je I
Tu You
Il He/it
Elle She/it
Nous We
Vous You (plural) and you (formal)
Ils They (m)
Elles They (f)

Tu/vous

In French, there are two words for "you" – **tu** and **vous**. You use the informal form, **tu,** when speaking to friends and family and the formal form, **vous,** when speaking to people you don't know very well (or when you are speaking to more than one person):

Comment vas-tu?
How are you? (informal)
Comment allez-vous?
How are you? (formal)

Il/elle/ils/elles

There are two words for "it" in French. You use **il** for masculine nouns and **elle** for feminine nouns.

Similarly, there are two words for "they". You use **ils** for masculine nouns and **elles** for feminine nouns.

You use **ils** when you are talking about masculine and feminine nouns together.

Ils sont grand
They are tall (masculine/masculine and feminine)
Elles sont grandes
They are tall (feminine)

If you don't know whether a noun is masculine or feminine in French, you use **il**:

Comment est-il?
What's it like?

However, if you know that the noun is feminine, you use **elle**:

Comment est-elle?
What's it like?

Possessive pronouns

There are three ways of saying "my" in French, depending on whether "my" is followed by a feminine, masculine, or plural noun:

Ma tante
My aunt
Mon oncle
My uncle
Mes livres
My books

Similarly:

Ta tante
Your aunt
Ton oncle
Your uncle
Tes livres
Your books
Sa tante
His/her aunt
Son oncle
His/her uncle
Ses livres
His/her books

Verbs

In French, verbs (action words) change according to the subject (the person doing the action).

Most verbs are regular (they follow a regular pattern). The two main types of regular verbs are those that end in **-er** and those that end in **-ir**. The two verbs shown below are written in the present tense. Verbs in the present tense describe the things you are doing now, or the things you do on a regular basis, eg, I'm watching TV/I watch TV every night.

Regarder To watch/see
Je regarde
I watch
Tu regardes
You watch
Il/elle regarde
He/she/it watches
Nous regardons
We watch
Vous regardez
You watch
Ils/elles regardent
They watch

Finir To finish
Je finis
I finish
Tu finis
You finish
Il/elle finit
He/she/it finishes
Nous finissons
We finish
Vous finissez
You finish
Ils/elles finissent
They finish

In French, there are a number of irregular verbs that don't follow these patterns. You will have to learn each one individually, but listed below are some of the most common irregular verbs:

Aller To go
Je vais
I go
Tu vas
You go
Il/elle va
He/she/it goes
Nous allons
We go
Vous allez
You go
Ils/elles vont
They go

Faire To do
Je fais
I do
Tu fais
You do
Il/elle fait
He/she/it does
Nous faisons
We do
Vous faites
You do
Ils/elles font
They do

Savoir To know
Je sais
I know
Tu sais
You know
Il/elle sait
He/she/it knows
Nous savons
We know
Vous savez
You know
Ils/elles savent
They know

Avoir To have
J'ai
I have
Tu as
You have
Il/elle a
He/she/it has
Nous avons
We have
Vous avez
They have
Ils/elles ont
They have

Être To be
Je suis
I am
Tu es
You are
Il/elle est
He/she/it is
Nous sommes
We are
Vous êtes
You are
Ils/elles sont
They are

Reflexive verbs

Reflexive verbs are often used to describe actions we do for (or to) ourselves, eg, **se laver** (to get washed) or **s'habiller** (to get dressed). Reflexive verbs use an extra pronoun (eg, **me**, **te**, **se**, **nous**, **vous**, **se**).

S'habiller
To get dressed/dress (oneself)
Je m'habille
I get dressed
Tu t'habilles
You get dressed
Il/elle s'habille
He/she gets dressed
Nous nous habillons
We get dressed
Vous vous habillez
You get dressed
Ils/elles s'habillent
They get dressed

S'appeler
To be called
Je m'appelle
I am called
Tu t'appelles
You are called
Il/elle s'appelle
He/she/it is called
Nous nous appelons
We are called
Vous vous appelez
You are called
Ils/elles s'appellent
They are called

Reflexive verbs can also be irregular:

S'asseoir
To sit down
Je m'assieds
I sit down
Tu t'assieds
You sit down
Il/elle s'assied
He/she/it sits down
Nous nous asseyons
We sit down
vous vous asseyez
You sit down
Ils/elles s'asseyent
They sit down

Ne... pas

To make a verb negative in French, you put **ne** and **pas** around the verb. **Ne** goes immediately before the verb and **pas** goes immediately after it:

Il n'est pas grand
He isn't tall
Elle n'aime pas le jus d'orange
She doesn't like orange juice

Past tense

You use the past tense to describe things that happened in the past. To form the past tense of most verbs in French, you use the present tense of **avoir** (eg, **j'ai**) with the past participle of the verb (eg, **joué**, **regardé**, **fait**). The past participle doesn't change – only the verb **avoir** changes depending on the subject (the person who has done the action).

This is how you form the past tense of regular verbs ending in **-er**:

J'ai joué
I played
Tu as joué
You played
Il/elle a joué
He/she/it played
Nous avons joué
We played
Vous avez joué
You played
Ils/elles ont joué
They played

This is how you form the past tense of regular verbs ending in **-ir**:

J'ai fini
I finished
Tu as fini
You finished
Il/elle a fini
He/she/it finished
Nous avons fini
We finished
Vous avez fini
You finished
Ils/elles ont fini
They finished

Some verbs, such as **aller** (to go), use the present tense of **être** plus the past participle (eg, **allé**) to form the past tense:

Je suis allé (e)
I went
Tu es allé (e)
You went
Il est allé
He/it went
Elle est allée
She/it went
Nous sommes allé(e)s
We went
Vous êtes allé(e)s
You went
Ils sont allés
They went (masculine)
Elles sont allées
They went (feminine)

With verbs that take **être** in the past tense, the past participle changes according to who has carried out the action. You add an "e" to the past participle (**allé**) (if the subject is feminine), an "s" (if the subject is plural), and an "es" if the subject is feminine plural:

Je suis allée au cinéma
I (feminine singular) went to the cinema

Nous sommes allés au cinéma
We (masculine plural) went to the cinema

Elles sont allées au cinéma
They (feminine plural) went to the cinema

Reflexive verbs

Reflexive verbs use **être** to form the past tense:

Je me suis brossé les dents
I brushed my teeth (masculine singular)

Nous nous sommes brossées les dents
We brushed our teeth (feminine plural)

The past participle changes to agree with the person who has carried out the action.

Ne... pas

To make a sentence negative in the past tense, you put **ne** and **pas** around the verb **avoir** or **être**:

Je n'ai pas joué au foot
I didn't play football
Je ne suis pas allée au cinéma
I didn't go to the cinema (feminine singular)

Nous ne nous sommes pas brossées les dents
We didn't brush our teeth (feminine plural)

I am going to...

One way of talking about what you are going to do in the future is to use **Je vais...** (I am going to...) followed by another verb:

Je vais voyager en avion
I'm going to travel by plane

Je vais faire mes devoirs
I'm going to do my homework

Je ne vais pas jouer au rugby
I'm not going to play rugby

Imperatives

To tell somebody to do something in French, you use a part of the verb called the imperative. Verbs that end in **-er** (as well as some other verbs such as **ouvrir**) drop the "s" in the **tu** form of the imperative:

Ferme la porte!
Shut the door!
Ouvre la porte!
Open the door!

Verbs that end in **-ir** don't drop the "s" in the **tu** form of the imperative:

Finis tes devoirs
Finish your homework

Reflexive verbs, such as **s'asseoir**, form the imperative by joining the pronoun to the verb by a hyphen:

Assieds-toi
Sit down

To make an imperative negative, you put **ne pas** around the verb:

Ne touche pas!
Don't touch!

Asking questions

There are various ways of asking questions in French.

You can make the statement **Tu aimes les bananes** (You like bananas) into an informal question by raising the pitch of your voice: **Tu aimes les bananes?** Do you like bananas?

You can also form a question by changing the position of the subject (**tu**) with the verb (**aimes**) and adding a hyphen:

Aimes-tu les bananes?
Do you like bananas?

Sometimes you can add **Est-ce que...?** to the beginning of the sentence. This is used for questions that are answered by the words "Yes" or "No":

Est-ce que tu aimes les bananes?
Do you like bananas?
Est-ce que tu aimes jouer au rugby?
Do you like playing rugby?

You can also use a word or phrase at the beginning such as **Que?** or **Qu'est-ce que?** (What):

Qu'aimes-tu faire?
What do you like doing?
Que font-ils?
What are they doing?
Qu'est-ce que tu aimes faire?
What do you like doing?
Qu'est-ce qu'ils font?
What are they doing?

Other words and phrases include:

Comment?
How/What?
Quand?
When?
Où?
Where?
À quelle heure?
What time?
Combien de?
How many?
Y a-t-il?
Is there/are there?
Combien de fleurs y a-t-il?
How many flowers are there?
Y a-t-il un chat?
Is there a cat?

Useful verbs

This section gives a list of useful verbs (doing words). Each verb is given in the infinitive (to...) of the verb. The most useful verbs, such as "to be" *être* and "to have" *avoir*, are written out so that you can see how they change depending on who is doing the action.

I = *je*
you = *tu*
he/she = *il/elle*
we = *nous*
you (plural/formal) = *vous*   they = *ils/elles*

We have also written out three of the most regular French verbs (*donner*, to give; *finir*, to finish; and *vendre*, to sell), so you can see how these change.
A reflexive verb is also written out. Reflexive verbs are often used where you would say "myself" or "yourself" in English. An example is *se laver* (to wash oneself). The verbs that are written out are shown in the present tense – they describe what is happening now.

to act
faire du théâtre
fair dew tay-a-truh

to agree
être d'accord
eh-truh da-kor

to allow
permettre
pair-met-truh

to appear
apparaître
ap-par-eh-truh

to ask
demander
duh-mahn-day

to bake
faire de la pâtisserie
fair duh la paht-eess-ree

to bark
aboyer
ab-wa-yay

to be
être
eh-truh

I am
je suis

you are
tu es

he, she is
il, elle est

we are
nous sommes

you (plural) are
vous êtes

they are
ils, elles sont

to be able to
pouvoir
poov-wahr

to be born
être né
eh-truh nay

to be called
être appelé
eh-truh ap-play

to be cold
avoir froid
av-wahr frwa

to be hungry
avoir faim
av-wahr fa(m)

to be scared of
avoir peur de
av-wahr puhr duh

to be thirsty
avoir soif
av-wahr swaf

to become
devenir
duh-vuh-neer

to begin
commencer
kom-ahn-say

to behave
se comporter
suh kom-por-tay

to believe
croire
krwahr

to bend
plier
plee-yay

to bird-watch
observer les oiseaux
ob-zair-vay layz wa-zoh

to bite
croquer
kro-kay

to block
bloquer
blo-kay

to blow
gonfler
gon-flay

to boil
bouillir
boo-yeer

to borrow
emprunter
ahm-pran-tay

to bounce
rebondir
ruh-bon-deer

to brake
freiner
fray-nay

to break
casser
kah-say

to breathe
respirer
ruh-speer-ay

to bring
apporter
ap-por-tay

to brush
brosser
bros-say

to brush one's teeth
se brosser les dents
suh bros-say lay dah(n)

to build
construire
kon-strweer

to bump into
rentrer dans
rahn-tray dah(n)

to buy
acheter
ash-tay

to camp
camper
kahm-pay

to carry
porter
por-tay

to catch
attraper
at-tra-pay

to cause
causer
koh-zay

to celebrate
célébrer
say-lay-bray

to change
changer
shahn-zhay

to charge (a phone)
recharger
ruh-shar-zhay

to check
vérifier
vair-eef-yay

to choose
choisir
shwa-zeer

to clap your hands
taper tes mains
ta-pay day ma(n)

to clean
nettoyer
net-wa-yay

to clear (a table)
débarrasser
day-bar-ra-say

to climb
grimper
gram-pay

to close
fermer
fair-may

to collect
collectionner
kol-lek-syo-nay

to come
venir
vuh-neer

to come back
revenir
ruh-vuh-neer

to come from
venir de
vuh-neer duh

to compare
comparer
kom-pa-ray

to complain
se plaindre
suh plan-druh

to contain
contenir
kon-tuh-neer

to continue
continuer
kon-teen-ew-ay

to cook
cuisiner
kwee-zee-nay

to copy
copier
kop-yay

to cost
coûter
koo-tay

to cough
tousser
too-say

to count
compter
kom-tay

to cover
couvrir
koov-reer

to crack
casser
kass-say

to crash
s'écraser
say-krah-zay

to create
créer
kray-ay

to cross
traverser
tra-vair-say

to cry
pleurer
pluhr-ay

to cut
couper
koo-pay

to cut out
découper
day-koo-pay

to cycle
faire du vélo
fair dew vay-lo

to dance
danser
dahn-say

to decide
décider
day-see-day

to decorate
décorer
day-ko-ray

to describe
décrire
day-kreer

to destroy
détruire
day-trweer

to die
mourir
moo-reer

to dig
creuser
kruh-zay

to disappear
disparaître
dees-par-eh-truh

to discover
découvrir
day-koov-reer

to dive
plonger
plon-jay

---

to do
faire
fair

I do
je fais

you do
tu fais

he/she does
il/elle fait

we do
nous faisons

you (plural) do
vous faites

they do
ils/elles font

---

to do one's homework
faire ses devoirs
fair say duhv-wahr

to do the gardening
jardiner
zhar-dee-nay

to draw
dessiner
dess-ee-nay

to dream
rêver
reh-vay

to dress up
s'habiller
sa-bee-yay

to drink
boire
bwahr

to drive
conduire
kon-dweer

to dry
sécher
say-shay

to earn
gagner
gan-yay

to eat
manger
mahn-zhay

to encourage
encourager
ahn-koo-ra-zhay

to enjoy
aimer
eh-may

to escape
s'échapper
say-shap-payto explain

to explain
expliquer
eks-plee-kay

to explode
exploser
ek-sploh-zay

to face
affronter
af-fron-tay

to fall
tomber
tom-bay

to fall down
s'écrouler
say-kroo-lay

to feed
nourrir
noo-reer

to feel
ressentir
ruh-sahn-teer

to fetch
aller chercher
al-lay shair-shay

to fight
se battre
suh bat-truh

to fill
remplir
rahm-pleer

to find
trouver
troo-vay

to find out
se renseigner sur
suh rahn-sen-yay soor

---

to finish
finir
feen-eer

I finish
je finis

you finish
tu finis

he/she finishes
il/elle finit

we finish
nous finissons

you finish
vous finissez

they finish
ils/elles finissent

---

to float
flotter
flot-tay

to fly
voler
vo-lay

to fold
plier
plee-yay

to follow
suivre
sweev-ruh

to forget
oublier
oo-blee-yay

to freeze
geler
zhuh-lay

to frighten
effrayer
eh-fray-yay

to get
recevoir
ruh-suhv-wahr

to get on (a bus)
monter
mon-tay

to get ready
se préparer
suh pray-pa-ray

to get up
se lever
suh le-vay

---

to give
donner
don-nay

I give
je donne

you give
tu donnes

he/she gives
il/elle donne

we give
nous donnons

you (plural) give
vous donnez

they give
ils/elles donnent

---

to go
aller
ah-lay

I go
je vais

you go
tu vas

he/she goes
il/elle va

we go
nous allons

you (plural) go
vous allez

they go
ils/elles vont

---

to go camping
faire du camping
fair dew kahm-peeng

to go home
rentrer
rahn-tray

to go on holiday
partir en vacances
par-teer ah(n) vak-ahns

to go out
sortir
sor-teer

to go shopping
faire les courses
fair lay koorss

to grow
pousser
poo-say

to guess
deviner
duh-vee-nay

to hang up (a phone)
raccrocher
rak-ro-shay

to happen
arriver
ar-ree-vay

to hate
détester
day-tes-tay

---

to have
avoir
av-wahr

I have
j'ai

you have
tu as

he/she has
il/elle a

we have
nous avons

you (plural) have
vous avez

they have
ils/elles ont

---

to have a shower
prendre une douche
prahn-druh ewn doosh

to have breakfast
prendre le petit-déjeuner
prahn-druh luh puh-tee day-zhuh-nay

to have fun
s'amuser
sam-ew-zay

to have lunch
déjeuner
day-zhuh-nay

to have to
devoir
duhv-wahr

to hear
entendre
ahn-tahn-druh

to help
aider
eh-day

to hide
cacher
ka-shay

to hit
frapper
frap-pay

to hold
tenir
tuh-neer

to hop
sauter
soh-tay

to hope
espérer
es-pair-ay

to hurry
se dépêcher
suh day-peh-shay

to hurt
blesser
bless-ay

to imagine
imaginer
ee-ma-zhee-nay

to include
inclure
an-klewr

to inspire
inspirer
an-spee-ray

to invent
inventer
an-vahn-tay

to invite
inviter
an-vee-tay

to join
joindre
zhwan-druh

to jump
sauter
soh-tay

to keep
garder
gar-day

to kick
donner un coup de pied
don-nay a(n) koo duh pyay

to kill
tuer
tew-ay

to kiss
embrasser
ahm-bra-say

to know (someone)
connaître
kon-neh-truh

to know (something)
savoir
sav-wahr

to land (in a plane)
atterrir
at-tair-eer

to last
durer
dew-ray

to laugh
rire
reer

to lay a table
mettre la table
met-truh la tab-luh

to leap
bondir
bon-deer

to learn
apprendre
ap-prahn-druh

to lie
mentir
mahn-teer

to lift
lever
luh-vay

to like
aimer
eh-may

to listen to
écouter
ay-koo-tay

to live
vivre
veev-ruh

to lock
fermer à clé
fair-may ah klay

to look
regarder
ruh-gar-day

to look after
s'occuper de
sok-ew-pay duh

to look for
chercher
shair-shay

to lose
perdre
pair-druh

to love
adorer
ad-or-ay

to magnify
grossir
groh-seer

to make
fabriquer
fab-ree-kay

to make a wish
faire un vœu
fair a(n) vuh

to make friends
se faire des amis
suh fair dez a-mee

to marry
se marier
suh mar-yay

to mean
signifier
seen-yeef-yay

to meet
rencontrer
rahn-kon-tray

to move
bouger
boo-zhay

to need
avoir besoin de
av-wahr buh-zwah(n) duh

to not feel well
ne pas se sentir bien
nuh pah suh sahn-teer bya(n)

to notice
remarquer
ruh-mar-kay

to offer
offrir
off-reer

to open
ouvrir
oov-reer

to own
posséder
po-say-day

to pack
faire les valises
fair lay val-eez

to paint
peindre
pan-druh

to pay
payer
pay-yay

to persuade
persuader
pair-swa-day

to pick up
ramasser
ram-ah-say

to plan
organiser
or-gan-ee-zay

to play
jouer
zhoo-ay

to play an instrument
jouer d'un instrument
zhoo-ay dan an-strew-mah(n)

to point
indiquer
an-dee-kay

to pour
verser
vair-say

to practise
s'entraîner
sahn-treh-nay

to predict
prédire
pray-deer

to prefer
préférer
pray-fair-ay

to prepare
préparer
pray-pa-ray

to press
appuyer sur
ap-pwee-yay soor

to pretend
faire semblant
fair sahm-blah(n)

to print
imprimer
am-pree-may

to produce
produire
pro-dweer

to promise
promettre
pro-met-truh

to protect
protéger
pro-tay-zhay

to provide
fournir
foor-neer

to pull
tirer
teer-ay

to push
pousser
poo-say

to put
mettre
met-truh

to put away
ranger
rahn-zhay

to rain
pleuvoir
pluhv-wahr

to reach
atteindre
at-tan-druh

to read
lire
leer

to realise
se rendre compte
suh rahn-druh komt

to recognise
reconnaître
ruh-kon-neh-truh

to refuse
refuser
ruh-few-zay

to relax
se détendre
suh day-tahn-druh

to remain
rester
res-tay

to remember
se souvenir de
suh soo-vuh-neer duh

to repair
réparer
ray-pa-ray

to rest
se reposer
suh ruh-poh-zay

to return
revenir
ruh-vuh-neer

to ride a bike
faire du vélo
fair dew vay-lo

to ride a horse
monter à cheval
mon-tay ah shuh-val

to ring
sonner
so-nay

to roll
rouler
roo-lay

to row
se promener en barque
suh pro-muh-nay ah(n) bark

to rub
frotter
fro-tay

to run
courir
koo-reer

to run after
poursuivre
poor-swee-vruh

to sail
faire de la voile
fair duh la vwal

to save
sauver
soh-vay

to say
dire
deer

to score (a goal)
marquer
mar-kay

to scratch (oneself)
se gratter
suh grat-tay

to search
chercher
shair-shay

to see
voir
vwahr

to seem
sembler
sahm-blay

---

to sell
vendre
vahn-druh

I sell
je vends

you sell
tu vends

he/she sells
il/elle vend

we sell
nous vendons

you (plural) sell
vous vendez

they sell
ils/elles vendent

---

to send
envoyer
ahn-vwa-yay

to shake
agiter
azh-ee-tay

to share
partager
par-ta-zhay

to shine
briller
bree-yay

to shout
crier
kree-yay

to show
montrer
mon-tray

to sing
chanter
shahn-tay

to sit
s'asseoir
sass-wahr

to skate (on ice)
patiner (sur glace)
pa-tee-nay

to skate (roller)
faire du roller
fair dew ro-lair

to ski
skier
skee-yay

to sleep
dormir
dor-meer

to slide
glisser
glee-say

to slip
glisser
glee-say

to smell
sentir
sahn-teer

to smile
sourire
soo-reer

to snow
neiger
nay-zhay

to sound (like)
sembler
sahm-blay

to speak
parler
par-lay

to spell
épeler
ay-puh-lay

to spin
tourner
toor-nay

to spread
étaler
ay-ta-lay

to stand
se tenir debout
suh tuh-neer duh-boo

to stand up
se lever
suh luh-vay

to start
commencer
kom-ahn-say

to stay
rester
res-tay

to stick
coller
kol-lay

to sting
piquer
pee-kay

to stop
arrêter
arh-reh-tay

to stretch
s'étirer
say-teer-ay

to study
étudier
ay-tewd-yay

to surf
surfer
soor-fay

to surprise
surprendre
soor-prahn-druh

to survive
survivre
soor-veev-ruh

to swim
nager
na-zhay

to take
prendre
prahn-druh

to take a photo
prendre une photo
prahn-druh ewn fo-toh

to take away
emporter
ahm-por-tay

to take turns
faire à tour de rôle
fair ah toor duh rohl

to talk
parler
par-lay

to taste
goûter
goo-tay

to teach
enseigner
ahn-sen-yay

to tease
taquiner
tak-ee-nay

to tell
raconter
rak-on-tay

to tell a story
raconter une histoire
rak-on-tay ewn eest-wahr

to tell the time
dire l'heure
deer luhr

to thank
remercier
ruh-mair-syay

to think
réfléchir
ray-flay-sheer

to throw
jeter
zhuh-tay

to tidy up
ranger
rahn-zhay

to tie
attacher
at-ta-shay

to touch
toucher
too-shay

to train
entraîner
ahn-treh-nay

to translate
traduire
trad-weer

to travel
voyager
vwa-ya-zhay

to treat (well)
traiter (bien)
tray-tay bya(n)

to try (on)
essayer
es-say-yay

to turn
tourner
toor-nay

to type
taper
ta-pay

to understand
comprendre
kom-prahn-druh

to undress
se déshabiller
suh day-sa-bee-yay

to unpack
déballer
day-bal-lay

to use
utiliser
ew-tee-lee-zay

to visit
visiter
vee-zee-tay

to wait
attendre
at-tahn-druh

to wake up
se réveiller
suh ray-vay-yay

to walk
marcher
mar-shay

to want
vouloir
vool-wahr

to warm
réchauffer
ray-shoh-fay

to wash
laver
la-vay

to wash (oneself)
se laver
suh la-vay

I wash
je me lave

you wash
tu te laves

he/she washes
il/elle se lave

we wash
nous nous lavons

you (plural) wash
vous vous lavez

they wash
ils/elles se lavent

to wash the dishes
laver la vaisselle
la-vay la vay-sel

to watch
regarder
ruh-gar-day

to wave
faire un signe de la main
fair a(n) seen-ye duh la ma(n)

to wear
porter
por-tay

to weigh
peser
puh-zay

to whisper
chuchoter
shew-sho-tay

to win
gagner
gan-yay

to wish
souhaiter
sway-tay

to wonder
se demander
suh duh-mahn-day

to work
travailler
tra-va-yay

to work (function)
fonctionner
fonk-syo-nay

to wrap
emballer
ahm-bal-lay

to write
écrire
ay-kreer

Useful phrases

Yes
Oui
wee

No
Non
no(n)

Hello
Bonjour
bon-zhoor

Goodbye
Au revoir
oh ruhv-wahr

See you later
À bientôt
ah byan-toh

Please
S'il te plaît
seel tuh pleh

Thank you
Merci
mair-see

Excuse me
Excuse-moi
eks-kewz mwa

I'm sorry
Je suis désolé
zhuh swee day-zo-lay

My name is...
Je m'appelle...
zhuh ma-pel

I live...
J'habite à...
zha-beet ah

I am... years old
J'ai... ans
zhay...ah(n)

I don't understand
Je ne comprends pas
zhuh nuh kom-prah(n) pah

I don't know
Je ne sais pas
zhuh nuh say pah

Very well
Très bien
treh bya(n)

Very much
Beaucoup
boh-koo

I like/I don't like
J'aime/Je n'aime pas...
zhehm/zhuh nehm pah

Let's go!
Allons-y!
alohn-zee

Happy Birthday!
Bon anniversaire!
bo(n) an-ee-vair-sair

How are you?
Comment ça va?
ko-mah(n) sa va

What is your name?
Comment t'appelles-tu?
ko-mah(n) ta-pel tew

Do you speak...?
Parles-tu...?
parl tew

Do you like...?
Aimes-tu...?
ehm tew

Do you have...?
As-tu...?
ah tew

Can I have...?
Puis-je avoir...?
pwee zhuh av-wahr

How much...?
Combien...?
kom-bya(n)

What's that?
Qu'est-ce que c'est?
kess kuh say

How many?
Combien?
kom-bya(n)

Can you help me?
Peux-tu m'aider?
puh tew meh-day

What time is it?
Quelle heure est-il?
kel uhr et eel

Help!
Au secours!
oh suh-koor

Stop!
Arrête!
ar-reht

Turn right/left
Tourne à droite/à gauche
toorn ah drwat/ah gohsh

Go straight on
Va tout droit
va too drwa

In front of
Devant
duh-vah(n)

Next to
À côté de
ah koh-tay duh

Where is/are...?
Où est/sont...?
oo eh/so(n)

Monday
lundi
lahn-dee

Tuesday
mardi
mar-dee

Wednesday
mercredi
mair-kruh-dee

Thursday
jeudi
zhuh-dee

Friday
vendredi
vahn-druh-dee

Saturday
samedi
sam-dee

Sunday
dimanche
dee-mahnsh

January
janvier
zhahnv-yay

February
février
fay-vree-yay

March
mars

April
avril
av-reel

May
mai
may

June
juin
zhwa(n)

July
juillet
zhwee-yay

August
août
oot

September
septembre
sep-tahm-bruh

October
octobre
ok-to-bruh

November
novembre
no-vahm-bruh

December
décembre
day-sahm-bruh

Acknowledgements

DK would like to thank the following people: Sarah Ponder and Carole Oliver for design help; Marie Greenwood and Jennie Morris for editorial help; Angela Wilkes and Lydia Yelo for language consultancy; Katherine Northam for digital artwork; Rose Horridge for picture research; Rachael Swann for picture research assistance; and Hope Annets, Mary Mead, Bethany Tombs, Todd and Sophie Yonwin for modelling.

The publisher would like to thank the following for their kind permission to reproduce their photographs: (Key: a-above; b-below/bottom; c-centre; f-far; l-left; r-right; t-top)

Alamy Images: Paul Horsted/Stock Connection Distribution 28bc; Janine Wiedel Photolibrary 16cb; RubberBall 28l; Corbis: Ronnie Kaufman 29c; Roger Ressmeyer 29l; Macduff Everton 85tl; Jason Horowitz / Zefa 89br; Anna Peisl / Zefa 89cr; Keren Su 1155b Mike Theiss/ Jim Reed Photography 28clb; Getty Images: The Image Bank 17cl, 48tl, 49tr; 89bl; Taxi 107tr; Photographer's Choice 48ftl, 48ftr, 48cla, 49ftl; Photonica 17fcl; Stone 16crb, 17ca, 17cr, 42tr; Taxi 10bc, 11tc, 11fcr, 48clb, 49ftr; Workbook Stock 16, 17tr, 17cra; Photolibrary: Rich Remsberg 49tl; SuperStock: Comstock 48bl; DK Images: Stephen Oliver 89tl; Jerry Young 3br, 89tc (iPod); Science Photo Library: Phototake Inc. 111tr

Answers to puzzles

Page 10
Bonne journée! = Toi aussi; Bonne nuit! = Bonne nuit!; Au revoir! = À plus tard; Bonjour, comment vas-tu? = Je vais bien, merci; Salut, ça va? = Ça va bien, merci.

Page 13
Ben is the oldest. Paul and Laura are the same age. Simone is ten. Eric is nine.

Page 14
1. = D, 2. = E, 3. = C, 4. = B, 5. = A, 6. = F

Page 16
1. = C, 2. = B, 3. = A, 4. = D

Page 18
1. = Isabelle;
2. = Philippe;
3. = Jean-Luc.

Page 21
La souris est sous la table. Le chat est dans la salle de bains. Le chien est dans la chambre. La télévision est à côté de l'armoire. L'armoire est derrière le fauteuil. La table est dans la cuisine.

Page 23
Sur photo 1: Il y adeux stylos; Il y a cinq crayons de couleur; Le stylo est bleu; La trousse est rouge. Sur photo 2: Il y a trois stylos; Il y a sept crayons de couleur; Le stylo est orange; La trousse est bleu.

Page 27
1. = C, 2. = A, 3. = D, 4. = B.

Page 28
1. = B, 2. = D, 3. = C, 4. = A.

Page 33
1. = David
2. = Danielle
3. = Giles

Page 37
A = Ils jouent au basket; B = Ils nagent; C = Il court; D = Elle fait du vélo; E = Il joue au rugby; F = Elle fait de la gymnastique; G = Elle danse.

Page 45
1. = F; 2. = C; 3. = E; 4. = A; 5. = D; 6. = B.

Page 50
1. = D; 2. = A; 3. = B; 4. = C.

Page 52
Pascal = C; Lucie = A; Etienne = B.

Page 54
1. = Eric; 2. = Antoine; 3. = Elisabeth.

Page 56
1. = le supermarché; 2. = le musée; 3. = la poste; 4. = la piscine.

Page 58
1. = Sophie; 2. = Michel; 3.= Pierre.

Page 60
A = Monique;
B = Christian;
C = Charlotte.

Goodbye!
Au revoir!